# TELFORD

## THE MAKING OF SHROPSHIRE'S NEW TOWN

*Telford town centre, looking east over Telford Bridge retail park and Sainsburys to the shopping centre, business park and Hollinswood residential area and the eastern primary road, now Queensway. On the far left is Stafford Park with the M54 motorway.* (Jefferson's Air Photography)

# TELFORD

## THE MAKING OF SHROPSHIRE'S NEW TOWN

*Maurice de Soissons*

SWAN·HILL
PRESS

First published in the UK in 1991
by Swan Hill Press

**A catalogue record of this book is available
from the British Library.**

ISBN 185310 253 9

Printed by Livesey Ltd, Shrewsbury.

# Swan Hill Press
An imprint of Airlife Publishing Ltd.
101 Longden Road, Shrewsbury SY3 9EB

# Contents

# Acknowledgements

Telfordians and Salopians of varied ages and backgrounds, including local authority councillors and staff, have helped with my research for this book. Most of them are mentioned in its pages, and I thank them all for giving me their time, their stories and opinions. Two whose names do not appear are Shropshire County Council's George Baugh of the *Victoria History of Shropshire* and Anthony Carr of the Local Studies Library in Shrewsbury. They were most helpful in directing me to material, particularly to do with the great days of the East Shropshire coalfield. Likewise, I should like to thank John Powell of the library of the Ironbridge Gorge Museum for assistance.

At Telford Development Corporation my grateful thanks go to the chairman, Frank Jones, and the general manager, Michael Morgan, for their help and encouragement with the project. Among many TDC staff who gave me assistance are David Wassell, Chris Mackrell, David Evans, Terry Bradshaw, Neil Griffiths, Joyce Nicholas (who typed the script), Marylin Allmark, Jeannette Drinkwater and Sue Campbell. My gratitude goes especially to the three members of the TDC editorial committee, who have worked so closely and tirelessly with me on all aspects of the book. Their interest and enthusiasm have been of major assistance. They are Keith Hadley, Gerald Chidlow and David Everington.

Numbers of ex-board members and former members of TDC's staff have also contributed to the book. Among them are Lord Northfield, Sir Frank Price, John Dugdale, Joseph Boyce, Laurie Buckthorp, Bill Wood, Michael Spratley, now of Tandy Associates, and Martin Horne, now of Martin Horne & Co. Finally, I would like particularly to thank Emyr Thomas, who gave me the benefit of his long, detailed and fruitful involvement with the town.

Maurice de Soissons

# *Foreword*

by Frank Jones
Chairman, Telford Development Corporation

The making of Telford has been a huge task. It has taken hundreds of millions of pounds of public money (much of it recovered by the sales of land and property) and involved vast land reclamation schemes, landscaping projects and civil engineering works on a scale which would have impressed the Pharoahs of ancient Egypt. Individual housing and industrial areas in Telford are larger than many of the smaller towns in a Shropshire which has gradually come to show a friendlier face to its extraordinary new child.

But this town has also absorbed the energies and ambitions of many talented people who have been members of the Board of Telford Development Corporation, its employees or residents who have campaigned and worked to create the sort of place in which they wanted to live. Many of them feel that they will be unlikely ever again to work on a project of such scale and breadth and sheer intensity. Some compare it to a period of service in the armed forces at a time of national struggle in pursuit of a great cause — a thing to be looked back upon with pride.

Maurice de Soissons has captured this exciting period in the history of East Shropshire in a way which is highly readable but at the same time very thorough in its chronicling of the pre-history of Telford and the story of the town itself. There will doubtless be other specialist books in much greater detail about this or that aspect of the development — but I believe this one will be the starting point for all subsequent research on a great achievement.

*Frank J. Jones.*

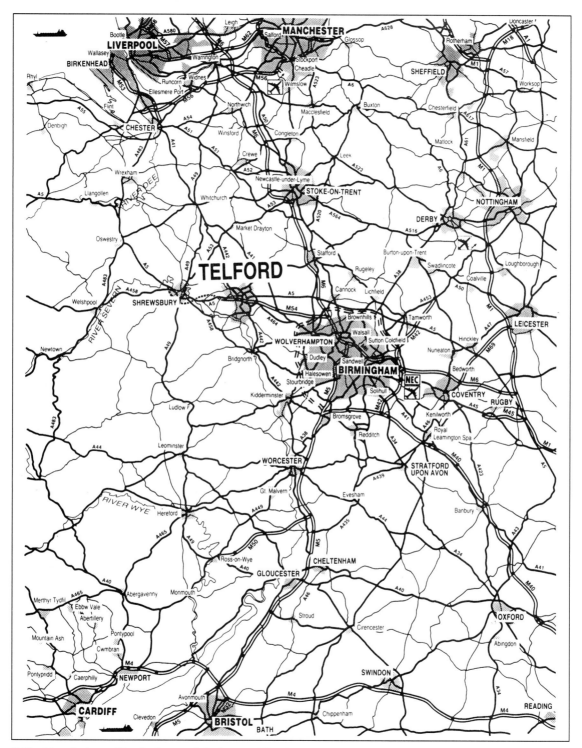

*Telford in relation to Birmingham and the West Midlands, Liverpool, Manchester and Bristol, and the motorway network.*

# *Prologue*

Public awareness of environmental matters in Britain is now, during the 1990s, at fever pitch. Chief among the worries is the disappearance, disfigurement or radical change of the countryside. Among a diversity of concerns are the ploughing up of flower-rich meadows, loss of habitat of many rare species of birds and animals, and over-use of national parks.

However, much closer to people's everyday lives is the anxiety about seemingly detrimental changes in landscape and in particular obtrusive, unsympathetic siting of out-of-character housing. The slogans read 'no more greenfield sites taken', 'redevelop the inner cities — no new settlements'.

The fact that Britain still needs more up-to-date, comfortable housing for its changing population — and demand is as always for suburban or quasi-country dwellings away from major conurbations — is too often played down or ignored. Attempts to provide something along these lines by adding on to existing towns and villages has led inexorably to long commuting hours and congested roads.

The Garden City movement said it all at the start of the century — 'live in a healthy garden environment, walk or bicycle to work, to school, to the shops'. The building of two widely-acclaimed garden cities by private enterprise led eventually to the New Towns Act after the Second World War, and Britain's new towns were created by government to provide families with houses and gardens in a green environment, with good schooling, shops and recreational facilities close to work. That aim remains unaltered.

Now comes pressure against more new settlements. It is the media's nature to ignore success stories and make much of disasters. Yet there are projects which embody a surprising number of the environmental good points of present-day popular thinking, in sensible and rational land use to satisfy the living, working and recreational aspirations of modern people. Some even provide a green environment where wood anemones, white admiral butterflies and badgers can also live in reasonable harmony with mankind.

Telford New Town is such a place. It has taken some green fields to be sure, but it has achieved what must be the most massive British land reclamation scheme, involving over 5,000 acres (2,025 hectares) of slag heaps, colliery tips, quarries, disused mine shafts and derelict works in what was once the East Shropshire coalfield. They were the visible and sometimes dangerously hidden signs of the extraordinary exploitation of coal, ironstone, clays suitable for pottery, porcelain, bricks and tiles, fire-clays, limestone, sandstone, bitumen tars, gravel and sand — worked to exhaustion by our ancestors at the forefront of the Industrial Revolution — and left as an enormous scar on the face of one of England's fairest counties.

The once-ravaged land now accommodates a dozen residential areas, modern industrial estates, a brand new extensive town centre, with parks, lakes, greenways, meadows and forest providing wildlife habitats and recreational areas, and linking older settlements with new ones. All is laid out with main highways and a network of feeder roads, and parking space and garaging for today's high-density use of motor transport.

# TELFORD
Shropshire

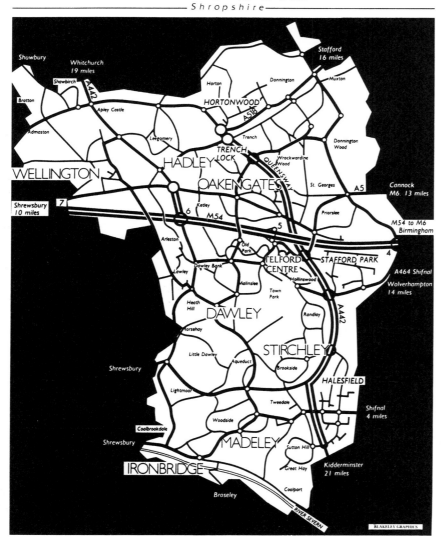

*Telford, showing its towns, villages, new residential and industrial areas, its town centre and road network in 1990.*


10

The designated area of Telford lies fifteen miles from Shrewsbury and twenty miles from Wolverhampton. It stretches ten miles from north to south, is three miles at its broadest, and covers nearly 20,000 acres (8,097 hectares). A watershed along the ridge where the Romans built Watling Street, drains the land north and south. To the south is an undulating plateau 400 feet to 600 feet (122 metres to 183 metres) in altitude with a high point of 700 feet (213 metres) at Dawley. Deeply-cut valleys take streams to the Severn Gorge in the extreme south. North of the watershed the land drains towards the Shropshire Plain. Much of the designated area lies on the coal measures which were so assiduously worked for 300 years with the inevitable legacy of run-down mining towns and villages, high unemployment and dying or dead industries. A vigorous hard life had bred an inward-looking people, intensely loyal to their own folk and settlement. Descendants of the colliers, ironworkers, brickmakers and quarrymen are still in Telford. They have been joined by many 'immigrants' from the West Midlands, the Black Country, Birmingham and Wales, and others from overseas. Now they work in international high-tech manufacturing, especially plastics and electronics, in service industries, warehousing and offices.

Today there are 120,000 inhabitants, and Telford provides work for 61,000 people. There are higher and further educational establishments, shops, offices, entertainment and sporting facilities in the town centre, and schools and simpler district facilities in smaller centres, some of them older settlements refurbished for today's needs. It is a third-generation new town built for 21st century people with rising expectations, which has benefited from the experience of earlier new towns, but has found its own solutions and innovations as changing economic and demographic circumstances have dictated.

The Telford story is not one of smooth-running success, unmarred by hostility, vested interests, personality clashes and all the other ingredients of most large-scale human endeavours. There were considerable economic setbacks, difficulties in attracting industry and commerce, political indifference, even a loss of faith in the whole concept for a time. Taxpayers' money went into 3,000 holes in the ground — the land reclamation was an act of governmental courage as well as sound environmental sense, but cost much more than was originally estimated. At first the towns and villages taken over were resentful of the new town, proud of their long virile smokestack industrial history or, in Wellington's case, its quiet and usually prosperous market town life.

Telford has sought by planning, landscaping, sociological and financial means to weld the old and new settlements into a well laid-out, extensive town with excellent living and working conditions for the gamut of social classes, where loyalties to individual villages and townships can flourish alongside a pride in the whole of Telford. Today, the new town is an industrial and residential force in the West Midlands, and has its own strong identity. Whether the welding process is complete or not, the story of the land's earlier history and of the creation of a 'town in a forest' from such unpromising material, is a story well worth the telling.

*The land now covered by Telford in 1611. Taken from John Speed's map of Shropshire in his atlas of the English counties. Coalbrookdale had yet to warrant a place, and Bratton appears to have changed its location.* (Shropshire CC Local Studies Library)

# 1 Early History
## before 1700

In the year of the Domesday census, 1086, the land from the Severn Gorge to the gentle slopes in the north down to the Weald Moors was in the King's forest of the Wrekin, later Mount Gilbert. The predominant heavy clay soils were thickly wooded. Lighter patches of sand and loam had been cleared by small independent Saxon farmers, and probably before them by the Cornovii, a Celtic people. Now, with the Norman Conquest, priories held most of the area under the manorial system of tenure and organisation further developed by the invaders. Forest law was designed to protect and continue the hunting and timber amenities of the woodlands for the benefit of the Crown.

Domesday records show that there were settlements at Wellington, Hadley, Horton, Ketley and Watling Street in the north, and at Madeley, Dawley, Lawley, Malinslee and Stirchley in the south. There were possibly isolated small farms in the countryside between the settlements, and rough roads linking them, most likely with the beginnings of a later road system — Shrewsbury to London along the Roman Watling Street, Wellington to Bridgnorth, and Shifnal to Little Wenlock via Madeley. The population was small. Apart from the inmates of the religious houses, the people were villeins, bordars, serfs and their families working the manors. Most of the cleared land was wood pasture where timber trees, often pollarded for firewood, dotted the grassland. Pigs were raised in woodland. Wheat and oats were grown on limited arable land. Forest places where coal lay at the surface were probably undisturbed until the next century. This is an example of how the Dark Ages forgot or ignored Roman technology. For coal was found in the heated air systems at Viroconium or Wroxeter, not far to the west.

Much of the forest at Domesday would have consisted of oak and ash, wych elm and lime, especially on the heavier soils, while birch and rowan, hawthorn, blackthorn, wild cherry and holly would have formed, with hazel, the under-storey and colonised the lighter soils. In 1086 this was an isolated, deeply-rural and near-primitive countryside. From that date until 1301, when the whole area ceased to be a royal forest, pressure of population began gradually to make itself felt. Many applications to assart or stump out patches of woodland for crops were made, and often refused. But it was the slow beginning of better farming and woodland management, and with it a concomitant exploitation of the exceptional natural resources below ground, both pursued with more and more sophistication until the Industrial Revolution truly began at the start of the 18th century.

As these changes evolved, the people of the area began to gain some of their livelihood from work in coal mines, iron foundries, lime quarries and kilns, while continuing farming and smallholding activities. Only in the 1600s did families begin to subsist entirely by some industrial form of labour. The working people's lives were simple and their pleasures homely. Their stories and those of the lords of the manors, the priests, the master craftsmen and entrepreneurial business people who were to evolve their skills and talents on the earlier exploitation of the riches are indicated in the outline histories of the parishes that were the first community authorities.

## Madeley

In the 8th century, clearings in the forest were first cut in Madeley. By 1086 the settlement had six villeins, four bordars and four serfs and their families. The prior and convent of Wenlock were lords of Madeley until the Dissolution in 1540 when the manor passed to the Crown, to be bought by Robert Brooke four years later, whose family held it for the next 200 years. Madeley — the Saxon origin of the name is uncertain but probably from Mada's lea or pasture — possessed a mill on the Washbrook, together with fishponds and later a windmill north-east of Madeley Court. There were horse pastures, dovecotes, a rabbit warren and an eyrie of swans. The settlement developed around the church from the 12th century. In 1235 forest jurisdiction brought stricter forest laws and any encroachments — cultivation or building without royal licence — were severely punished. In 1267 the rector of Madeley was licensed to hunt in the royal forest. Nearly twenty years later the Bishop of Lichfield had to rectify misappropriations of tithes in sheep and corn. Madeley was not then regarded as a 'fat' living for its priest, nor for the hierarchy above him who took some of the tithes. A Tuesday market was licensed in 1269 and a new town laid out east of the original settlement, along the road to Shifnal.

*Madeley Court, mainly Elizabethan and with a Jacobean gatehouse. The house was the home of Abraham Darby III. This photograph was taken before restoration by Telford Development Corporation, and shows pit mounds to the left, planted with oak, birch and pine in the last century.*

Only after 1301 did agricultural development take place more rapidly. Cultivated open fields lay round Madeley town where corn was grown, with pastures and woodland beyond. By 1332 coal was being mined. The Wenlock priory granted Walter de Caldebrook for the sum of 6s the right to dig coals in the Brockholes for one year. Caldebrook, later Coalbrookdale, was first mentioned as having inhabitants in 1274, but the population of the parish of Madeley was still very sparse, for in 1327 only eleven adults paid taxes. During these years increasing acreages of woodland were being coppiced for charcoal production and firewood. Charcoal provided the intense heat necessary to smelt iron. As ironworking grew — smiths were recorded in the parish in the 14th century — so woods were managed to provide cordwood. Oak, ash and beech were probably used at first, with hazel, hornbeam and sycamore brought in during the centuries ahead. Depending on the speed of growth of the coppicing species, the woods were separated into twelve to twenty parcels and each year one parcel was cut.

By 1536 there was a bloom smithy water-powered by the Caldebrook at Coalbrookdale, and ironstone quarries were being worked on some scale. Later that century, blastfurnaces and forges were described. In 1579 John Brooke, lord of the manor, employed colliers and Madeley coal was shipped to Worcester. Transport on the Severn was by then steadily developing, and building stone — probably carboniferous limestone — was exported downriver in 1588. With the next century, mineral extraction and ironworking expanded. Hearth plates dated 1602 have been found at Coalbrookdale. Sir Basil Brooke established an ironworks in Coalbrookdale where a cast-iron beam bearing the date 1638 and his initials still exists. His mines in Madeley Wood were mostly horizontal insets into the hillside up to 1,000 yards (914 metres) long. Seams of coal varied from eighteen inches (45.72 centimetres) to three feet (0.914 metres) thick, and he had water problems and had to drain the mines. Longwall adit shafts were later developments. During the Civil War, when the opposing forces were active in the region, the Parliamentarians captured the ironworks and ousted a Royalist garrison from Madeley. After the Battle of Worcester in 1651, Charles II is reputed to have passed a night and a day in a Madeley barn belonging to a supporter.

Quarries, sandpits and stone mines were opened up in the parish. Limestone was quarried and there were limekilns at Lincoln Hill (probably Limekiln Hill) in the 1600s. Wooden railways with wooden wagons, drawn by horses, mules and oxen began to be built between mines, forges and furnaces around 1605. Otherwise, packhorse trains shifted coal in panniers at 3½ hundredweights (177.8 kilograms) a horse, with 35 hundredweights (1,778 kilograms) carried by ten horses known as 'a stack'. Ironstone was transported by twelve horses carrying a total of 42 hundredweights (2,133.6 kilograms) known as 'a dozen'. By 1700 the wagonways linked mines with wharfs on the Severn. Gradients were eased by embankments, cuttings and stone bridges over streams.

By 1630 Madeley had small soap- and candlemaking industries, both important to miners. But although minerals exploitation was increasingly important, the parish still remained largely agricultural, with many colliers and ironworkers also with smallholdings. Animal husbandry took pride of place, cattle often being the most valuable possessions of a family. Pigs were commonly kept and there were sheep and bees. Apples were widely grown, and so were hops.

15

Already cottages were being built on 'waste' rough land, on commons and along roads. In Madeley Wood especially there was haphazard building of colliers' cottages. In 1677 owners of cattle and swine were brought to the manorial court because their animals were nuisances on the highways and lanes, and 'oppressed' the commons. There were fifteen ale sellers in the parish and the populace were accused of 'tippling, gaming, and desecration of the Lord's Day'. Other cases brought before the court included assault, keeping swine unyoked and unringed, illegal land enclosure and encroachment, trading offences, sheep stealing — and defaulting suitors.

Apart from Madeley Wood there were settlements of ferrymen, boatmen and trowmen along the Severn's edge, and a hamlet at Coalbrookdale which in 1700 consisted of a furnace, several forges and five houses, and was described as 'very barren and little money stirring'. Madeley itself had by then become a small market town with mercers, tailors, a glover, butchers, carpenters, coopers and a bowyer. Smiths, nailers, platers, a pot founder and a gunsmith were evidence of a proliferation of metal-working trades. In 1660 the numbers of men who earned their living entirely as colliers or metal-workers was still quite small, but in the next forty years specialisation in industrial trades grew. By the turn of the century the parish of Madeley contained about 450 people.

*Rose Cottage in Coalbrookdale, built in the 1640s. It was a farmer's or smallholder's dwelling, and would probably have been occupied by one of the increasing number of men who worked in the mines and foundries and had smallholdings during the early years of industrialisation.*

## Dawley

The parish of Dawley had from early times settlements at Great and Little Dawley and at Malinslee. Dawley is thought to originate from Dealla's lea or pasture, while Malinslee's name is obscure, possible Maelden's lea. The Domesday Book of 1086 mentioned ten villeins in Great Dawley, and one villein, two bordars and a serf in Little Dawley. The parish was thickly wooded, with the Loamhole and Lightmoor brooks flowing through their valleys to the head of Coalbrookdale. Almost all the parish lay over the coal measures. A certain Richard of Dawley is recorded as early at 1180 as operating a forge. But there appears to have been little change in the way of life of the few inhabitants until the late 13th century when more land was brought into arable cultivation. Great Dawley in 1327 had only sixteen inhabitants. In 1340 Malinslee, by this time in the manor of Leegomery as was Little Dawley until the 16th century, reared horses, goats, pigs and cattle. The names Horsehay and Hinkshay, enclosures for horses and stallions, pointed to considerable horse rearing. In 1406 Malinslee contained six smallholdings and four cottages.

Mining is recorded in Dawley in the early 1500s. In 1526 it was evident from the rents charged that ironstone was more highly prized than coal. A bloom smithy was operating at the Ridges near Lightmoor in 1580, and by 1631 Sir George Hayward, lord of the manor of Great and Little Dawley, worked ironstone and coal, employing day and weekly labourers. He had an ironstone mine on the Ridges farm. Limestone quarries and limekilns were operating in Little Dawley from 1653. The Eyton family of Leegomery worked minerals at Malinslee. The countryside of small hamlets and scattered farms of a largely wood-pasture economy was gradually changed from the 16th century by the haphazard building of industrial workers' cottages. Their tenure was ratified by payment of rent to the lord of the manor. Most were of brick and tile, but some were constructed in sandstone from the mines. They are described as being one storey and a half, sometimes with a hipped roof.

Great Dawley slowly developed with a cluster of dwellings round the church — there is evidence of a chapel there before the 12th century — the parsonage and the manor house, known as Dawley Castle and probably fortified. In 1543 there were three alehouses in the parish and reports that these 'harboured illegal gambling'. Little Dawley in 1580 contained mostly timber-framed houses, a large smallholding, eight 'tenements' and one cottage. Open fields are recorded round Great Dawley in 1612, the larger known as Common Field lay along the boundary with Little Dawley, together with large enclosures for stock.

During the Civil War when Dawley manor was held by the Cromptons, there were apparently both Royalist and Parliamentarian members of the family which caused much pain and friction. The Roundheads are reputed to have destroyed Dawley Castle. By 1672 there were twenty-five householders in Great Dawley who paid hearth tax, with fifteen each in Little Dawley and Malinslee. Conditions in the parish as it reached the 18th century were much as in Madeley, still largely pastoral with many smallholdings run by men with other trades, and farms from seventy to 180 acres (28 to 73 hectares) in extent. Woodland covered big areas, much of it coppiced for charcoal, probably with twelve to eighteen standard timber trees, mostly oak, to the acre. Over the parish the miners' and iron-workers' cottages were forming small settlements.

## Lilleshall

Only the south-west portion of the ancient parish of Lilleshall — the hill of Lil — lies within the Telford designated area. Recorded history here begins with the Romans who built Watling Street to Wroxeter from London, and in the 1st century established a post at Red Hill, probably known as Uxacona. When the Normans came there were likely to have been isolated Saxon farms. In 1086 there were twenty-two inhabitants in the parish. Donnington — Dunning's or Deora's farm — where there were large tracts of ancient woodland, was mentioned in 1180, and Muxton — Muxcel's farm — existed by 1186. Trench Way was recorded in 1288. Lords of the manor were the abbots of Lilleshall. In 1341 there was a disease that wiped out the sheep population. The Black Death evidently took its toll, although in 1345 the abbots built houses on smallholdings, and some cottages and crofts were enclosed for landless families.

Already by 1277 exploitation of mineral resources had begun. There was a smithy at Quam Pool, and ironworking at Donnington Wood, with a coal mine there by 1330. In 1539 Donnington was the most populous settlement with fourteen 'able' men for the militia against Lilleshall's eleven and Muxton's eight. At the Dissolution of the monasteries the Leveson family bought the manor, and by 1563 there was eighty-four households in the parish. Seventeen years later Walter Leveson owned water-driven hammers on the Humber brook, a neighbourhood known as The Hammers, later changed to The Humbers. By that time leasehold tenures for holdings were common, and by 1598 a quarter of the arable land in open fields was enclosed, although arable holdings open to common grazing still continued. Small tenants worked land at Donnington and Muxton. All had alternative employment — there was a clocksmith, wheelwrights, weavers, a finer of iron, tailors and a surgeon. About that time the name Coalpit Way first occurred, a bloom forge is mentioned, small-scale founding and nailmaking developed.

By 1625 limestone extraction at Lilleshall was well-established and limekilns existed, using coal from Donnington Wood. The surface coal seams were exhausted and underground mining had commenced. By 1676 there were 428 adults in the parish.

## Stirchley

Away to the east on the edge of the coalfield, Stirchley — stirks' or young bullocks' pasture — was most likely uncleared woodland well into medieval times, gradually being opened up to pastoral farming in the 12th and 13th centuries. The church was built in the 12th century. Buildwas Abbey owned the manor in the 13th century and there was an outer settlement at Oulmeyre, later Holmer Farm, when Stirchley consisted of a cluster of cottages and smallholdings round the church. By the end of the 1400s most of the land was in three large freehold blocks and already cleared, with timber and 'coaling' wood going to early ironworks in Madeley, Coalbrookdale and Dawley. By 1563 the parish contained only seven households, and in 1612 comprised just the three farms and five cottages. Hearth tax was paid by eleven people sixty years later, and when the century drew to a close Stirchley subsisted on a pastoral economy with much permanent pasture and little early industrialisation.

## Wellington

Founded about the year 800 by the Saxons, Wellington — a farm or enclosure of a descendent of Weala, hence Wealingtun — was quite well-developed agriculturally by 1086. Woodland had been cleared and the aspect was of open country with crops, pastures and herds of cattle. At Domesday there were thirty-three inhabitants of the ancient parish, including a priest. Within the parish lay Hadley, Horton, Lawley, Leegomery, Watling Street, Ketley, Dothill and Arleston, and there were certainly small settlements at these places in the 11th century. A Thursday market was granted in 1244 where agricultural produce surplus to subsistence was sold and craft goods purchased by the inhabitants. Livestock fairs were later instituted. Cloth and leather trades were established by the early 1300s by which time the early street pattern had also been laid down. Lying off the coal measures itself Wellington slowly developed as an agricultural market town, although carboniferous limestone outcropped in the little settlement of Watling Street and limekilns were first mentioned in 1240. In 1327 Wellington, with some of the outlying settlements, had twenty-nine taxpayers. Also around that year Apley Castle was built, probably a moated house. By now most of the settlements had open arable fields nearby, there was woodland and rough pasture in Arleston, and waste and commons towards the Weald Moors.

By the 15th century Wellington tanners sold hides at the market, and there were many leather workers. Carpenters and coopers plied their trades. Spinning and weaving developed using local hemp, flax and wool, and cloth was sold in the town. Bell founding and ropemaking came to Wellington, and in 1601 a maltings was established. But earlier than this, in 1543, a grammar school was founded and by 1563 the parish had 219 households.

In these early years Wellington was often second only in size and importance in Shropshire to Shrewsbury. Civil war strife came to the town and it was fought over and captured several times. In 1676 the parish contained 1,544 adults with Wellington itself 725. Arleston — probably Eardwulf's farm — lay on the coal measures and coal and ironstone were mined in the 1680s. In 1688 Leegomery, bought by James Leveson 140 years earlier, passed to a relative named William Gower. A condition was that he attach his name to Leveson, thus founding the Leveson-Gower dynasty of Leegomery and Lilleshall. Leegomery's name is difficult to assess, possibly from lea and an earlier Norman owner Alured de Cambrai or Cumbre. For most of the 17th century farms had been held on lease, and more sophisticated practices employed in general farming. Turnips were widely grown by the 1660s and dairying developed with cheese sold in commercial quantities.

By 1697 local government by the jury of the manorial court seems to have been well in hand. In addition to the bailiff, leather inspectors, sealers, swine ringers, yokers and haywards (until the final enclosures) Wellington boasted two street scavengers and a common crier. When the Wrekin wakes — the Wrekin lay within the old parish — were begun is not known precisely, but they were well established by the beginning of the 18th century on the first four Saturdays in May. They traditionally ended in fights between the various trades and settlements — a pastime that was to continue into the 20th century.

## Hadley, Horton, Ketley and Lawley

Hadley — Headda's lea — was poor and wooded in 1086, while Horton — probably a 'muddy farm' — contained large areas of waste. Coal and ironstone with fireclay lay in deep strata at the extreme south-east. Tiles were made at Horton in 1681, but at the end of the 17th century the district was still largely agricultural. Hadley had its share of weavers.

At Ketley — Cytel's lea — sandstone was quarried as long ago as 1269. Coal and ironstone were taken near the surface by 1584, while Coalpit Bank, later Ketley Bank, was so named in 1613. However, the area remained well-wooded with many smallholdings and small farms. Miners' cottages were evident along Watling Street by the late 1600s. Smallholders practised a trade as well, but there were increasing numbers of families living entirely on coal mining. In 1688 some residents of Coalpit Bank complained that poverty forced them to send wives and children to work in the pits.

At Lawley — Laua's lea — there were four serfs and a villein in 1086, and only four 'able' men in 1542, while in 1672 twelve households paid hearth tax. In the early Middle Ages there was much woodland and waste, and three main farmsteads. Coal and ironstone were being mined by 1589, and ironstone may have been sent to a furnace in Coalbrookdale in 1685.

## Wombridge and Oakengates

The origins of the name Wombridge are obscure, either womb-ridge, a lake ridge, or a bridge either at a corner or in a hollow. The place developed from the Augustinian priory of St Leonard founded around 1135, and Priorslee was a pasture of this priory.

Oakengates was a late medieval hamlet — the name either literally an oaken gate or derived from Uxacona, the Roman staging post on Watling Street, or ochr/ockren, a hillside, and gate or yate, a road or street. The priory exploited coal and ironstone from the early 1500s and at the Dissolution there was an iron mill at Wombridge. Settlement grew with industry and mining, and hamlets sprang up alongside mines and ironworks, notably at Coalpit Bank. There were three alehouses in Oakengates, one at Coalpit Bank around 1618. Mining was established at Snedshill by the 1600s. By then what woodland remained in Wombridge, Priorslee and Snedshill was almost certainly coppiced. A mill and furnace at Wombridge owned by the Foley family produced 239 tons of iron in 1669 and 289 tons the next year. In 1672, hearth tax was paid by eleven households in Oakengates and three in Wombridge. About 1690 there were said to be a total of eighty families in the two settlements.

## Wrockwardine Wood

Detached from Wrockwardine parish and manor — which included Admaston and Bratton — Wrockwardine Wood was reputed to be well-stocked with oaks and underwood, probably hazel, in 1235. The origins of the name are not clear, perhaps derived from Viroconium, the Roman town now called Wroxeter, or from Wrocc's estate or village. By 1290, clearances had begun in what was then known, and until about 1577, as the King's Wood. There was an iron-ore mine in 1324, and the easily-available surface coal was opencast mined in the early 1600s, underground mining beginning at the end of the century. Straggling roadside and crossroad settlements were built by colliers and iron miners. In 1650, fourteen smallholdings and thirty-five cottages were occupied in the wood, including twelve cottages at Pain's Lane, now St George's. In 1666 a document referred to Rocardin Wood.

## The 1690s

In the last decade of the 17th century, the pressure on woodland and on charcoal supplies for smelting iron turned many men's thoughts to the use of coal. Cutting fifteen to twenty acres (six to eight hectares) of coppice annually to sustain the forty days in a year when an average charoal furnace was operated took about 240 acres (97 hectares) of coppice in a coppicing cycle of twelve to sixteen years. East Shropshire was now an important source of iron for these furnaces. Yet despite the pits, quarries and ironworks situated on streams from north of Watling Street to the Severn Gorge, the economy at the dawn of the 18th century was still predominantly agricultural. Many men still worked as weavers, tanners, coopers, wheelwrights, ropemakers and maltsters. There were clothiers, colliers, blacksmiths, foundrymen, limekiln workers, and carters and packhorse carriers. But most kept a pig or a cow, grew corn and flax at the least, and some managed with their family's aid to run dairying and cheese-making enterprises, raise sheep, rear and train horses and draught oxen.

Inventories of goods owned by recently-deceased inhabitants give an insight into their lives. Yeoman collier Walter Hartshorne of Malinslee died in 1696. He left sheep, cows and pigs worth £49, farming implements and crops, £5, pit equipment and coal stocks, £20. He had a house with six rooms and a cellar, a feather bed, and twenty small cheeses in a cheese chamber. John Duddell of Dawley was a carpenter. He left tools worth £6, boards worth 10s. He farmed several acres, had five cows, two pigs and four horses. Edward Aston of Muxton was a lymeman tending a lime kiln. He left estate valued at £12. 15s. 6d, of which £9. 9s was in cattle.

Beds were the most valuable items of furniture. Poor men had to be content with straw bags and wooden slats, and with benches and simple tables, while their richer neighbours had soft beds, chairs, chests of drawers, coffers, linen sheets, screens and hangings, fowling and birding guns, brass and pewter tableware and dishes. Table cutlery was rarely mentioned — people used their fingers. Coal was cheap for heating and cooking, and beer the common beverage.

In most ways the people of this corner of Shropshire must have led a satisfying, largely peaceful, isolated country existence, in small hamlets and villages far from strident authority and wars — except the Civil War. They had food, relatively clean water from streams, wells and ponds, they were warm in winter, and they had work, and in hard times most could fall back on their land for sustenance and support. Industrialisation had been gradual, but soon greater demand for coal and iron, new inventions and influxes of people were to alter their lives and their landscape radically.

# 2 Industrial Growth and Decline 1700 to 1900

The catalyst for East Shropshire's expansion of coal mining and ironworking was the successful use of coke from coal in iron smelting. Abraham Darby leased a derelict blastfurnace at Coalbrookdale in 1708 and began experiments the next year, probably mixing coke with charcoal, raw coal and peat, before being satisfied with his methods by 1713. The next year substantial cokemaking hearths were built at Dawley mines, yet Darby's innovative techniques were not widely appreciated or copied for another thirty years. He added a second blast-furnace, made large castings for civil and mechanical engineering projects, plates and rods, and parts for Newcomen steam engines. These provided an alternative source of power to water and brought enormous benefits in keeping mines dry. Mining was still a hazardous occupation from gas, roof falls and broken ropes, but Newcomen's engines dramatically reduced deaths by drowning in flooded mines.

By now, the estimated 1711 population of the coalfield was 11,500, presumably including the bargemen, ferrymen, trowmen and shipwrights living in the Severn Gorge. River transport was still superior to road transport and wagon railways were increasingly built, taking coal and ironstone from mines to forges and furnaces, and coal for export to Bristol and Shrewsbury. About 1729 iron-flanged wheels were introduced, followed by iron sleepers and rails. On the river were trows carrying from forty to eighty tons, mostly ironstone, and square-rigged single-masted barges and wherries moving respectively twenty to forty tons and five to six tons of coal. They went downstream with the current, upstream by means of bow hauliers until later in the century towpaths were built and horses used. The bow hauliers had a reputation for pilfering the cargoes of trade goods, and poaching game along the banks. By the 1720s attempts were made to improve the roads. Responsibility for upkeep was taken from the parishes and toll companies were formed. Roads in East Shropshire began to be turnpiked from 1726.

## Iron industry expansion

In the 1740s and 1750s, the first swift expansion of ironmaking and iron forming took place. Abraham Darby II began Horsehay works in 1755, leasing mines at Great Dawley and Ketley. Two years later iron smelting began at Ketley. Clusters of shallow coal pits were dug at Old Park, and along the valley sides of Lightmoor. The 'lunar' landscape of these workings remained until Telford's land reclamation schemes. Iron ore from Donnington and Wrockwardine Wood was brought by wagon railway to ironworks in the south. The Madeley Wood Company built two blastfurnaces beside the Severn in 1758, known as the Bedlam furnaces. The third Abraham Darby, grandson of the first, took over the Bedlam works in 1776. He also built the Lightmoor works, where men from

Madeley and Dawley worked. There is a report which indicates that the Coalbrookdale Company of the Darbys was alive to the need for some reclamation work in the 1750s when it planted conifers, probably Scots pine, on broadleaved woodland sites which had been stripped for pit props and charcoal furnaces. As mines and quarries were developed, much coppiced woodland was cleared. By 1760, the estimated population of the coalfield was over 20,000.

Earl Gower and Company was formed in 1764 to exploit resources in the north of the coalfield and invested heavily in drainage and new equipment. Two years later, deep strata coal mining was undertaken at Hadley. Between 1776 and 1806 the Shropshire iron trade enjoyed its most prosperous time. About forty per cent of national production, some 12,000 to 13,000 tons a year, came from the county. Some furnaces produced up to forty tons a week, and steam engines replaced bellows for blowing air into the blastfurnaces, while steam winding brought greater mining abilities for the deep seams. John Wilkinson was a leading ironmaster of the 1770s who introduced many innovations. He became a folk hero and was commemorated in song, and is reputed to have given pensions to old workmen who had served him well.

By now most major ironworks were linked financially and by wagon railway to brickfields such as those at Madeley Field, The Lloyds, Blists Hill and Hollinswood. Both coal mining and ironmaking required large quantities of bricks, and the cheaper more sulphurous or 'stinking' coal was used to fire them. White limestone was used for fluxing in the blastfurnace, while grey limestone was crushed for agricultural use or cement making. In the 1790s Horsehay produced clay drainage pipes, pits for forging processes and ground clay for glass and porcelain making. Large-scale ironmaking began at Donnington Wood in 1785, while new coal pits were exploited at Blists Hill and Old Park in the next decade. By 1797 the Coalbrookdale Company was one of the largest ironmakers in Britain. Other leading ironmasters were William Reynolds, Banks and Onions, Alexander Brodie, Wright and Jesson, Addenbrooke and Homfray, the Botfields, and John Bishton.

## Economic boom and distress

During the 18th century, with an overall booming economy in the coalfield and a labour shortage, ironmasters and mine owners appeased their workers, fearful of damage to their installations, a situation that was to change in the next century. But there were periods of economic distress. Food riots broke out in 1756, and farmers were 'persuaded' by colliers and ironworkers to sell their produce at earlier, more reasonable, prices. By then a substantial proportion of the industrial workers had no other means of livelihood, and probably only an allotment to help with subsistence. Poor harvests affected those with small-holdings. Often times were hard in the 1770s and 1780s, and in 1795 food scarcity reached famine proportions. One Madeley writer, evidently well-fed himself, ascribed the famine to the habit of eating four meals a day — breakfast, dinner and supper, and now tea as well, 'which wastes both Meal and Time and makes a difference (in consumption) in the Parish of Madeley of 3,234 lb of flour'. Meetings expressed 'alarm at the scarcity of corn and dearness of all kinds of other provisions'. Many Madeley families were in dire circumstances and colliers were only prevented from rioting by the assurances of 'men of property' that they would help, which they did by buying 2,000 bushels of Indian corn.

As the final land enclosures began, the smallholders that relied on commons and wastes found their rights extinguished, and many became day labourers or sought work in industry. There was a heavy and increasing burden on parishes which had become directly responsible in 1787 for succouring the poor. An enlightened ironmaster, Richard Reynolds, encouraged small allotments by leasing land to his men. Later, others leased farms outside the coalfield so that they would have food for their workers. One curious custom that persisted well into the 19th century and which worried ironmasters whose installations needed constant attention, was the twice-a-year exodus when workers downed tools and went into the countryside to bring in the hay and cereal harvests. As more and more land disappeared for mining, the surviving coalfield farms became

*Part of John Rocque's map of Shropshire, dated 1752, showing the exploitation of the coalfield well under way.*

(Shropshire CC Local Studies Library)

*Coalbrookdale in the mid to late 18th century. The ironmasters' houses are at the head of the dale with the road up Jigger's Bank. The great warehouse, furnaces and furnace pools, and an early use of tracked transport are shown. Note the still heavily wooded slopes.*

(Ironbridge Gorge Museum Trust)

geared to produce for adjacent industry's needs, particularly in providing pasturage and fodder for the huge number of horses at ironworks, pits, and on the wagon railways, and later the canals.

The 1760s saw the rise of evangelical protestantism in the coalfield. The vicar of Madeley from 1760 to 1785 was John Fletcher, who began the strong methodist influences which were to be a powerful force in the mining and metalworking villages for eighty years and more. Together with Richard Reynolds he opposed the increasing violence and drunkenness of the colliers and ironworkers. Fights on market days between various factions, including bargemen, were regular occurrences, as were bull-baiting contests with dogs. Reynolds laid out promenades in his woods above Coalbrookdale and encouraged villagers to use them on a Sunday. Concern to have a stable, skilled workforce brought attempts to control festivals and wakes so as to avoid the more violent pastimes. Sunday and other schools — Dawley had a free school in 1777 — began to be established. But the twin influences of alehouse and chapel were in the future to battle for the communities' souls, and there would be some settlements dedicated to the one and some to the other.

## New settlements

As the ironworks and mines proliferated, so settlements grew and new ones came into existence. The scattered groups of squatter cottages on roadsides, woodland edge and commons were bases for expansion. Many new dwellings were built in the early years of the century by the colliers and craftsmen themselves, others by speculative builders. Houses grew with additional rooms as families enlarged. Land was subdivided. Freehold and leasehold tenures became common. Occasionally there was enough land for a smallholding or allotment. A large squatter community of bargemen, shipwrights and other trades was in the gorge. Ketley had many cottages with irregular enclosures and the largest squatter settlement away from the Severn. The Wellington-Newport road at Trench Lane, and the commons at Lawley and Snedshill were quickly built up. Priorslee Hall was built about 1728, and by 1752 there was a small village beside it, with squatters' housing towards Snedshill Coppice.

By now companies had begun to put up rows of houses and cottages for their employees. They reckoned to have a greater degree of social control over their workers so housed, and as the houses were almost invariably of higher standard, they were expected to be an inducement during times of labour shortage. Coalbrookdale Company built cottages at Coalbrookdale from the early 1750s, the best known of which were Nailers' Row, Tea Kettle Row and Carpenters' Row, and at New Dale in Lawley township in 1759. The company also erected cottages at Horsehay in the 1790s, while two redundant brick ovens were turned into homes in 1793, the trend of using old industrial buildings as dwellings becoming quite widespread throughout the coalfield. By the 1790s Beveley, Coalpit Bank (Ketley Bank), Red Lake and Low Wood had settlements, some of the housing built precariously on pit wastes. Holywell Lane in Little Dawley grew rapidly. Old Park ironworks built fifty cottages at Hollinswood. Many other company houses were constructed before the century's end at Gravel Leasows, Burroughs Bank, Stoney Hill and The Finney, all in the Lightmoor area. Most houses were of brick, but a number used coal measures sandstone.

## The canal era

During the second half of the 18th century, the area's tub-boat canal systems were begun. The first was the Donnington Wood canal in 1767, built for Earl Gower and Company of Lilleshall. In 1788 a canal linked Ketley with mines in Oakengates, and by 1792 there was a network serving mines, quarries and ironworks, including a branch to Coalport on the Severn. The name Coalport dates from 1794, and three years later there were several pottery and porcelain factories and thirty houses. From the outset of the building of East Shropshire's canal system there were water problems, particularly in high, broken and already disfigured land. The engineers found it difficult to establish water storage points, especially close to mining works. Flights of locks to scale steep gradients were, therefore, not practicable. So tunnels, aqueducts and especially inclined planes were utilised. Inclined planes, where the tubs were hauled up and let down from one stretch of canal to the next, were built at Brierly Hill, Lincoln Hill, Blists Hill, Windmill Farm, Ketley, Trench and Donnington Wood. The famous Hay inclined plane at Coalport was constructed in 1791. There were substantial water reservoirs in the Randlay and Stirchley areas.

The old wagon railway still ran from Sutton wharf below Coalport north to Hollinswood, with spurs off to numerous mines and ironworks. It was built at a tenth of the cost of the canal and carried goods more cheaply. It was closed under an 'arrangement' with the canal owners. The canals did, however, open up the markets for East Shropshire coal and iron. Before their advent, coal from the north of the coalfield had been sold locally within a ten-mile radius, while coal and iron from the south had been exported by river. As mines and quarries close to ironworks were worked out, so the canals brought in coal, ironstone and limestone from elsewhere in the coalfield.

*The inclined plane at Trench Lock, where tubs were hauled up and down between stretches of canal. The canals, started in the 18th century, declined rapidly with the coming of railways in the 1850s.*

## The Iron Bridge

The settlements along the Severn, and their industries, all grew. A wooden bridge was built across the river at Coalport, and in 1779 the famous Iron Bridge, the first in the world, was constructed further upstream. It was largely designed by a Shrewsbury architect, Thomas Pritchard, although it is likely that the iron working skills of the Darbys of Coalbrookdale contributed to the design. The structure soon gave the growing settlement its name and became a great spectacle, drawing early tourists as well as engineers, scientists, businessmen and academics. Across the river at Broseley and Caughley, coal was mined and exceptional clays were used in pottery and porcelain works from the 1770s. In 1796 John Rose was the guiding spirit in establishing what was to become a famed maker of fine porcelain at Coalport in the next century. Also at Coalport during the 1790s bitumen was made up from a nearby tar source. But it was on the iron trade that the East Shropshire coalfield depended for its prosperity at the end of the century as the war with France, begun in 1793, escalated.

*The Iron Bridge was opened in 1779. This late 19th century photograph shows the toll keeper's house to the right of the bridge, a Severn trow, and riverside housing with shops.*
(Ironbridge Gorge Museum Trust)

## The 1800s — expansion and depression

As the new century dawned, some 34,000 people lived on and worked the coalfield and its industries. War kept demand for iron high. In 1802 the Lilleshall Company was formed out of the Leveson-Gower family interests. Ketley's six blastfurnaces produced 7,500 tons of pig iron in 1804, while the next year the Lilleshall Company's pits at Donnington Wood produced 6,750 tons of coal and 1,300 tons of ironstone. By 1809 there were twenty-four active pits in Hadley, and the next year the roll-call of fully-operative ironworks was Donnington Wood, New Hadley, Wrockwardine Wood, Ketley, Snedshill, Queenswood, Old Park, Hollinswood, Horsehay, Dawley Castle, Lightmoor, Madeley Wood and Coalbrookdale. Old Park, owned by the Botfield family, was the largest ironworks in Shropshire, and the second largest in Britain.

By now ironworks depended chiefly on steam as the source of power, although Coalbrookdale still operated most machinery with water power, using steam to return water to high-level reservoirs. Goods made at Coalbrookdale included bedsteads, bookcases, engine cylinders, stoves, ovens, salt pans and window frames, and many different castings, shipping around 1,000 tons of these a year. Ketley foundry specialised in heavy industrial castings, doors for steam engines, bridges, puddling furnaces, pipes, cylinders, anvils, wheels, cannon stoves and shot furnaces. At the other end of the range of industrial enterprise, three potteries and porcelain factories at Coalport employed 400 people in 1814.

After 1815 and the defeat of Napoleon at Waterloo, economic reaction was swift. Depression fell on the coalfield. Colliers accustomed to taking home 4s. (20p) a day found themselves with 1s. 6d (7½p). The friendly societies that had begun their operations in about 1812 were unable to cope. Many men sought parish relief. Ketley ironworks closed in 1816 and for a time the ironworkers and colliers thrown out of work threatened to become 'an appendage to the Wellington workhouse'. During that year and the following one, many paupers were sent back to their parishes of settlement or origin — in Wales, Lancashire, the Black Country, and other parts of Shropshire. The Coalbrookdale Company came close to closure. In 1817 Wrockwardine Wood had 1,938 inhabitants, 703 of them receiving poor relief. Local men demobilised from the army added to the unemployment. Fortunately, Ketley re-opened in 1818, producing pig and bar iron. But hard times continued elsewhere on the coalfield with rising food prices. In 1820 there was a strike of colliers protesting at wage reductions, and the yeomanry — the peace-keeping force of the time — was attacked with stones and bludgeons at Wombridge and Wrockwardine Wood.

The year 1821 saw the beginning of another religious revival with the rise of primitive methodism in the industrial settlements. Meetings on pit mounds and even inside furnace buildings were held. That year, too, there was a serious labour confrontation known as the Cinderhill riots when 3,000 colliers defied troops on a slag mound at Old Park. Two rioters were killed when the soldiers opened fire, and a ringleader was later executed. Years later, in 1839, 4,000 primitive methodists gathered for a great open-air meeting on Cinderhill.

From 1822 to 1830 there was a gradual return to full employment and some measure of prosperity. East Shropshire's ironworks were largely obsolete and investment in more modern plant was necessary. Another ironworks opened at Wombridge. Randlay blastfurnaces with later forges and rolling mills were erected in 1826. But wages were said to be fifteen per cent below other areas with more modern ironworks, and in 1831 there were strikes for higher wages. New blastfurnaces were built by the Madeley Wood Company, under the control of the Anstice family, at Blists Hill in 1832, 1840 and 1844. Three new furnaces went up at Madeley Court. In Dawley in 1831 collieries and ironworks employed 1,379 men, and supported ninety per cent of the parish's families. The Coalbrookdale Company bought the Lightmoor ironworks in 1839. By then the plant at Coalbrookdale itself was old, but the company's Lawley and Horsehay works were more modern. The Muxton Bridge pit opened in 1840 and in Donnington and Muxton during the decade there were over 400 acres of pits and tips, and annual average producton was 100,000 tons of coal and 50,000 tons of ironstone. More deep mines were opened such as Hills Lane, Meadow, Hales, Blists Hill and Shaw. The late 1830s saw some profitable times, but these were short-lived and by 1842 wage reductions brought more strikes. In the settlement of these the authorities used more restraint and tact and most strikers returned to work quite soon. In 1851 the Lilleshall Company built four blastfurnaces at Priorslee which were operated by hot rather than cold blast with consequent greater ironmaking quality and efficiency.

## Uneasy stability

There was an uneasy stability in East Shropshire in the middle years of the 19th century. Ironworks working from 1840 to 1870 were the New Yard, Ketley, The Lodge, Donnington Wood, Wombridge, Snedshill, Lawley, Priorslee, Old Park, Stirchley, Randlay, Hinkshay, Langley Field, Horsehay, Dawley Castle, Lightmoor, Coalbrookdale, Madeley Court and Blists Hill. The Lodge at Donnington Wood was famous 'the world over' for the quality of its iron — ironfounders far and wide were said to consider it essential to include some Lodge iron in the blend when they made a chilled roll.

*Where Coalbrookdale and Iron-bridge meet. Severn Row in the foreground, now demolished, was typical of the late 18th and early 19th century company housing for foundry workers. this late 19th century photograph shows the straggling housing up the hillside and the scar of limestone quarrying on Lincoln Hill, formerly Limekiln Hill.*
(Ironbridge Gorge Museum Trust)

*The Blists Hill ironworks, built in the 1840s. A photograph taken in the late 19th century.* (Ironbridge Gorge Museum Trust)

Meanwhile, more housing was built, new settlements arose, schools and institutes of learning were provided, more places of worship constructed and the railways came. The conditions under which the ordinary people lived were altered, often but not always for the better. Single-storey barrack houses were characteristic of the north part of the coalfield. Waxhill barracks, with twenty-seven dwellings, were built in 1804, and Donnington barracks of sixty-seven houses in about 1810. A T-shaped row of twenty-nine barracks went up at Snedshill in the 1820s. Earlier and haphazard housing with little provision for clean water and sanitation brought a cholera epidemic to Lincoln Hill, Madeley, in 1832.

The employers redoubled efforts to provide better housing. Rows at Hinkshay which had been begun in 1815 were substantially added to in 1833. About the same time long rows of over sixty cottages were built in Dark Lane. Canal-side cottages for workers were put up at Blists Hill in the 1830s, and housing at

Lightmoor in 1838. Horsehay terraces were dated in the 1840s. Many had no garden, so provision was made for allotments. Where possible, pigsties and brewhouses were built so as to provide two of the notable components of families' diets at the time — bacon and beer. Brick houses were built at Priorslee in 1839 and further terraces in 1857, when the village had a population of 393.

Redundant engine houses, brick kilns and even old blastfurnaces were adapted as dwellings. Eleven tenements were made out of a Wrockwardine Wood blastfurnace, and were inhabited until 1912. Former potteries at Horsehay were turned into twenty-four dwellings in 1843, and a patternmaker's shop into two cottages. In 1842 a surgeon reported that most settlements were healthier than in the past, that the poor clothing and food, and bad nursing in infancy had been rectified. Cheaper soap had helped with clothes and linen, while better ventilation in housing, cheap salt and Epsom salts, and vaccination against smallpox had all played their part.

At Horsehay in 1851 the average density per dwelling of the Old and New Rows of company housing was 5.66. Despite this evidence of overcrowding, Shropshire colliers and ironworkers were reputed to be better housed than in industry elsewhere, with dwellings grouped in dozens rather than hundreds. However, there was often no shop, and sometimes no chapel or pub. The settlements developed a reputation for being inhospitable to strangers, and especially hostile to the market towns of Wellington and Shifnal. One commentator described the Donnington Wood settlements as 'a frontier society'. The short life expectancy of the miners and industrial workers must have contributed to this atmosphere. Dangers to life and health were everywhere. If a collier survived the dust, damp and accidents, he was nevertheless asthmatic by thirty and finished by fifty. Although most ironworkers' lives were less dangerous, a puddler's work days were over by the time he was forty. Church, chapel and the companies tried to encourage thrift, but with such a life expectancy, in good times the workers spent their wages on better food, especially tea, and

The Lilleshall Company's New Yard engineering works at Wrockwardine Wood close to St George's were opened in 1861. The caption reads 'The Lilleshall Company's Great Foundry and Engine Factory, Where Steam Hammers, Locomotives, and all kinds of Steam Engines are made.'
(Shropshire CC Local Studies Library)

pleasures such as they were, particularly in the pub. The vicar of St George's said of his flock that 'money got at the hazard of their lives was spent to the ruin of their souls'.

## The public house

Certainly the public houses were everywhere. In 1847 Madeley parish contained fifty-three of them. The Golden Ball in Madeley Wood dated from 1728, the Three Furnaces at Madeley Court had the worst police record. A rough and brutal life bred equally tough recreations. Cockfighting was common in the early 19th century until about the 1830s, while bullbaiting using specially-bred bull terriers continued until the mid-1820s despite efforts by the authorities to stamp it out. On the credit side for the pubs, the growing number of friendly societies met in them, as did sporting clubs and teams. At the wakes and fairs, blood sports were gradually superseded by funfairs, sports events, horse and donkey racing, and firework displays. But by all accounts gambling and fighting between groups of men continued. Prize fighting was popular, and public executions at Shrewsbury were well-attended. Temperance societies were founded in the villages to counter the influence of the pubs. Mechanics institutes were established in Ironbridge, Wellington and Donnington, and the Coalbrookdale Literary and Scientific Institution formed, all providing the populace with books, papers and lectures.

## Schooling and child labour

The Sunday school system of minimum schooling developed into a more effective organisation which sought to educate a majority of the young. It grew alongside a continuing employment of children in the area's mines and industries. Boys over six worked at the coal seams, fewer at the ironstone bands. One man, later a leading primitive methodist, went down a pit at Donnington Wood in 1827 at the age of seven and a half. Not until 1842 was there legislation to ban women and children working underground, and only in 1910 were boys under thirteen stopped from going down mines. Girls even in 1851 began work on the ironstone banks with their mothers and elder sisters at the age of ten, separating ore from the clays and shales. A more attractive way of earning money for East Shropshire girls was to join bands going to London to pick fruit and vegetables in the market gardens. They often came back with their marriage dowries earned from their labours. This annual migration lasted until the 1870s.

Typical of the schools was a national school opened at Snedshill Coppice with 100 pupils in 1818. It had 120 pupils in 1824 and 150 by 1838, and was a free school supported by the church and by subscription, until 1860 when it was taken over by St George's Church school, where the costs were met by the Lilleshall Company. Elsewhere by the 1830s there were public day schools. Some were built by the ironmasters as at Coalbrookdale and Pool Hill, Dawley, others by church and chapel authorities. A county primary school was opened in Lilleshall parish in 1844. By 1852 each pupil paid 2d a week. A Church of England school was founded in Donnington Wood in 1847 and by 1850 had 160 mixed pupils. In Wellington in 1833 there were nine Sunday schools out of which national schools developed. In 1872 the Wellington school board was formed — the first in Shropshire — to take over most voluntary schools. Wellington College was founded in 1880, later to change its name to Wrekin College.

## The charter master system

Despite slack periods, breakdowns in equipment and fluctuations in their pay packets, few able-bodied men sought relief from the poor law societies, except in dire circumstances. A majority of miners and the less-skilled ironworkers were employed by subcontractors who operated on monthly contracts, so their income and the number of workers contracted to them went up and down. This 'charter master' organisation extended into keeping pubs and running shops. Little family 'empires' were built up under the system and an applicant for work had to have the right surname. To get a job at Donnington Wood, for instance, a man had to have one of half a dozen surnames, notably Proudler, Pidgeon or Lawrence.

There were frequent demarcation disputes between the skilled and the less skilled. Most workers did a twelve-hour shift with forty minutes for dinner and 20 minutes for lunch. Colliers were paid by the fortnight, a system which was attacked in the 1840s — it was one of the reasons for an 1842 strike — but survived into the 20th century. In the 1850s in slack times some employers, notably the Leveson-Gower interests, found alternative work on farms, timber felling, road and bridge repair, and afforestation of pit mounds for their workers.

## The railway age

In the far south of the coalfield back in the 1830s, Ironbridge was still a busy port and by 1841 had a population of about 3,000. There were numbers of potteries and porcelain works on either side of the Severn which had not suffered in the post-war depression. Many young women found skilled work as painters in the Coalport porcelain works, which imitated designs of Sèvres in France. By 1851 Coalport employed 500 people. Nevertheless, the advent of the railways saw the beginning of a long decline in employment and population in the gorge.

Already in 1837 the Grand Junction Railway passed fourteen miles away from the coalfield, but was initially little used. The Shrewsbury-Birmingham line through Oakengates opened in 1848 and was taken over by the Great Western Railway (GWR) in 1854. By 1849 most of the area's canals were fighting competition from the railways. Subsidence and water shortages added to their difficulties. The Wellington to Stafford line crossed the northern townships, and Wellington was linked to Shrewsbury. The Wellington and Severn Junction Railway put out lines to the south. A branch line was laid to Madeley and Lightmoor in 1854/55 from a junction with the GWR between Oakengates and Shifnal. Companies like the Shropshire Union Railway and Canal Company tried to combine the two methods of transportation in an economic partnership. By 1860 all the major ironworks had direct access to standard-gauge railways. In 1862 the Severn Valley line opened to Coalport and Coalbrookdale, run by the Oxford, Worcester and Wolverhampton Railway, known locally as 'Oh Worse and Worse'. In time the small companies, in many cases in direct competition with each other, were taken over by two giants, the GWR and the London and North Western Railway (LNWR). Eventually, both GWR and LNWR had branch lines serving all the major ironworks, mines and settlements.

In 1851 the estimated population of the coalfield was 50,000. There was still no recognised centre, although Oakengates had begun to rival Wellington as a market. Both towns had benefited by the arrival of the railways. Wellington was a contented English market town, and progressive. Gas had been laid on in 1823 and the town was well-lit by 1835. The Wellington Water Company was established in 1851. Between 1826 and 1850 Oakengates developed from a dozen houses and pubs surrounded by a quagmire in wet weather. By 1856 there were shops, including a bookseller and stationer, and trades such as blacksmith, cobbler, barber and watchmaker. The railway brought access to the township from the surrounding settlements. Gas and other services such as dispensaries and post offices appeared to have spread only slowly. Ironbridge had a dispensary in 1828 and a post office the next year, while gas reached it in 1839. Madeley had to wait until 1842 for a post office and Dawley until 1848 for gas-lit streets. Donnington Wood only received a post office in 1855 and gas in 1870. Outlying settlements had none of these refinements. For all except Wellington, water came from streams and wells, increasingly polluted, and there was little or no sanitation.

## Slow decline

Three new deep coal mines were developed, the Granville in 1860, the Grange in 1864 and Halesfield colliery in 1870. But in general the raw materials began to give out. The ironstone, low in ferrous oxide content, was less suitable for use in hot-blast furnaces. Only those ironworks which were able to diversify into the more sophisticated steelmaking or engineering and manufacturing were able to weather the economic storms ahead. The ironworks of C. & W. Walker established in 1837 developed a business in manufacturing stamps, presses and tools and later became famous for its gas holders and gas equipment. Wombridge made wire and wire billets after 1852, while Snedshill specialised in heavy castings and bridge girders.

The Lilleshall Company, which in 1856 still had eight furnaces and employed 5,000 people, in 1861 opened its New Yard engineering works in Wrockwardine Wood, close to Pain's Lane and St George's. Locomotives and large gas engines were made there. In 1871 the Castle Ironworks was established by Nettlefold

*The engine house and blastfurnaces of Priorslee in the 1850s, owned by the Lilleshall Company.*
(Shropshire CC Local Studies Library)

and Chamberlain based on Karl Siemens' designs. In 1878 the Great Western Nail Works began business, later making cycle and eventually motor car parts. By 1879 Lilleshall had installed basic Bessemer converters for steelmaking at Priorslee with primary rolling there and secondary rolling at Snedshill, which also possessed a plate mill. Typical of numbers of small manufacturing companies was the Eagle Company of St George's, making shovels from 1890.

In the south, Coalbrookdale also diversified further but contracted gradually back to its works in the dale. Lawley furnaces were shut down about 1864. In 1878 and 1883 respectively, Lightmoor and Dawley Castle furnaces closed. Old Park shut down in 1887. The Lodge furnaces went the next year. Horsehay was sold by Coalbrookdale to other interests which developed bridge-making activities which kept the works viable well into the next century. From 1870 onwards, the skilled men emigrated, the colliers to new deep mines in Staffordshire and the ironworkers to more prosperous iron-and-steel centres. Dawley, whose morale must have been boosted in 1875 when one of its sons, Captain Matthew Webb, became the first man to swim the English Channel, suffered a typical population loss. In 1881 there were 9,200 people and ten years later only 6,996. By 1885 iron production was a quarter of the 1869 figure of 45,000 tons and back to that at the turn of the century.

Throughout this period the clay industries continued to do well, brickfields were prosperous. Blockleys of Hadley was founded in 1894 at Bloxwich. Factories made more specialised sanitary war, pipes and drains, and the potteries and porcelain makers in the gorge did well. But the agricultural depressions that had been regular occurrences since 1860 became more acute in the 1870s and 1880s and added to the miseries of East Shropshire. There was widespread poverty, and in Malinslee and Stirchley the churches ran soup kitchens for over ten years. Despite these problems sport began to be established. Wrockwardine Wood was said to have had one of the earliest professional football clubs in the country. Wellington Town Football Club was founded in 1879. Cricket came to Hadley and Trench Lock in 1882. Dawley, Madeley and Priorslee all had teams.

*Snedshill brickworks belonging to the Lilleshall Company, taken from Greyhound Hill. Priorslee church is at the top right and St George's church at top left. Some of the brickwork's buildings still exist and have been renovated by Telford Development Corporation.*

## Fewer houses required

During the 1850s and 1860s new company housing in terraces had been constructed in several villages and townships, notably St George's, by the Lilleshall Company for their New Yard and Priorslee workers. As closures and emigration began to have their effect on population, much of the squatter housing and ill-built speculative cottages disappeared, leaving the better-constructed company terraces. After 1881, construction of new homes virtually ceased until the late 1920s. A survey in 1965 showed that only 6.5 per cent of houses in the Telford designated area were built between 1881 and 1925.

*Stone Row, a group of 1830s cottages at Malinslee, built of sandstone from the coal and iron-stone mines. The photograph was taken in 1963. The cottages were demolished to make way for Telford town centre.* (RCHM England)

## Water and sanitation

Throughout the 19th century water supplies and sanitation, except in Wellington, had left a great deal to be desired. As late as 1890 Madeley relied on water from a spring on Sutton Hill and on local wells. In Dawley during 1896 some forty per cent of the population obtained water from public wells, the rest from wells on their premises. Supplies were all liable to be contaminated. Until 1897 Ketley's water came from a spring that became progressively more polluted.

In 1892 water in Oakengates was described as 'as bad as it can be . . . scanty, inaccessible . . . contaminated or liable to be, from rainwater butts, dip bucket wells and a few mechanically-pumped wells'. The area was sewered either not at all or ineffectively. New Lilleshall Company housing had sewers but these passed into open ditches that ran through older housing before going into settling tanks. Many cesspits were open, ash and rubbish was often thrown into yards and streets.

The formation of district councils towards the end of the century had a markedly good effect on these two vital concomitants to good health. For example, Wellington Urban District Council was formed in 1874 and the Rural District Council in 1882. Madeley became a ward of the Borough of Wenlock from 1889. Dawley Urban District Council was established in 1894 while Oakengates UDC began in 1898 and covered Wombridge, Priorslee, St George's and Wrockwardine Wood. New water works and sewerage began to be supplied by the local authorities before the century ended.

But living conditions on the coalfield for many were poor, the long decline in mining and metalworking industries continued. From the Severn Gorge to the edge of the Shropshire Plain in the north, save for the clay industries and the engineering firms which still made a living for themselves and their employees, gradual dereliction proceeded, bringing with it added hardships to the settlements. The early 1900s were to see the decline accelerate.

*Left: The rebuilt Priorslee furnaces around the turn of the century, with a group of foundry workers.*

*Below: The Donnington brickworks of the Lilleshall Company with its circle of brick ovens and central chimney stack. Built in the late 19th century, the works were photographed here in the early 20th century. They have since been demolished.*

# 3 Qualifying as a New Town Site 1900 to 1963

In 1900, although the nation was at war with South Africa, there was no boom in basic metal-producing industries on the East Shropshire coalfield as there had been a century earlier. Prosperity had moved to areas better endowed with raw materials. Waxhill Barracks colliery closed, ironmaking and coal mining in Stirchley ceased. There were only three blastfurnace plants operating, at Priorslee, Madeley Court, which closed down in 1902, and Blists Hill, which lasted until 1912. The Lawley pits shut in 1901. Wombridge ironworks, which had blown out its furnaces and become a foundry, closed in 1902.

The trend begun in the 1880s for engineering and clay industries to have the most viable companies was accentuated. Although the Lilleshall Company mined 400,000 tons of coal in 1900, and installed a Siemens open-hearth steel converter at Priorslee which could take scrap in the metal charge, its New Yard engineering works was its pride, and most profitable enterprise. By then the yard boasted a dining room for employees and a cottage hospital, and close social concern for its workers. At Horsehay from 1900 to 1903 the Sentinel steam wagon was developed, a form of transport that was already being overtaken by petrol-engined cars. On the site of the Castle Iron Works at Hadley, the Castle Car Works built 701 tramcars in 1901 but shut in 1904 for lack of tramcar demand. The works reopened in 1905 making railway carriages, but closed again in 1908, and the site was bought by Sankeys who specialised in motor vehicle wheels and bodies, and chassis frames. At last the works had found the mode of transport that was to prove a world-beater. In 1906 the Crucible works had also found a niche by producing cycle and motor castings, as well as hobs and grates, steel toe-caps, rivets and nails. It employed 300 people. Other firms produced chains, gates and bedsteads. At Ketley, when the foundries shut in 1903, Nettlefolds manufactured light castings for the building industry, and rainwater 'goods'. Using furnace slag from Priorslee, a concrete works at Snedshill started in 1903 making blocks, fencing posts and slabs. The slag mounds from disused ironworks all over the area were gradually utilised as demand dictated, for agricultural fertiliser, cement and roadmaking materials. The GWR removed slag from Horsehay in 1913 for hardcore on its railway lines. Blockleys opened new brickfields in 1901 and 1902. Brickworks at Donnington Wood, opened in 1878, were by 1909 producing three to four million bricks a year.

Against the steady closure of the old, businesses attempted to diversify, to bring new industry to employ the increasing numbers of those without work. The Madeley Court ironworks site was taken over in 1912 by an electrical engineering company specialising in iron castings for the electrical industry. Numbers of small works in the Madeley/Dawley area engaged in metal finishing, pressing, welding and steel fabrication. Also in that year the Lilleshall Company opened at Priorslee its asphalt plant, using tar from the plant's coke ovens, and a plant producing benzole from coal distillation. Its New Yard works was by then producing gas engines and a big range of products with some 4,000 workers. Horsehay works was by 1913 producing gas plant, while its brickworks were still operating satisfactorily.

## Little new housing

With a falling population overall, the East Shropshire coalfield saw only small amounts of house building before the First World War. In order to house workers at the reinvigorated Hadley Castle works, some 94 houses were built by Sankeys and said to resemble those at Port Sunlight, Lever's 'ideal' workers' village in Liverpool and one of the early influences on the garden city and new towns movements. Wellington, with its agricultural market town base and its malting and brewing, timber yards, farm machinery engineering, and its brick and tile manufacturers, continued to be prosperous and built its first council housing, a block of sixteen in 1902, although no more were constructed until after the war. The town's attractions equalled those of similar small market towns. Cricket, football, bowls and athletics were well established. A swimming pool was opened in 1910. Bands, orchestral and operatic societies, arts associations, festivals and a small theatre graced the town. These activities were also being developed at Oakengates, where the first cinema opened in 1912, and indeed, the Hadley and District Orpheus male voice choir had been established as long ago as 1901.

*The market place at Wellington in the early 1900s. Lying off the coalfield, Wellington was a quiet market town with an agricultural hinterland.*

Despite these evidences of a civilised life, the industrial settlements remained largely run-down and unloved. The years of stagnation in Ironbridge prompted a visitor to describe it in 1912 as 'tiers of dirty cottages above riverside tips — a dull and squalid little town'. Until the war came to bring some relief with more employment, times were periodically very hard. *The Hadley Book* (see Bibliography) of reminiscences quoted people recalling the 'year of agony' of 1905, 'when there was no money and no one to turn to as there is now'. Billy Brown, later a puddler at the Shropshire Iron Works, describes how his father earned 19s 6d (97½p) a week at the same ironworks. His rent was 3s 6d (17½p) a week, and a typical shopping list of Mrs Brown's contained bread, ham, bacon, butter, lard, cheese, an onion, tomatoes, tea, sugar and sausages, which cost 5s (25p). They had few pleasures, adults or children. Billy recounted how bathing in the canal — presumably stagnant and polluted — was forbidden. 'Our Dad caught us in the water. He didn't say a word, just gathered up our clothes and took them home so we'd got to go home naked. Yes, and the strap was waiting for us, too, then off to bed, also, no tea.' Cliff Turnock, a miner, described how in 1910 they were paid on the tonnage they mined, some coals being much harder to win than others. Miners still had to buy their own pick, shovel and drill rods, and candles or oil lamps. There were no safety helmets or safety lamps.

*Wellington station in 1909 with the town's dignitaries awaiting the arrival of Princess Marie Louise of Schleswig-Holstein.*
(Wrekin Photo Services)

The abandoned pit mounds, quarries and derelict buildings must have provided the children of the settlements with an adventure playground of huge proportions and many hidden dangers. Councillor Iris Butler, born and bred in St George's, remembers life for a miner's family in the 1920s, and confirms this. One particularly popular pastime was sliding down the slopes on pieces of cardboard. She also recalls two evidently fatal incidents involving the dangerous aspects of the 'playground'. 'A boy blackberrying at Snedshill disappeared and was never found, while a young man also failed to return from a place with old shallow mine workings.' One mound near the Woodhouse pit did give the children a useful 'dividend'. Coals from the engine house would be dumped on it. The children would wait until they were cool and then carry them back to their own hearths. 'There was plenty of life still in those coals.' The 'wilderness', by now often overgrown with self-sown vegetation, also provided courting couples with their lovers' lanes. Further attempts at land reclamation had taken place by planting mounds with trees. By 1901 all the spoil heaps at Madeley Court had been covered with oak and birch.

The pit mounds also provided secluded places for that old coalfield pastime of fighting. Harry Baugh was born in Dark Lane and moved to Lodge Row in Malinslee, becoming a template maker at Horsehay works. He describes a dip, a natural boxing ring, among the mounds between Lawley Bank and Old Park where, so his father told him, the men of the settlements fought each other barefist, two by two on a Sunday. 'At the end of the day they would stand round in a circle on the edge of the dip and choose their opponents for next time — "I'll fight thee next Sunday" — pointing a finger across the dip.' There was apparently no ill-feeling. Fighting was a sport still often indulged in during the early years of the 20th century. According to Harry Baugh, football and cricket were later popular games — he himself played football for the Dark Lane Prims from the primitive methodist chapel congregation.

High Street showing Market Hall, Dawley.

*Dawley High Street some time in the early 1900s. The town's narrow streets were to become congested 'with a pet herd of heavy lorries', as one resident described it.* (Ironbridge Gorge Museum Trust)

Improvements in water supplies and sewerage were slow to come. Reservoirs at Dawley Bank and Lawley Bank were filled with water from Madeley in 1909. Few had piped water laid on to their homes. For the southern part of the coalfield the local authorities put sewage into streams such as the Washbrook, and so into the River Severn. Except in Wellington, conditions were little better in the northern part, although Oakengates Urban District Council opened the Trench Farm sewage works in Hortonwood in 1904–1905, and clean water supplies also improved.

*Horsehay Works became well-known for its iron bridges. Here is the lathe workshop photographed at the turn of the century.*

## The First World War

The 1914–1918 war brought relief of a sort with more employment, but took its toll of the depressed villages, heaping extra hardships of food and other shortages on communities already in difficulties. At Lilleshall's New Yard works, 183 men joined up immediately, and others were later drafted. Women were employed in their stead, and also did night shifts. Munitions were made, and a wide range of metal requirements were manufactured for the war effort, from horseshoe nails to motor vehicle parts. Walkers produced steel plates for ships. Wellington and all the mining settlements sent their men to France, Gallipoli and other theatres of war. The overwhelming majority of those joining the army went into the King's Shropshire Light Infantry. Some measure of the sacrifice and of the numbers involved can be gauged from the roll of honour for the District of the Wrekin. A total of 1,143 lost their lives, including Major Charles Yate VC, son of the vicar of Madeley. From Oakengates and Wombridge alone, fifty-two men were killed in action, twenty-six of them serving with KSLI battalions.

The homes that many of the survivors returned to were hardly 'fit for heroes' as the Lloyd George slogan went. And as the mines and works geared down for peace, many of them shed workers. Dawley UDC tried to tackle insanitary and overcrowded housing conditions, estimating in 1920 that 240 new houses were needed. Only in 1927 did major building take place, with some 390 houses built between that year and the start of the Second World War. Most were two-storey dwellings in pairs or blocks of four, built to standard government-approved designs in local brick and tile. Slum clearance took place at the same time, the inhabitants moving to the new houses. But in 1936, 106 houses in Dawley were still classified as overcrowded. In Madeley the pace of building was slow until 1933. A total of forty-four council houses were built between 1925 and 1930 at the west end of the town, with forty-six going up in Coalbrookdale to relieve congestion there. Between 1933 and the first year of the war, before a halt was called to all house building, over 200 houses were erected as areas of slums were demolished.

After its small 1902 building programme, Wellington UDC built no more council housing until 1920 to 1925 when a total of 136 were constructed. An increasing population thereafter caused over 2,000 dwellings to be built until 1963. From the 1920s private developers also built houses. In Donnington there was no council house building until the 1930s. Towards the end of the decade a total of 844 houses were begun by Wellington Rural District Council for staff at the Central Ordnance Depot, and building continued during the war. The estate was first called New Donnington and later just Donnington. Hadley and Horton received about 200 council houses between the wars. In Oakengates, the settlements of Ketley Bank, Snedshill and Priorslee were gradually drawn towards each other by council estates built at Trench, Snedshill — on the site of the old Snedshill barracks — Ketley Bank and Wombridge. Slum clearance also took place and by 1935 Oakengates UDC had built 313 houses. An estate of seventy-four houses was stopped by the war with sixteen completed.

*Oakengates in the 1920s, with the huge Charlton Mound over-shadowing its streets. The mound was removed by the International Voluntary Service for Peace in the late 1930s.*

Between the wars some progress was made in bringing gas and electricity to the settlements. For instance, Stirchley — quite a small grouping — received electricity in 1933. But piped water supplies to individual housing in many settlements had to wait until after the war. During 1935 to 1937 a sewage disposal works was built in the Washbrook valley at Coalbrookdale for the western part of Madeley. The second phase for Aqueduct and the eastern part of the town had to wait until 1961. In Dawley a sewage disposal scheme was begun in 1930 which culminated in the Castle Fields and Stirchley works in 1934. Further north, Wellington continued to use its Admaston disposal works at Dothill built in 1898, and Oakengates its Trench Farm works dating from 1905. Donnington used the Lilleshall Company's 1905 sewage works at Donnington Wood until 1939, when Donnington and Muxton were put on mains sewerage with a new works at Donnington.

## The Depression

The East Shropshire coalfield suffered particularly badly in the recession after the First World War, since its obsolescent industries again found themselves uneconomic, and the raw materials on which they had been based continued to fail. In 1920 Priorslee's coke by-product and benzole plants closed. The steel-works was struggling against imports of cheap steel and wrought iron from abroad and closed its steel converters, leaving only its steel rolling mills. Five years later the Snedshill ironworks shut down, leaving a stock of 16,000 tons of pig iron which was only disposed of finally in 1928. The Shropshire Iron Works shut in 1927 and the Trench Iron Works in 1931, making around 400 men redundant. Also in that year there was an even bigger blow. The New Yard engineering works of Lilleshall shut down with 1,000 thrown out of work. For years no capital had been put into new machinery, and its huge range of products made rationalisation difficult. Numbers of small engineering works also went to the wall, and the larger ones such as Sankeys and Walkers were forced to retrench. *The Hadley Book* recounts the story of Len Rappit, who was on the dole for so long that eventually his dole money was stopped, and officials came round to see what his circumstances were at home. 'Furniture and ornaments — any possession you'd got, you had to sell to live.' In the book *Oakengates in the Words of Oakengates People* (see Bibliography) it is recorded how a single man over the age of twenty-one was paid 15s 3d (76p) a week on the dole, and under twenty-one, 8s (40p). After six weeks out of work there was a tribunal and if further dole was refused then there was no recourse but to the parish for 'just a bare existence'. The Liverpool to London hunger march of 1929 passed through Oakengates. Meanwhile, on the transport front, the rationalis-ation of the railways in the area was effected from 1923 with the formation of the London Midland and Scottish (LMS) that took over the lines and joint running interests of the GWR and LNWR.

While the general trend was towards closure and dereliction, there were bright spots. Labour surpluses and vacant buildings attracted several firms from Birmingham and London both before and after the Second World War — during the 1930s these were mostly engineering companies. Small steel fabricators set up at Lightmoor, where clay mining and manufacture of refractory bricks, sanitary pipes and salt-glazed stoneware pipes had continued during the Depression. The Horsehay Company found its niche in producing bridges and bridge equipment, the Hadley Castle Works built up its specialisation in motor vehicle wheels and chassis. Gradually the economic situation improved for many of the coalfield's inhabitants. The greatest boost was the choice of Donnington in 1936 as the site for the Central Ordnance Depot moving from Woolwich. The depot was moved from London so as to be away from the threat of bombing in the event of war. The move was also deliberately designed to provide employment in a depressed area. Begun in 1938, it was operative in 1939 with several thousand employees, including local ex-miners and 600 civilians transferred from London in 1940.

The between-wars period also saw some changes in the ravaged landscape. Using slag, the Snedshill concrete works had expanded in the 1920s, but towards the end of the next decade most heaps had been removed. From 1928 to 1934 some of the pit mounds of Dawley's Paddock, Portley and Parish collieries were planted with conifers. Other pit mounds were levelled by unemployed men for playing fields. During the late 1930s Charlton Mound, which overshadowed Oakengates, was removed by the International Voluntary Service for Peace. The Rev. J. E. Gordon Cartlidge wrote in that decade in his book *The Vale and Gates of USC-CON* (see Bibliography) of the Oakengates area 'what trace is this present generation going to leave of its passage downstream?' It should 'secure the removal of the scars and debris of the industrial era . . . and thus restore some at least of the valley to its former usefulness and beauty'. Shropshire County Council levelled an area for a new senior school and playing fields. Volunteers made a public recreation area out of flattened pit mounds and planted trees. The Rev. Cartlidge called for a Shropshire Land Reclamation Society, but no record of its having been formed has been found. In 1936 the Lilleshall Company began filling in mineshafts — 230 in St George's, Donnington Wood and Priorslee. Since 1872 mine owners had by law to deposit plans of mines they proposed to abandon with an appropriate government department. Waste material from mounds was bulldozed into the shafts until they would hold no more. Subsidences did occur in heavily waterlogged shafts.

The difficult international situation of 1938 brought Air Raid Precautions and a host of other war preparations to the notice of East Shropshire inhabitants. Not even the discovery of the Donnington treasure in March of that year could have dispelled the anxiety of the times. The treasure consisted of 517 coins spanning the reigns from Queen Mary, 1554, to Charles I, 1648. About 300 of them were Elizabeth I coins. Opinion had it that they had been buried during the troubled Cromwellian period.

## At war again

Once more the area was on a war footing. Many joined the forces and there was a labour shortage. The remaining coal mines were worked 'flat out'. The Lilleshall Company's facilities re-rolled steel, made tank-track links, rivets, shell caps and aircraft parts. They also repaired railway wagons. The last war contract was to dismantle and segregate war equipment for scrap, with Italian prisoners-of-war drafted in to do the work. The Trench Iron Works that had closed in 1931 was reopened in 1942 by K. J. & A. Sommerfeld Ltd to make emergency runways and portable roadways, and continued after the war manufacturing building components and furniture. Walkers again made steel plates for ships, and heavy steel shields for large guns, bomb casings and mine destruction gear. The company also repaired bomb-damaged gas holders. Horeshay produced material for landing barges.

At the Central Ordnance Depot some 4,000 civilians were employed. Donnington Farm was turned into a honeymoon hotel for soldiers at COD. The depot had its 'skirt' of Nissen hut camps for army personnel, displaced persons and prisoners-of-war. One St George's man, Des Guy, played football as a youth at Donnington towards the end of the war. He has two overriding memories — the piled baked beans on toast his Oakengates team was treated to after the match, and the spotless condition of the displaced persons' camps and their cheerful atmosphere. They were Poles, Czechs and Hungarians, many of whom are still there in flats rebuilt on the camp sites, and whose children have grown up and gone into the local communities.

*Malinslee station pictured just after the Second World War. It and the railway line were to be removed in the early 1960s.*
(Ironbridge Gorge Museum Trust)

As part of the country's ARP District No 3, air-raid shelters were constructed, walls of sandbags built round gasworks and waterworks. Food committees, Dig for Victory campaigns, and a long progression of fund-raising 'weeks' such as those for Spitfires, war weapons, the Red Cross and Aid to Russia, followed. The Home Guard battalion serving the coalfield area and Wellington was the 11th Battalion of the KSLI. Enemy action was limited. Bombers on their way to Manchester and Liverpool tended to overfly rural Shropshire. On November 9, 1940 there was extensive superficial damage to buildings at Benthall Edge woods in Ironbridge from bombs dropped by a Junkers 88 bomber. In March 1941 high explosive bombs fell at High Ercall, Wellington and Donnington, doing little damage but putting the electricity supply out of action. Later in the war a stick of incendiaries fell somewhere on the site of Telford Town Centre. There were no casualties from any of these incidents. But war elsewhere took its toll of the inhabitants. A total of 317 men and women from the District of the Wrekin lost their lives in the armed forces.

## Housing shortages

As in many parts of Britain there were housing shortages in some towns and villages of East Shropshire when the war ended. Immediate panaceas were prefabricated single-storey dwellings, the famous 'prefabs'. Some of these, of concrete and aluminium, were erected in Oakengates, while Madeley had a small estate of twenty-seven. Otherwise, new housing was slow to come in the difficult post-war economic times. Slum clearance got under way in Dawley and Madeley. The 1954 Housing Act pinpointed nearly 500 houses in Dawley as still being sub-standard. Nevertheless, some 800 council houses were built in Dawley, and about the same number in Madeley from the mid-1950s until the early 1960s, when talk of a new town caused house building to be postponed until the future was clearer. While most of the houses were for local people, Dawley did provide 100 dwellings between 1958 and 1961 for Birmingham overspill families. Some 500 houses were built in the parish by private interests. The biggest local authority housing programme in Madeley took place between 1962 and 1966, with 500 houses built. Another and bigger sewage scheme became necessary and the works at Cuckoo Oak resulted. The number of houses in Dawley UDC without exclusive use of a w.c. dropped from over fifty-one per cent in 1951 to twenty-three per cent in 1961.

Further north, new housing was also added to the existing towns and villages. Donnington received 285 new council houses in the early 1950s, while the War Department created an estate for army personnel north-east of the COD. The local authorities built 676 houses at Hadley, Horton and Haybridge between 1947 and 1968, and some 374 houses and flats between 1957 and 1966 at Ketley Brook. In Oakengates during the 1950s over 250 council dwellings were built, including single-storey housing for the elderly. Considerable private housing was built in Trench and Wombridge in the 1950s and early 1960s. It was competitively priced and people moved from Wolverhampton and the Black Country, commuting to work elsewhere. The housing was said to have contributed to surface drainage problems only solved by TDC's new drainage works in the 1970s. Wellington UDC completed by 1963 its council estates which totalled over 2,000 dwellings including those from pre-war days, and virtually met its requirements.

*Dark Lane, a settlement of sixty miners' cottages, built in the second half of the 19th century, and demolished to make way for Telford town centre.*

Schools gradually developed in line with population. Shropshire CC assumed responsibility for many, although some church schools developed and maintained their pupil numbers. As a case history, Coalbrookdale Boys' School, established before 1816 by the Coalbrookdale Company, had an attendance of 126 in 1903. The county council took it over in 1916 as the Coalbrookdale Boys' County School and in 1928, reflecting the hard times, there were eighty-seven pupils. As numbers dwindled it closed in 1938 and the remaining boys went to the dale's church school. Meanwhile, Coalbrookdale County High School, begun at Dale End in 1911 for seventy-five boys and seventy-five girls, in 1965 amalgamated with the 1937 Madeley Hill Top Modern School to become the Abraham Darby Comprehensive School.

The change from all-age schools to primary and secondary schools — recommended by the Hadow Report of 1933 and required by the 1944 Education Act — was not always as swift as it might have been. Dawley only received its secondary school in 1956. However, in technical education the area had a 'first'. In 1927 the Oakengates Science and Arts Committee was succeeded by Walker Technical College, sponsored by C. C. Walker, and heralded the start of continuous technical education in East Shropshire, becoming the county centre for mining engineering.

## Some new industry

Piecemeal and uncoordinated in any larger and overall plan for the old coalfield area, the housing patterns were repeated by sporadic new and expanding industry dictated largely by an unemployed labour force and spare buildings. Madeley's small engineering works were joined by garment makers, especially of pyjamas, by a soft toy manufacturer, a firm making rubber matting from old tyres, and a maker of steel-supported staircases. In neighbouring Dawley, engineering works, dry cell battery manufacture, clothing, medical supplies, ice cream and an expanded football manufacturing company kept its inhabitants in work. Hadley Castle Works became the largest producer of vehicle wheels in Europe, and several new iron foundries started up, one on the site of Langleyfield brickworks, making manhole covers, gully gratings and cisterns in 1947, and two in Oakengates in 1952 and 1960 making grey iron and nickel castings for all trades. The Horsehay Company went from strength to strength

*An Old park coal mine photographed just after the Second World War. The piles of pit props, the simple temporary buildings and the pit mounds give the scene a 'frontier' atmosphere. Today Telford's retail park is on this site.* (Ironbridge Gorge Museum Trust)

48

specialising in heavy and travelling cranes, bridges and mining equipment. The Nettlefolds engineering works at Ketley continued in operation and joined Allied Ironfounders. Snedshill foundry found a new lease of life making pipe fittings and commercial vehicle parts. The COD, Walkers, and the various brickworks contributed to the relative prosperity of the late 1940s and 1950s. At Priorslee the Lilleshall steel interests had been briefly nationalised from 1951 to 1953, to be repurchased by the company. However, the remaining furnace was blown out in 1959, although the steel rolling mills were electrified in 1960.

So engineering and electrical goods, metal and clothing manufacturers, car industry parts manufacture, the clay industries, and a small regeneration of the old metal-forming industries kept unemployment down. Coal mining also proved profitable just after the war with five major pits in 1947, taken over by the National Coal Board in 1948, although there was only one by 1967. But despite all the gallant rearguard actions of primary industry and the beginnings of meaningful secondary industry, the area's long-term decline continued, in the face of steadily vanishing resources, a poor location with regard to major conurbations, and very inadequate transport systems. The intricate railway networks between foundries, mines, brickworks and main lines had been allowed to rot away. Since 1947 under British Rail the passenger and freight lines had shown ever-decreasing economic viability and all but the main line from London and a freight line to Buildwas power station on the south bank of the Severn were to close before the 1960s were halfway through. The road systems both within the area and to the outside world were in a very poor state.

By 1963 the East Shropshire coalfield from the rundown riverside town of Ironbridge, through the old mining areas of Madeley and Dawley, the ironworking sites in Coalbrookdale, Lightmoor and Horsehay, to Randlay, Malinslee, the sites of Old Park and other long-closed ironworks, the Dark Lane cottages, and north to Hadley and Ketley, Donnington, Wombridge and Oakengates, presented an extraordinary landscape. It was a dense pattern of settlement and industry, set amid tumbled mounds, quarries and claypits, with old buildings, long-disused canals and railway tracks, with occasional woods and fields of smallholdings and the last surviving farms. On the north-western edge of the coalfield was the traditional English market town of Wellington, doing business with its sprawling 'neighbour', but standing aloof from the old industrial area's considerable economic, social and identity problems, and its major disadvantages in terms of poor transport and inability to participate in the economic life and greater prosperity of the West Midlands of which it was a geographical part.

If the smoke and fire, the clanging of mine gear and foundry, and the pall of polluted air had largely disappeared, the blackened grimy houses and the confused broken landscapes remained. In the terms of the early 1960s, the inhabitants lacked much in the way of amenities enjoyed by others, and their 'quality of life' — difficult though that is to assess accurately — would have been considered to be far less than adequate by the standards of the time.

The old East Shropshire coalfield, after 200 years of exceptional history, was ripe for some further huge metamorphosis. It was to come, born out of the need initially of Birmingham to find homes for its people, and as part of the New Towns movement, begun in 1946 but with much older antecedents, to bring a healthy, green, pleasant and efficient urban environment to British people.

# 4 New Town Principles

The new towns set up in Britain under the 1946 New Towns Act were an integral part of post-war planning strategy of the wartime national government, and brought in by the then Labour government. The aim was to avoid piecemeal enlargement of towns and villages by building integrated towns with their own commerce, industry, shopping and recreational facilities. Not only would slums and overcrowding, and mean living conditions in polluted air, be a thing of the past, but the new towns would herald social change in which everyone could share a better quality of life in green and pleasant surroundings. There had been earlier attempts at new towns and villages, especially the two garden cities in the 20th century, but in none was the authority and finance of government deployed on such a huge scale.

Most of the earlier essays in planning were designed to relieve overcrowded, insanitary and miserable living conditions, and some to counter the sprawling unplanned and distorting growth of existing towns during the Industrial Revolution. Others were specifically meant to provide better conditions for workers and thereby a stable, happy workforce leading to greater and more efficient production. Between 1801 and 1901 the population of England, Scotland and Wales rose from 10.5 million to 37 million. Many country people moved to towns and the quality of town and city life deteriorated. It has been said that the conditions brought together unlikely allies who tried to alleviate the situation. On the one hand were those who feared the conditions would breed riots and insurrection, and on the other those appalled at the exploitation of the working class. Only a few of their schemes were ever built, most foundered because they were impractical or financially improvident.

As early as 1759 the Coalbrookdale Company began a community project with a row of back-to-back housing at a new foundry established at Newdale on the East Shropshire coalfield, but this was not developed further. Coalport was built as a 'new town' by Richard Reynolds in 1792.

Elsewhere, in 1790 a community was built round a cotton-spinning factory by Samuel Oldknow. The concept of the industrial village was used by Robert Owen for social improvement at New Lanark and other locations in Scotland. His villages held 1,200 people and were grouped in clusters, each with their own food and goods stores and a church or chapel. Garden villages within ten miles of London were planned to house an incredible 350,000, many of whom would commute to the city by the new railway lines. The scheme was put forward by an architect named Moffatt. The estimated cost was £10 million and the year was 1845. Nothing came of the project since it held nothing of interest to investors. But gardens and railway links were to be dominant factors in future plans. Another pipe-dream about this time was that of a village at the heart of 1,000 acres (450 hectares) of prime agricultural land where 300 families would make their living by crafts and an agricultural or horticultural smallholding.

In 1849 James Silk Buckingham sought private venture capital of £3 million to buy 10,000 acres (4,050 hectares) and another £1 million to fund industries for a town of 10,000 people. The town would be built on the central 1,000 acres with the industry on the periphery and green belt stretching round all sides. An association would own the freehold of the land, operate shops and services, and every householder would own shares in it. This again was never built, but some of the ideas came down to future projects. With numbers of other projects, some of which were built, Buckingham's town banned alcohol and public houses, and provided instead recreation grounds and a community club.

The most notable of these was Titus Salt's Saltaire, influenced by an earlier village scheme called Copley, built by Edward Ackroyd, who later built a second called Ackroyden. Saltaire was constructed in 1853 on a 'greenfield' site round a wool factory. Houses had three to six bedrooms and there was good drainage. Saltaire had wide streets and pleasant squares with gardens and a recreation ground, a covered market, schools and a church, an infirmary, baths and wash houses. But there were no individual gardens and no pubs. Bromborough Pool garden village had been started in the same year on Merseyside by a candle company, but it was not until thirty years later that another scheme close by at Aintree was begun by a jam manufacturer. These no doubt prompted William Hesketh Lever's Port Sunlight, a most important 'evolutionary' development since it deliberately combined social purpose with visual attraction for the first time. Round the soap factory in long terraces of houses, with adjacent land used as allotments, several architects achieved a village of charm, practicality and good living standards of 1,000 houses on 140 acres (57 hectares). In 1898 George Cadbury started building Bournville just outside Birmingham for his workers. This village also proved influential as every house had a garden, and houses were set back from the streets, with wide pavements and grass verges. Most houses had front gardens, while avenues of trees and shrubs were planted.

## Garden City

From all these schemes and from writers and artists such as William Morris, John Ruskin, Walter Crane, Henry George and Edward Bellamy, a brilliant synthesis in the form of Garden City was produced by Ebenezer Howard. He set out the concepts very simply and clearly in a book, *Tomorrow: A Peaceful Path to Real Reform*, published in 1898, which was reissued in 1902 with certain changes of emphasis as *Garden Cities of Tomorrow*. Howard wrote, 'I have taken a leaf out of the books of each type of reformer and bound them together with a thread of practicality.' Contemporary opinion of Howard suggests that he believed in the essential co-operativeness and egalitarianism of mankind, only given the right environment. His Garden City was for him that right environment where the land was publicly owned, where private enterprise flourished, and economic and social advantages were for all citizens. The book was only incidentally concerned with better housing, much more with fundamental problems of urbanism and overcrowding, of town growth without planning, and the poverty of community life. Sir Frederic Osborn, who worked closely with Howard at Letchworth and then Welwyn Garden City, wrote that Howard believed that traditional values of family life, love of countryside and human neighbourliness could be reconciled with the huge benefits promised by science, association of labour, and good organisation. Garden City was to provide the proof.

His self-contained new town was to be built in the central 1,000 acres (405 hectares) of a 6,000 acre (2,430 hectares) estate, and would have a population of 32,000, where eight-five per cent of householders would work in the town. Garden City was circular in plan with six boulevards dividing it into wedge-shaped wards. Public buildings, shops and a park were at the centre, and on the perimeter were industrial premises with a ring railway connected to the main line. With electricity as the power, there would be no pollution. The wards contained about 5,000 people with housing, schools, community centres with small shops, and were the schematic forerunners of neighbourhood units. The rest of the land was for agriculture, woodland and various community institutions. A great deal of interest was shown in his book, and the ideas appealed to many.

Ebenezer Howard next founded the Garden Cities Association in 1899, hoping to create the conditions for a real garden city to be built. By mid-1903 land had been acquired at agricultural prices at Letchworth and an operating company was formed with a share capital of £300,000. Designed initially for a population of 35,000, much along the lines laid down in Howard's book, the garden city suffered from the start from financial problems which in turn led to planning and architectural conformity difficulties. Only a few local inhabitants were friendly to the enterprise, while somewhat unusual and idealistic people were attracted by the novelty and the sociological nature of Letchworth to become its first residents. Some of these hoped they could build a community free of the evils of old cities. Letchworth was an outstanding achievement in the climate of the times against great odds. Yet it did not become well-known or appreciated before the First World War, and its garden city principles were not clearly defined from the superficially similar garden suburbs.

When the war ended, Letchworth's influence and that of the GCA, now the Garden Cities and Town Planning Association, was not enough to move government in the direction of more garden cities. This was despite the fact that the Unhealthy Areas Committee of the Ministry of Health strongly recommended the establishment of garden cities as one of the principal means of solving the problems of congested slums. Under the 1919 Housing Act, houses were mostly constructed where immediate demand was most pressing. Although built to better specifications than before, there was little town plan-ning, resulting in untidy sprawl and ribbon development. However, there were some garden suburb-type housing schemes built under the Act, which have survived quite happily to the present day.

## Welwyn Garden City

Howard, meanwhile, without faith in government to act along planned town lines, founded his second private-enterprise garden city on farmland between Hatfield and Welwyn in Hertfordshire. Learning from many of the difficulties Letchworth had encountered but bedevilled by financial problems in the post-war and depression years, the second garden city benefited from being closer to London. In its early years the difficulty of attracting industry meant that housing had to be built in advance of people to occupy them in order to act as a bait. For the latter years of the 1930s expansion took place quite rapidly, with industry and housing keeping pace with each other.

Planned with a formal town centre and residential units following contour lines and winding country roads, with many cul-de-sacs, Welwyn Garden City also drew unusual and innovative people to live in it, and a strong social and cultural family life was soon evident. Begun long before the dominance of the motor car, the garden city was deliberately of a size where people could walk or bicycle easily to their work, to school, to the town centre to shop, and be out in the countryside as quickly. The first population target was 35,000, later increased to 50,000. Although it never achieved Howard's aim of eight-five per cent of householders working in the town, the principle that family, sporting and hobby life would benefit from the lack of commuting was well-founded here. Wide verges, tree-lined avenues, small 'village' greens, formal town centre gardens, as well as the gardens of individual houses, all contributed to the firm justification of the town's name. In addition there were wild woodland areas on the periphery where garden citizens could take their exercise and ease.

The garden city's town centre amenities — it had the first major department store built outside the great cities — had difficulty keeping pace with development in providing recreation and a full range of competitive shops. This experience later pointed the way for larger new towns in order to have big enough populations to warrant full facilities. Although Welwyn Garden City was obviously not the prototype for the post-war new towns, it has often been described as the inspiration for them. Just as it had benefited from the Letchworth experiment, so Welwyn Garden City provided many object lessons for the future new towns. On its success as a community, Osborn once summed up the personal advantages of community building in the early days — 'a wider circle of friends and companions, a sense of partnership in a great enterprise with permanent results, a deepened consciousness of community, a share in another kind of culture springing from voluntary activity and personal creativeness'.

## Post-war planning

The Ministry of Town and Country Planning had been set up in 1943 and the next year the Town and Country Planning Act empowered local authorities to acquire land for planning constructively and not just zoning the various uses of land, which had been the case before. But to the advocates of garden cities and new towns — now together in the Town and Country Planning Association, formerly the GC&TPA — a great moment came when the Labour government in October 1945 appointed the New Towns Committee chaired by Lord Reith. The committee's brief was to consider the establishment, development, organisation and administration of new towns. These towns would be part of a policy of planned decentralisation from congested urban areas, and would be developed as self-contained and balanced communities for work and living. Its work culminated in the New Towns Act of 1946.

In general terms the Ministry of Town and Country Planning, after consulting local authorities, would decide the new town sites. Each new town would have a development corporation with a board of part-time paid members including a chairman and vice-chairman. A full range of professionals would lay out and develop the new town. Projects would be funded by the Treasury through national loans. The development corporations would have the power to buy land by a simplified form of compulsory purchase. In theory the price would exclude any rise in the value of the land brought about by the building of the new town. Development corporations would hold the freehold of all land save for schools and some private housing. Their powers were limited to providing housing, commercial and industrial premises, appropriate infrastructure of water, sewerage and minor roads, and some community facilities. They could where appropriate contribute to funds of local authorities and statutory undertakers of services to the new town, and the local health authority. All major plans and projects had to be submitted to government for approval. Once this was given the development corporation became in effect the planning authority. As development corporations found out, there was no formal mechanism set down for co-ordination between government departments on industrial relocation, and on major health and transport expenditure.

The legislators did not appear to be worried about the new towns' ultimate financial status. They hoped development corporations would balance their books. The New Towns Committee stated, 'Any profit after meeting interest and amortisation would go to benefit the town generally . . . but the matter would be unlikely to need a decision for some twenty years'. In the event, as the potential for new towns to yield substantial profits — increments of land values and facilities — began to manifest itself, pressure increased on development corporations to organise for a financial break-even point at a foreseeable date.

## First generation new towns

The first generation of new towns included Stevenage, Crawley, Hemel Hempstead, Harlow, Aycliffe, East Kilbride, Peterlee, Welwyn Garden City (taken over by government against the will of the private company that had created the town), Hatfield, Glenrothes, Basildon and Corby. A diversity of circumstances brought the new towns into existence. While many were designed to rehouse Londoners and Glaswegians, some such as Corby, Peterlee and Aycliffe were to provide housing for existing centres of employment, while Glenrothes was built to house coal miners at a mine which later closed. All attempted to have a substantial majority of householders also working in them.

From the start there were teething troubles. Hostility came from local authorities who objected to the non-elected nature of the development corporations' boards — they were largely appointed from local people but did not invariably include a local councillor. The intention was always to have a varied mix of housing — public housing for rent, housing association homes for rent, and private housing for both rent and sale. All were aware of the necessity to have a spread of social classes living in and interested in the new towns, which dictated the need for different types of housing. In fact the hard economic times from 1946 meant that nearly all new town housing was built for rent by the development corporations, and so housing was very much subject to central government control as to moneys available, layout, building materials and, above all, densities. Housing, built to minimum standards of space and finish, had to have central government approval.

In the first four years of the post-war new towns movement there was much disillusion about the feasibility of new towns, and some outright hostility to the mechanism for carrying them out. Development corporations were covered by the Rent Restrictions Act, repealed in 1968, which prevented the raising of rents once houses were occupied. So the corporations had to fix rents to allow for increases in maintenance. High rents resulted and there had to be rent income pools to give rebates to the low paid. Restrictions on capital investment, especially for the vital infrastructure of roads, drainage and services, and the slow and difficult process of obtaining licences and industrial development certificates were added to often unhappy relations with local authorities. As the garden cities had found, the building of the town centres with a comprehensive range of facilities had to follow the build-up of adequate populations.

*Family housing in Stevenage New Town, Hertfordshire, the first of the new towns after the New Towns Act of 1946. The terraced houses are staggered across a slope and have a good standard of landscaping.* (Commission for the New Towns)

Although they all set out with the aim of being 'complete' towns, some inevitably tended to be part housing estate or dormitory town. Ebenezer Howard's sociological precepts, bringing a new healthy and happy life to people previously living in miserable conditions were, if without the earlier paternalistic overtones, implicit in the new towns. In face of such difficulties as were encountered, this visionary element was hard to maintain. Government interest in new towns waned during the 1950s. The Conservatives believed that development of existing towns under the 1952 Town Development Act was a better and cheaper alternative. The essential low-density element of garden cities and the early new towns — giving those green, pleasant, uncluttered living and working conditions — were increasingly under fire. Critics said that towns should be compact, made up of streets, and were for people who essentially wanted to live close together. Higher density and high-rise developments, taking up fewer precious acres, began to find favour, and new town building followed suit. So in the later stages of the first generation towns and for the second generation, higher densities became normal as at Cumbernauld. A severe limitation on new town management was the level of loan charges. High interest rates and inflation later made financial planning very difficult.

*First-generation Harlow New Town. The Market Square was built by the development corporation in the late 1950s. It was an early and celebrated example of a pedestrian shopping area.*
(Commission for the New Towns)

## Commission for the New Towns

In 1959 the Conservative government set up the Commission for the New Towns. Once the development corporation had done its task of creating the new town and had been disbanded, this body was intended to hold and manage the land, housing, industrial and commercial assets, and these would be managed to the advantage of the British taxpayer. The commission would have no compulsory purchase powers and be subject to the local planning authority. It could acquire land, contribute to local amenities and services, offer mortgages, and finally, dispose of property. In later years this last function was to become paramount.

*Built in the early 1960s at Crawley New Town in Sussex were these substantial semi-detached houses.* (Commission for the New Towns)

After 1960 came a renewal of interest in new towns. Population increases were causing concern. The south-east's population was expected to increase by three-and-a-half million between 1961 and 1981, with 350,000 new houses required. Renewed efforts had to be made to draw off part of this increase to alternative growth centres. The idea implicit in new towns, that they should be centres of commerce and industry themselves, was again stated by government. The Town and Country Planning Association, as the guardian of the new town ideal, was as always to the fore in campaigning for new towns, although with strictures of its own as to how changes were being effected that altered the ideal, particularly as to housing density. The second generation new towns began with Skelmersdale in 1962, with Dawley, Runcorn, Redditch and Washington following.

The Shopping City at Runcorn New Town in Cheshire. Built in the late 1960s, it has multi-storey car parks, service at ground floor and shopping at first floor levels. (John Mills Photography Ltd)

## The Midlands situation

In the Midlands, the Birmingham conurbation's housing needs were as pressing as those further south. The primary task in the late 1950s was seen as rehousing those living in slums and congested areas. The existing slums were high density, and if there were to be improved standards a great deal of housing at lower densities elsewhere would be necessary to provide for a regional increase by 1981 of at least half a million. A journalist from Dawley, A. W. Bowdler, is credited with the idea of developing the town for an overspill population. He set out his views in an article in the *Birmingham Gazette* in February 1955, entitled 'Here's a place for overspill'. In April 1960 the Ministry of Housing and Local Government rejected Birmingham City Council's plans for the conurbation to grow on its southern boundary. The minister called for a report on Dawley and announced in November that year the possibility of a new town there. There was then an urgent need for new housing to accommodate an initial 150,000 people. The 'overspill' problem was also addressed in a housing policy memorandum published in September 1961 by the TCPA and the Midlands New Town Society. The criteria on which government policy was based were that potential new town sites would present no major problems of water supply, drainage and communications, and would not occupy first-class agricultural land.

The memorandum proposed that the overspill should go into two and possibly three new towns and that several small towns outside the conurbation should be expanded. The new towns proposed were Dawley, a second in the

Woofferton/Orleton district of the Shropshire/Herefordshire border, and a possible third at Swynnerton in Staffordshire. The first two new towns would each have 50,000 incomers and another 150,000 would go to the expanded small towns. At the same time as the memorandum was published, the Birmingham city architect, A. G. Sheppard Fidler, was making a survey of Dawley. He reported that despite site difficulties there was a good potential for Dawley as a new town. While the town certainly did not occupy good farming land, its problems of drainage and water supplies in such disturbed terrain, and its communications left much to be desired. Evidently the sociological, industrial and commercial deprivation epitomised by the derelict aspect of the Dawley environment found a sympathetic government ready, despite the huge extra costs that land reclamation would incur, to proceed with the site as a new town. The accepted principle of bearing the costs of reclamation limited the need to take in good agricultural land. In September 1962 Sir Keith Joseph, Minister of Housing and Local Government, issued a draft designation order for Dawley New Town, and this was confirmed in January 1963. Selwyn Lloyd, who was Chancellor of the Exchequer at the time, later maintained it was he who accepted the need for additional costs for the land reclamation. He remembered the area well from travelling through to his constituency, and felt the money would be well spent in the national interest.

## Support for Dawley

Shropshire County Council early supported the idea of a new town at Dawley. According to Neville Jones, chief executive from 1966 to 1987 and before that in the legal department from 1954, the county council believed it had a moral duty to help relieve Birmingham's housing problem, and the expected population explosion throughout the country. However, as far as Dawley was concerned, the worse the social problems the higher the costs in social work and education. There was no way in which the county council could fund the reclamation of the East Shropshire coalfield itself. 'Just to update the drainage systems of the area was quite beyond our resources.' In all matters of expenditure the council had to be seen to be even-handed throughout the county. While approving the new town in principle, the county council supported the National Farmers' Union and the Country Landowners Association in putting forward detailed objections to the proposed designated area so as to limit the amount of agricultural land taken. In the long term the county council saw the new town as improving Shropshire's economy.

Dawley Urban District Council also welcomed the new town. It was after all the only way government moneys in sufficient quantity could be brought into the area to give Dawley what it so conspicuously lacked. Reservations that the UDC had about the development corporation continued throughout the life of the corporation and ensured they were the best of sparring partners — each acting as a spur and goad to the other. Costs and benefits to local authorities in new towns were always a subject of debate. Since 1959 local authorities had had to buy land at market prices, reflecting value with planning permission, while development corporations often sold land to local authorities at very advantageous prices, but after 1962 government obliged them to sell land at midway between existing use and market value. Land for roads was transferred at the purchase price plus development costs.

## Private sector involvement

In the new towns movement up to 1960 the principal private sector involvement was manufacturing industry and a slow expansion of retail and service industries. With the start of the decade and better economic times, new towns became keener to attract employment and especially to diversify social class employment. Development corporations could make arrangements that enabled private capital to be used, while still providing the corporation with revenue, usually by means of 'lease and lease-back' arrangements.

The new towns up and down the country have earned their fair shares of bouquets and brickbats; some were demonstrably more successful economically and sociologically than others. Their layouts and their architecture had both critics and admirers. Many people who moved to them found their lives markedly bettered, and settled in quickly. The experience of others led to the so-called condition of 'new town blues'. Except where they had been sited to provide housing for established industry, they were all fighting to get more industry, and trying to balance jobs and housing. They were up against a somewhat unco-ordinated government support system where there was little co-operation between transport and health, the Board of Trade, and the ministries responsible for planning and new towns.

This then was the new towns situation, and the Shropshire and West Midlands scene when Dawley was designated. The Minister of Transport as early as 1962 had given an undertaking to improve communications. Dawley was founded on the hope that Birmingham would release some of its industry to go with the 50,000 'overspill' people that the new town was to accommodate.

The designated area of Dawley New Town comprised 9,168 acres (3,712 hectares) of which 3,775 acres (1,528 hectares) were derelict. It would have an ultimate population of 90,000, and had an existing population of 21,000. It was not a 'greenfield' nor a 'brownfield' site, but a 'blackfield' site, as Emyr Thomas, later general manager of Telford Development Corporation, put it. Dawley New Town ran from just south of Oakengates to a narrow strip on the south bank of the River Severn. It contained Dawley, Madeley, Ironbridge, Coalbrookdale, and the smaller mining and industrial settlements close to these centres. The A464 from Wolverhampton to Wellington crossed the northern boundary. The A442 from Bridgnorth to Wellington ran through Dawley. The B4380 ran near the southern boundary and the B4373 near the western limits. The main railway line from Wolverhampton to Wellington passed close to the northern boundary. The Severn line and three connecting links to main lines provided what some people contended then was a good rail system on which to build, but which was allowed to disappear a few years later. The remnants of primary industry were still working, there was some light engineering, clothing and other factories. It was an area in great need of redemption.

In many ways 1963, apart from the wickedly cold winter that gripped the country in 1962/63, was a difficult time to be born.

# 5 First Dawley then Telford 1963 to 1968

Sir Reginald Pearson, chairman, Dawley Development Corporation, 1963 to 1968.

Sir Reginald Pearson, the first chairman of Dawley New Town, wrote in his first annual report that 'it is confidently expected that Dawley will prove most attractive to industry and commerce'. He detailed 'satisfactory' discussions with all kinds of authorities, including Shropshire County Council, the five local councils over whose districts the designated area stretched, and the National Farmers' Union, regional hospital board, the GPO, and water, electricity and gas undertakings. The local authorities were Dawley UDC, the Madeley Ward of the Borough of Wenlock, Wellington and Shifnal RDCs and Oakengates UDC.

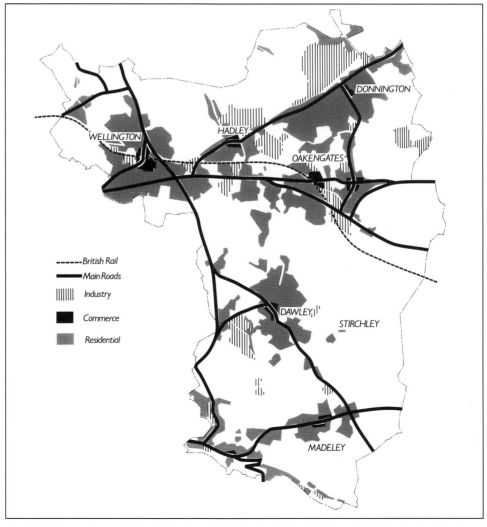

*TELFORD — GROWTH OF DEVELOPMENT 1963. Although Telford was not yet in being, here is the Telford New Town designated area showing the residential, industrial and commercial development, and the transport systems, when Dawley New Town was designated. This figure can be compared with those on pages 122 and 167 for 1980 and 1990 respectively.*

Assurances of help and co-operation came from all. Sir Reginald concluded that the development corporation was 'particularly fortunate in the ready acceptance of the new town by everyone concerned and the genuine desire that the scars of the Industrial Revolution should be properly healed'. He evidently believed in travelling hopefully.

Dawley's chairman had had a distinguished career in the motor industry, joining Vauxhall in 1919 as an apprentice and retiring as deputy chairman in 1962. He was a Black Country man from Dudley. Robert Penrhyn Owen, general manager of the development corporation, was a lawyer with considerable service in local government, latterly with Lancashire County Council. Already their chief officers had been appointed and staff in administration, planning, engineering, finance, legal and social relations were being gathered for the big task ahead. In September 1963, John D. Madin & Partners of Birmingham, had been appointed to prepare the new town's master plan. Of the total designated area of 9,168 acres (3,712 hectares) that the consultant planners had to work with, only 35 per cent or 3,209 acres (1,299 hectares) were unaffected by mining, quarrying or instability. Some 1,600 acres (684 hectares) or 17.5 per cent were already built on. The area affected by landslip, spoil heaps, shallow mining or open-cast workings was 41 per cent, or 3,758 acres (1,521 hectares). At March 31, 1964 the development corporation's land acquisition programme was barely under way. Only five acres (two hectares) had actually been bought, although 385 acres (156 hectares) were under negotiation. Three houses had been purchased and three were in course of being bought. One of these was Priorslee Hall on the northern edge of the designated area, which was bought from the Lilleshall Company for £11,510 as the corporation's headquarters.

*Robert Penrhyn Owen, general manager, Dawley Development Corporation, 1963 to 1968.*

The first fourteen months of Dawley Development Corporation's (DDC) life was full of hope, enthusiasm, and initial preparation, and perhaps a dawning realisation of the complexity and difficulty of building a new town at Dawley. In this first and calm period, forces and pressures were building up within and without the newest, the eighteenth British new town. Already, just to the north, Wellington UDC was looking at possibilities for the redevelopment of the town's centre, in distress from a poor road system and inadequate access. Oakengates had already completed a town centre development with town hall, market and shops.

*Typical pit mounds and cottages in the Old Park area of Dawley New Town, taken in 1964.*
(Wrekin Photo Services)

During 1964, Dawley Development Corporation bought land. Much of it was in small parcels — 31.5 acres (12.7 hectares) at Heath Hill, Dawley; 32.5 acres (13.1 hectares) at Park Lane, Madeley; 23.5 acres (9.5 hectares) at Cuckoo Oak, Madeley — and by October that year some 2,000 acres (810 hectares) had been purchased. About sixty farmers and smallholders were affected and were considered to be reasonably satisfied with the terms. The development corporation brought in compulsory purchase orders only as a last resort. Tenants were paid normal compensation for tenant rights and disturbance, and could be offered discretionary payments of up to two years' profits. Owner occupiers were paid the vacant possession value of their property and received only legal and removal expenses. However, if they could show that, regardless of the new town's influence, there was a demand for their land for development purposes, the appropriate value was paid by the corporation. Since there was as yet no master plan, land bought but not immediately needed was licensed for temporary agricultural occupation. Before 1964 was out Sir Reginald was able to thank the farmers for the amicable negotiations. However, the land now occupied by Sutton Hill, DDC's first residential unit, was earmarked for early use and planning went ahead before the master plan was published.

## 'Like beads on a necklace'

Early in 1965 the consultant planners, who had worked closely with the corporation's professional staff, produced their draft master plan, and this was presented to the public. This was an adaptation of Gordon Cullen's theoretical new town 'Alcan' which was planned in linear form on either side of a dual carriageway primary road designed to motorway standards. Housing and industrial estates were planned along this primary route with road junctions at optimum distances to suit convenient access and traffic safety considerations. Business, administration, education and recreation areas would be at suitable points along the route, all threaded on to the primary road 'like beads on a necklace', as Ceri Griffiths, DDC's chief architect/planner, put it. Dawley was the first new town to be planned since the Buchanan Report 'Traffic in Towns', in which was the prediction that one in three of the population would own a motor car in fifty years' time. Thus a new town should be planned with a capability to take a trebling in the volume of traffic, with a 'hierarchy' of roads comprising primary, secondary, distributor, local distributor and local estate roads.

Dawley's master plan envisaged a 'curvilinear' city, with a U-shaped urban motorway, the northern open end to be closed eventually by a proposed A5 bypass. Distributor roads would feed the primary circuit road from residential and industrial areas, where pedestrian traffic would be separated from vehicular traffic as far as possible. Pedestrians would have freedom of movement to walk in safety along pleasant walkways and greenways. Only roads with slow-moving traffic would have to be crossed by pedestrians. Flyovers, underpasses, multi-level junctions and subways would make all this possible and accommodate inevitable increases in all traffic in the years ahead. There would be nine residential units each with approximately 8,000 people, grouped in threes, and in the north of the site would be a town centre. Three major new industrial sites were planned. While an independent footpath system traversed the whole town, at the other end of the scale heavy commercial traffic had direct access to industrial sites without going near the town and district centres or residential units. A town park was planned, covering several hundred acres of open grassland, woodland and lakes, just south of the town centre. The main urban motorway would be set in parkland, and tree- and bank-fringed to limit the effect of noise and fumes.

As early as August 1964, Bill Yates, MP for Wrekin, had initiated a debate in the House of Commons for a university at Dawley. Birmingham City Council supported the idea, Wolverhampton Corporation opposed it, suggesting Shrewsbury as the site of any Shropshire university of the future. From time to time, the university issue was to surface in the history of Telford. Meanwhile, a site above Coalbrookdale of 310 acres (125.5 hectares) was set aside for a university campus.

The draft plan made clear that the best qualities of the existing settlements would be preserved and integrated into the new town structure. Although the consultants pointed out that a significant portion of the existing houses were in poor condition, they considered it important that the character of the settlements was kept. Of the approximately 7,000 dwellings in the designated area, a staggering forty per cent were then considered to have a further useful life of up to five years only. Many of these were the rows of industrial workers' cottages built by the companies, which had few if any modern conveniences, and were in a state of dilapidation. Later there were to be critics of the development corporation, who accused it of demolishing too many of these. In fact as the story of Telford unfolds the development corporation's concern to keep and refurbish the best of past buildings becomes a continuing prominent theme, and many of the demolitions were the result of slum clearance under the housing acts.

*Priorslee Hall, the headquarters of Dawley Development Corporation and later of Telford Development Corporation. The house was built in the first half of the 18th century in the English renaissance style, and had an attic storey added in Victorian times. For many years before the new town it was the headquarters of the Lilleshall Company, and it is expected to become the home of Telford and Shropshire's polytechnic.*

Dawley, Madeley and Stirchley would be the three district centres, each with two 'satellite' residential units. The district centres would have churches, schools, recreational and social facilities and a shopping precinct, while the residential units would have their own small centres including shops, primary schools, a church or church hall, public house, community centre, doctors' and dentists' surgeries, and maternity clinics. Between each group, and within the groups, and between industrial areas and the town centre would be greensward, woodland and forest, much of it made up of the most difficult-to-reclaim devastated land, which would be suitably landscaped and planted with trees and shrubs. Although some of the derelict land was unsightly with hidden mineshaft hazards and burning tips, other stretches had been well clothed by nature and there was a great variety of shapes and contrasts in vegetation. D. G. Fenter, later to be chief architect of Telford, describes many of the abandoned workings as 'full of interest and character'. DDC's concern to begin landscaping work as soon as possible resulted in the appointment of a consultant landscape architect. By the end of March 1965 the corporation owned 2,114 acres (856 hectares) and was in the process of buying a further 2,126 acres (861 hectares).

*Early in Dawley New Town's life, massive new drainage and sewerage works were undertaken. This photograph of surface water drainage at Tweedale indicates the big capacity of the network in the southern part of the town, catering then for an eventual population far greater than was finally settled on.*

## First things first

It was already plain that any development would need substantial new drainage and a new large and modern sewage installation. The most up-to-date of the nine works within the designated area was at Cuckoo Oak, and this was capable of some expansion. The other eight were obsolete, overloaded or malfunctioning.

The land drained naturally, except for the Lightmoor area, towards the Severn Gorge, and during 1965 the corporation searched for and found a suitable site of 23.5 acres (9.5 hectares) south of the river at Gitchfield, just outside the designated area. Works would be built here to cater initially for 60,000 people and eventually up to 180,000.

Drainage works, new roads to carry traffic away from the centre of Madeley, were begun, as were the preliminaries for bringing services to the sites of proposed development, notably at Tweedale for industrial purposes, and Sutton Hill for the first of the residential units. In order to have land for roads, and eventually to refurbish the centre of Madeley as a district centre under the plan, some properties had to be demolished and their inhabitants moved to other accommodation. Inevitably, there were upsets. Press reports showed the sadness of people, especially the old, having to move from homes that many of them had lived in for a lifetime. But the reports also showed the pleasure of numbers of them with their new homes, modern and labour-saving. One old lady described development corporation flats as 'like little palaces'. In what became a *cause célèbre*, the only baker then operative in Madeley, George Moore, refused to move from his shop and bakery, where his family had been bakers for sixty-two years. The land was needed for road-widening works. He stood his ground for three weeks, claiming both inadequate compensation and poor alternative premises offered. In Dawley, George Chetwood and his wife built a house with their own hands over seven years while living in a caravan alongside. Unfortunately, it was in the town park and had to be demolished. One inhabitant of a condemned cottage at Blists Hill was said to have threatened a DDC official with a shotgun.

In those early days few people in the settlements welcomed the new town unreservedly, although most accepted that change was inevitable. They saw the new town as upheaval, demoliton, mud, and the beginning of radical changes to landscape, town- and streetscapes that they had known all their lives. The younger generations to whom the greatest benefits would accrue were also lukewarm, and an opinion poll among youngsters in Madeley and Madeley Wood pointed this up. The enthusiasm, dedication and patience of the DDC staff must have been tried by all this, and by considerable sniping at the corporation from local councillors who naturally resented the fact that, despite consultations, so many of the decisions on the physical changes taking place were outside their control.

## The West Midlands Study Group report

Government had, early in 1965, formed regional economic planning councils to look at the broad strategy of regional development. In July, while the draft master plan of Dawley was being studied by the Ministry of Housing and Local Government, the West Midlands council had a study produced by the Ministry of Economic Affairs referred to it. This threw into sharp focus the needs of Wellington and the northern portion of the old East Shropshire coalfield and that area's relationship with the new town at Dawley. The study proposed a series of projects west of the Birmingham conurbation each taking 50,000 overspill population by 1981. These were in or near Worcester, Wellington/

Oakengates, and an area between Stafford and Stoke-on-Trent. The Wellington/ Oakengates expansion would not be part of Dawley New Town, but would be planned in concert with it, and effectively 'twinned'. Another recommendation significant to the eventual outcome was that of considering a centre for the region based on Shrewsbury and Dawley 'to create a new axis of national growth along the Severn Valley'. The report also emphasised the need to promote greater industrial mobility within the region, and the speeding up of roadworks required to encourage development.

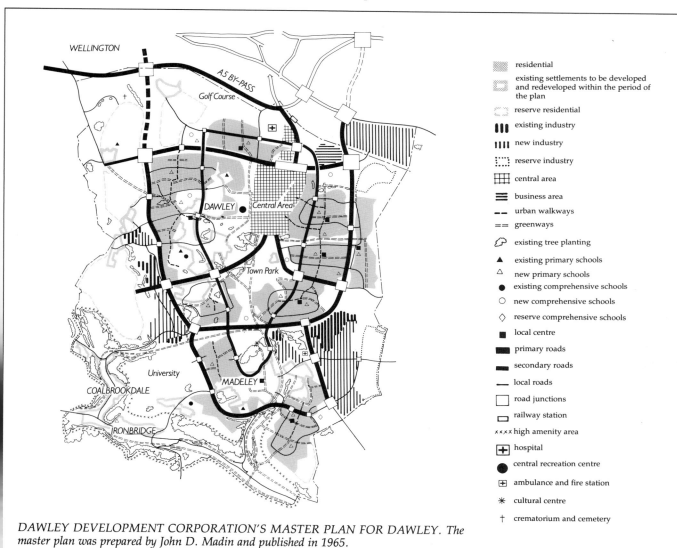

residential

existing settlements to be developed and redeveloped within the period of the plan

reserve residential

existing industry

new industry

reserve industry

central area

business area

urban walkways

greenways

existing tree planting

▲ existing primary schools

△ new primary schools

● existing comprehensive schools

○ new comprehensive schools

◇ reserve comprehensive schools

■ local centre

primary roads

secondary roads

local roads

road junctions

railway station

xxxx high amenity area

⊞ hospital

● central recreation centre

⊞ ambulance and fire station

✳ cultural centre

† crematorium and cemetery

*DAWLEY DEVELOPMENT CORPORATION'S MASTER PLAN FOR DAWLEY. The master plan was prepared by John D. Madin and published in 1965.*

Before the end of 1965 the Ministry of Housing and Local Government had commissioned the Madin group 'to study and define a possible site for an overspill town of 50,000 in the Wellington/Oakengates area', and then produce a master plan for this, combined with Dawley. Work on the Dawley plan had earlier been suspended, but the minister let DDC know that the momentum of building should be maintained during the period of considerable uncertainty as to the eventual future that the enlargement plans had produced. He asked what areas could be developed over the coming four years without prejudicing the overall 'greater' plan. The development corporation's own professional team of architects, engineers and planners therefore went ahead with Sutton Hill and Tweedale, with Halesfield and Woodside, within the scope of a continuity plan which was eventually published in April 1966, which confined development to the south of the designated area. Following the West Midlands report, the press continually referred to the 'twin-town' proposal, which Wellington supported, fearing that its own town centre rejuvenation would take second place in an enlarged single new town. The county council also had misgivings, viewing with some trepidation a combined town of 200,000 or so, which would claim county borough status.

The minister was Richard Crossman who, according to his memoirs published in 1975 (see Bibliography), had already expressed surprise at both the seeming 'opulence' of the Dawley Development Corporation's Priorslee Hall operations, and what he thought of as the somewhat open-ended commitment to a new town among the pit mounds. He wrote 'money could have been no object in (Evelyn Sharp's) mind since it will cost a fortune to turn this into a modern urban area'. Evelyn Sharp was the Permanent Secretary to the Ministry of Housing and Local Government. He went on to say, 'in time, the perspicacity behind choosing difficult rather than cheap sites may be revealed, but it is extraordinary that powerful arguments to back such a leap in faith were not marshalled for use if need be'. This is presumably a reference to the lack of commitment from the government departments responsible for public infrastructure and the direction of industry. And the local newspapers regularly carried reports of meetings, of statements by Sir Reginald and his general manager, the local MP, and local councils and councillors, in which all aired their trenchant views on the paucity of industry moving to the new town, and the total lack of any hard news on a major motorway link. The Board of Trade was still giving priority to development areas, yet a statement by Robert Mellish, minister responsible for the new towns, in August 1966 said that Birmingham and Black Country firms would have no difficulty getting industrial development certificates (IDCs) for new factories in Dawley, and he tried to allay fears that the government's economic squeeze would affect the new town.

When Dawley was designated there were no fewer than five local authorities. During 1965 the county council rationalised the situation by creating a new Dawley UDC with its boundaries the same as those of the designated area.

DDC mounted exhibitions in Birmingham and conurbation centres trying to encourage industries in need of room to expand, to move to Dawley. An earlier slogan, 'Dawley — the town of the 21st century' — was superseded by 'Dawley — for people on the move'. Local councillors criticised this, saying that the people could be 'on the move out'. They suggested first 'Dawley — for people of the future' and then second, with strong support, 'Dawley — for people on the move to better things'. The corporation continued to use its new slogan unchanged, and this was later adopted by Telford.

## Continuity plan

Meanwhile, the development corporation produced its continuity plan, showed it to the public — over 400 people attended a meeting in Madeley and 'it was quieter than a church meeting' according to one Madeley resident. In essence the small industrial estate of Tweedale and the first housing unit of Sutton Hill, together with access roads and all services, with a bypass for Madeley, were all to continue. Sewerage and drainage work for the eventual new system connecting with Gitchfield was stepped up. As the drainage work, begun in the south, advanced north, so would developments. Tweedale consisted initially of eight small 'nursery' factories. Jobs would be created if possible before the first houses at Sutton Hill were ready. As it happened, the winter of 1965/1966 was very wet, and the start-up of building work at both sites was delayed. The Tweedale site appeared to be suitable for development, but a disused and filled-in canal was later found to cross it. Fenter said, 'as perverse chance would have it, none of the site investigation trial holes had struck the line of the canal'. Earlier subsidence with the canal bed being built up to compensate caused considerable problems and extra expense for the foundations of factories and roads. The second building phase consisted of six larger factories and was later followed by purpose-built units designed to clients' requirements.

*Small factory units built by the development corporation at Twee-dale, in advance of need. They were steel-framed with 'monitor' roofs and projecting single-storey office accommodation, and became the first 'seedbed' of industrial development in the new town.*
(Pisces)

## First residential unit

Sutton Hill, to be built on agricultural land east of Madeley, was a mixed development for rented housing and houses for sale, and was planned at first for 2,039 houses. In 1965 prices there would be 133 at £6,000 to £10,000, 466 in the £4,000 range and 1,440 in the £2,000 plus range. Effort was therefore being made to attract a cross-section of income groups as residents. Density of the public housing was to be about fourteen houses to the acre (thirty-five to the hectare) with some maisonettes rising to thirty-three dwellings to the acre (eighty-two to the hectare). In fact, a total of 1,233 development corporation houses for rent were built. The golf course that now abuts the southern boundary was planned at the same time.

*Aerial photograph showing the start of construction of the first residential estate, Sutton Hill, in the centre foreground. Tweedale industrial estate is in the centre, with Madeley at left, and the Blists Hill valley.* (Aerofilms Ltd)

The local centre was sited geographically almost in the centre of the housing so that people would have a quarter to a third of a mile to walk to it for everyday simple needs. It consisted of a community centre, a pastoral centre, branch library, play centre, junior schools, public house, premises for medical and dental practices, and shopping which comprised a mini-supermarket for groceries, a chemist and a newsagent. Sites were reserved for a youth club and a public lavatory. There was parking for forty cars. This large local centre was not repeated in later schemes — these became smaller as district shopping centres at Madeley, Dawley and Stirchley were developed or redeveloped, and building began on the town centre. With an eye to the primacy of the motor car in the future, the original plan was that each dwelling would have a garage and a parking space. In the event, government controls and economies did not quite allow for this generous treatment.

Housing design in the 1960s was dominated by 'Radburn' planning, based on an original concept carried out at Radburn in New Jersey, USA. Groups of dwellings were arranged in a series of cul-de-sacs within a 'superblock' which was encircled by a main perimeter road. Pedestrian and road traffic systems were independent of each other. There were no through roads and a resident could walk everywhere without crossing a road. Sutton Hill, Woodside, and later Brookside, were all based on the Radburn principle, although modified by site restrictions, high densities, and increasingly as experience and 'feedback' from residents dictated. The more expensive houses were sited outside the superblock and next to the golf course.

Government decreed that Sutton Hill should be built as rapidly and as cheaply as possible, although the Radburn layout meant extra costs. Since the original Radburn layout had been for detached dwellings, the higher-density public housing at Sutton Hill had shorter access roads and these did not reach all houses. Garages were in terraced blocks along and at the ends of access roads, which meant that many residents had up to 150 feet (45.7 metres) to walk to their cars. In order to achieve rapid building, an industralised building process was chosen. This was a timber-framed design with external wall faces in weatherboarding, brick and tile, described at the time as 'rationalised traditional'.

*Designed by Dawley Development Corporation Architects' Department, the Sutton Hill housing is timber-framed and clad in brick, tile and timber, with sturdy timber fencing. This shows a pedestrian way threading through the housing to the shops, pub, school and play centre.* (Derek Peters)

Being on a large scale and to a repetitive layout, with mono-pitch and 'butterfly' roofs, the houses as they were being built gave an impression of monotony, and were quick to find critics, especially among Dawley councillors. One castigated the poor access to some houses, the difficult house numbering systems. Another said the houses were 'like Victorian slums with dark passages leading up to them'. However, others praised the spacious, light and airy houses set in potentially pleasant surroundings. When the excellent landscaping did eventually grow up to soften the outlines of buildings and dampen the sameness of the houses, and residents became used to the unusual layout and the habits it engendered, many householders — ten years later — were happy at Sutton Hill and sprang readily to its defence.

Much larger than Tweedale was the Halesfield industrial site to the east of the primary motorway, where development began soon after the Tweedale start. Covering a total of 460 acres (186 hectares), Halesfield included the buildings and spoil heaps of Kemberton colliery, with one big mound known locally as the Madeley Matterhorn, often on fire from combusting coal shale. Some 350 acres (142 hectares) were able to be developed for factories. The remainder was utilised for woodlands, roads and noise baffle banks. In the early stages factories were speculative small and medium units, but were soon followed by larger ones and those made-to-measure for specific clients. Many of the earlier units were built in clearings in existing low-grade woodland which was improved and managed to form an attractive landscape setting, with woodlands walks and sitting-out areas.

## Woodside

Before construction began at Sutton Hill, design work for the Woodside residential unit west of Madeley was undertaken. This was on a larger scale and originally consisted of 2,400 rented houses within a Radburn superblock, lozenge-shaped with the local centre almost in the centre. Two small general purpose 'round-the-corner' shops were planned in the eastern and western sectors of the block, so as to keep everyday needs within easy walking distance. Densities were much the same as at Sutton Hill. Again with government pressure — the national house-building programme had become a political issue — a timber-framed industrialised building system was chosen. Working on cost yardsticks which severely limited the money available, Woodside is largely of two-storey terraces with only one grouping of three- and four-storey maisonettes and flats to give a taller scale and different roof line. Some twenty houses were built with five bedrooms to accommodate large families. Again the careful planning of trees and shrubs was to give a welcome visual break to elevations and roof lines before too long. The experiences of large-scale housing — social, visual and functional — with the early housing units was to bring radical changes in later development corporation housing.

The third residential unit would in the future be the reconstituted Madeley with more traditional housing layouts to the south-west of the town, which together would make up the 8,000 people to give a complete district of 24,000 people with its work places in Madeley and at Tweedale and Halesfield. Primary schools in the residential units and secondary, later comprehensive, schools in Madeley, were planned and built by Shropshire County Council.

## The Queen visits Dawley

In these early years before decisions were taken on the Madin Report on Wellington and Oakengates, DDC and its new town projects were subject to disruption, abuse, antagonisms, mud and continuing lack of commitment by the industrial and transport powers-that-be. It slowly became obvious that Birmingham was unwilling to let any of its industry go, and if the truth were known at the time, was already considering other solutions to its housing problems. Boosting morale, Dawley received a visit from the Archbishop of Canterbury in July 1966, who dedicated a stone on the site-to-be of the Sutton Hill social centre and the Sutton Hill ecumenical centre. His visit was followed by the arrival of the Queen in February 1967, to see the first complete houses and their residents at Sutton Hill and open a factory at Tweedale.

*Dr Michael Ramsey, Archbishop of Canterbury, blessing the stone outside what was to become the pastoral centre at Sutton Hill. Taken in July 1966.*
(John Rea Studios)

The annual reports of the corporation are couched in official language which gives the facts but little of the small human dramas, the setbacks to enthusiasm for DDC staff, the difficulties encountered by the incoming families, the resentment of the original inhabitants — and their anguish, too, as familiar landmarks and a way of life were altered or disappeared. The local newspapers chronicled much of this as well as statements by local councillors and the replies by the sometimes embattled corporation chairman and general manager. The plain fact was that designing and building a new town round existing settlements was not easy. The huge engineering works of sewers, drains and roads, the beginnings of reshaping tangled landscapes, the lack of immediate amenities for the new residential units, the constant worry about not enough jobs for the new town's inhabitants all presented a situation where those living through it needed to have the pioneering spirit. Many evidently were not used to or able to be conditioned to a pioneering existence and some resented having to be pioneers at all.

*In March 1967 the Queen visited Dawley and went to Sutton Hill. She is here seen talking to Mr and Mrs Dawes, the first residents of the new estate. Sir Reginald Pearson, DDC's chairman, is at her side.*

Mindful of the need to fill the new houses and allay industry's professed fears of labour shortages at Dawley, the corporation sent out a total of 350,000 leaflets and questionnaires asking the conurbation's council house tenants and all on housing waiting lists, 'do you want to come to Dawley?' Reading the newspapers of the time, it was evident that some incomers from Birmingham found rents and rates high and facilities lacking, others said they were better off, worked well and happily with Shropshire people, and were patiently waiting for better things to come in terms of street lighting, bus services, community activities, and a calmer atmosphere.

## Ironbridge

Ironbridge presented the development corporation with a special problem. Derelict property was said by many to be a disgrace and a danger to the young. Sewerage problems were paramount — and even the Iron Bridge was in dire need of repairs to its abutments. The DDC came up with a plan to refurbish as many of the buildings and houses as possible in the riverside town and Coalbrookdale, and to turn the Severn Gorge area into a special amenity area for the new town, including a new road bridge. It would be 'no Blackpool for outsiders' residents were assured, although some voices were already talking of the tourist potential.

About this time the first call was made for a new general hospital to serve the new town, and it was included in the government's hospital plan for 1967.

During 1967 figures for the month of January showed that 900 people lived at Sutton Hill. A total of 376 houses had so far been completed, and 776 were in course of construction. But there were empty houses and some of these had been vandalised. For the year approximately 5,700 people were employed in the new town, of which 4,490 worked in thirty-two companies. Over 4,000 commuted to Wellington and Oakengates to work, while miners from the exhausted coal pits in Madeley were travelling to work at the Granville mine between St George's and Donnington, which was said to have a tremendous future and be producing 600,000 tons of coal a year. There were around 6,000 construction workers working on Dawley New Town.

*Sir Frank Price, new chairman of Dawley Development Corporation, and the first chairman of Telford Development Corporation (1968 to 1971), looking at planning proposals for the enlarged new town with John D. Madin, the planning consultant.*
(John Rea Studios)

## New chairman

In this year, despite the work already done, the then Minister of Housing and Local Government, Anthony Greenwood, castigated Dawley Development Corporation for slow progress. He appears to have ignored governmental strictures on industrial development through IDCs and a lack of any help with improving road communications. Sir Reginald Pearson resigned at the end of March 1968, having indicated for some time that he wished to do so, and the minister appointed Sir Frank Price. The new chairman was leader of the Labour group on Birmingham City Council and a former lord mayor, and would, so the minister believed, be 'very energetic' in the post.

Meanwhile, in December 1967 a draft designation order for Dawley with Wellington and Oakengates had been published, based on the Madin group's report. The press labelled it 'the triple-town' report, but it was clear that an attempt was being made to weld the huge area into one extended town. The county council asked not to be hurried for its comments. Although developments on such a scale might be expected in due course to create rateable values out of which it would ultimately recoup costs, in the meantime the county would have to provide schools and other services which were very costly. Public enquiries were held in April and May 1968. The farmers' organisations objected to the amount of agricultural land being taken, and the minister accepted a reduction of 1,872 acres (758 hectares) and confirmed the designation order in December 1968.

The Wellington/Oakengates area designated covered 10,143 acres (4,106 hectares) and added to Dawley's 9,168 acres (3,712 hectares) made a total of 19,311 acres (7,818 hectares). The existing population of the enlarged new town was about 70,000. It would take 100,000 people from the West Midlands, and with growth by natural increase the population was calcuated to rise ultimately to 220,000, with 89,000 employed, by the late 1980s. The proposals showed in essence the same principles of primary motorway, major and minor distributor roads, with residential and industrial developments still hung more or less like beads on a necklace, given the dense pattern of older settlements in the northern section of the new town. The primary road circuit would be completed close to the northern limits, while the town centre was moved slightly further north to be more centrally placed, and the town park enlarged to approximately 450 acres (182 hectares).

## Naming the enlarged new town

When it became obvious that the 'twin-town' and 'triple-town' ideas had coalesced into a 'one-town' new town embracing all the old settlements, Wellington made a play for its own name to grace the larger whole. Others put forward the name Wrekin, from the great hill which, while being outside the designated area, overlooked almost the entire town. The name would have been sufficiently neutral to have found favour had not Anthony Greenwood himself come up with the name Telford. With Shropshire and Madeley connections, Thomas Telford's name conjured up innovation and engineering — both facets of the area's proud earlier history and its hoped-for future — as well as sound planning and good organisation, which Telford Development Corporation expected to provide.

Earlier in 1968 a mixed bag of happenings serve to show how the new town was often taking two steps forward and one step back as it struggled to maintain momentum in uncertain times. In January, Dawley New Town's population actually went down by 120. A team of language specialists came to trace, identify and record the old Dawley 'broad' dialect which in fact varied from place to place in the town, serving to emphasise how disparate the settlements had been. Horsehay was pronounced 'ouse-A' and Lawley 'Louley'. Sir Frank Price exhorted Dawley to make itself attractive and asked government to help persuade a big company to come to the town. Strangely, the Lord Mayor of Birmingham in opening the Sutton Hill social centre, actually pledged that the

## THOMAS TELFORD  *1757–1834*

In a well-known play on words, the poet Robert Southey called Thomas Telford the 'Colossus of Roads', and certainly his road building benefited Britain for 200 years. But in a long and productive life he also built public buildings, canals and bridges, designed harbours, and brought to civil engineering projects an enhanced architectural quality. His connection with Shropshire began in 1784 with a commission to restore Shrewsbury Castle, and was to continue for many years with his appointment in 1787 as surveyor of public works for the county.

Born in Dumfriesshire in 1757, Telford was the son of a shepherd, who died soon after his son was born. He was brought up in poverty, and apprenticed to a stone mason at the age of fourteen. With help from well-meaning local patrons he early developed a passion for reading, and for writing poetry. In 1780 he travelled to Edinburgh to work at his trade, and there studied architectural styles and building methods, before taking the 'high road to England' in 1782. He was a mason on the construction of Somerset House in London, and by 1784 was building superintendent of the naval dockyard at Portsmouth.

In Shropshire, Telford was responsible for the design of Shrewsbury jail, and bridges at Buildwas and Montford. He built the new Madeley church, opened in 1797, and a church at Bridgnorth, and is thought to have been responsible for the design of Malinslee church which was built by another in 1805. By the mid-1790s he was already heavily engaged in canal work. The Ellesmere canal of 1795 with aqueducts over the Ceiriog and Dee rivers was followed in 1801 and 1802 by the building of the Caledonian canal in Scotland.

Harbours, roads, bridges and canals up and down the land received the benefit of his mastery of civil engineering principles and ability to put technical advances into practice. His organisation of work was exemplary. In 1820 Telford was elected president of the newly-formed Institution of Civil Engineers. By 1822 his integrated transport system of roads, canals and bridges for the Highlands was complete. His great suspension bridge across the Menai Straits was opened in 1826. He was responsible for the improvements to the London-Holyhead road which included alterations to the highway at Ketley Bank. During that decade he was engineer to the government body set up to ease unemployment — after the end of the Napoleonic Wars — through grants of financial aid to civil engineering schemes.

A dominant personality, Telford was a man of great talent, energy, and intellectual curiosity. He is depicted in contemporary accounts as very thorough in his work, well-organised, and able to infect others with his own inexhaustible fund of enthusiasm. He died in 1834 at the start of the railway era, still unconvinced of the merits of steam power on rails with a costly special track and a restricted range of movement. These views perhaps explain the relative obscurity to which he was consigned in the later 19th century. Telford believed then that the future lay with steam road carriages utilising the nation's 'common road', a belief perhaps vindicated a century after his death.

*Thomas Telford, engineer and architect, 1757 to 1834. A portrait belonging to the Ironbridge Gorge Museum Trust and attributed to a member of the circle of Samuel Lane, painted in the 1820s.*

city would give all possible assistance in getting industry to move to the town. The biggest Midlands carpet manufacturer brightened the new town's world by announcing it would build two factories. A further six other companies also said they would come.

A study of the possibilities of district heating, initially for Sutton Hill, and later for Brookside, was undertaken. To counter 'new town blues', two social workers welcomed new families and started play groups, youth centres and clubs for children and young adults. Although almost all families moving in from outside had a car, often this was taken to work by the breadwinner, leaving wives with only an as yet inadequate bus service to take them outside their own locality.

As 1968 drew to a close, Telford Development Corporation faced a veritable stewpot of problems. It had inherited DDC's sound start in providing adequate sewerage for the southern half of the designated area, together with the planning and some building of residential and industrial units. Sewerage drainage northwards for all the old settlements now drawn into the new town was in great need of major reconstruction. The town centres of Wellington and Oakengates, as well as those of Madeley and Dawley, required replanning. The new road system — Sir Frank had opened the Madeley bypass — needed to be extended as rapidly as possible. There was still no firm commitment for a motorway link with the M6. The economic situation of the country was deteriorating, Birmingham was distancing itself and it seemed that what industry was coming to Telford was from the Black Country rather than Birmingham.

One bright spot was that, after an application for the new town to be an intermediate assisted area to give an effective 'carrot' to encourage industry had been refused, the Board of Trade did acknowledge Telford's appalling employment situation. It temporarily allowed the new town to recruit industry from the whole of the West Midlands region, rather than the Birmingham conurbation only.

Sir Frank Price, the ebullient, well-connected and energetic new chairman of TDC, told the press in a typically confident and defiant mood, that whereas Dawley might have earned its sometimes evoked soubriquet of 'Dawdling Dawley', Telford would never earn such a title as 'Tottering Telford'.

---

## DAWLEY DEVELOPMENT CORPORATION 1963 to 1968

In the five years of its existence, Dawley Development Corporation spent £9.8 million on the purchase of land and buildings, and the creation of new assets. All the money used was borrowed from government at an average interest rate of 6.48 per cent. At March 31, 1968, the position was as follows:

| | |
|---|---|
| Total spent on purchase and development of land and buildings, where development had been completed | £3.0 million |
| Total spent on 4,908 acres (1,987 hectares) of land awaiting development | £2.7 million |
| Total spent on the creation of assets still to be completed | £4.1 million |
| Total | £9.8 million |

Of the £4.1 million spent on creation of assets still to be completed, £0.6 million had been expended on sewerage and sewage disposal, and £0.1 million on roads. Buildings purchased or built were:

| | Purchased | Built | Cost |
|---|---|---|---|
| Dwellings | 198 | 292 | |
| Industry in square feet (square metres) | 29,624 (2,752) | 73,950 6,870) | £0.7 million |
| Commerce in square feet (square metres) | 36,232 (3,368) | 1,601 (149) | £0.1 million |
| Admin. in square feet (square metres) | 22,000 (2,044) | 19,471 (1,809) | £0.2 million |
| | | | £3.0 million |

Major industrial employers for the Dawley workforce were: GKN Sankey, Lilleshall Company, Adamson Alliance, Allied Ironfounders, John Maddock, Ever Ready, Chilcotts, Worth Buildings, Pyjamas Ltd., Automatic Pressings, Haybridge Steel/Flatherbright Steel, Alycast Ltd., Court Works, Glynwed Foundries, COD Donnington, J. C. Hulse Ltd, C. W. Walker Ltd, Owen Organisation Foundry Ltd, Coventry Gauge & Tool Co, Blockleys Ltd, Coalmoor Refractories, Nuway Manufacturing, Russells Rubber Co, Chad Valley Co Ltd and Merrythought Ltd.

# 6 Telford Struggles to Succeed 1969 to 1973

While developments in south Telford continued, plans were laid for the first phase of the town centre, seen to be a major factor in the creation of Telford as an entity. Also vital both structurally and politically to the eventual oneness of the enlarged new town were plans for the centres of Wellington and Oakengates. These would form two of the district centres in the north. Surveys of Ketley, Hadley and Donnington were set in train. The two latter settlements, with Trench, formed a relatively modern and quite dense urban belt along the northern edge of the designated area, with the Central Ordnance Depot and Sankey's bolstering north Telford's economy. The surveys were important so that the planning outlines of the larger new town could soon be fleshed out in detail once the basic plan had received government approval.

The realisation soon came that Telford New Town and Milton Keynes, designated six months after Telford, were quite different from any British new town to date. They both covered about four times the superficial area of the others, and were aiming then for eventual populations of 220,000. So second-generation Dawley New Town with its relatively high-density new residential units, became a third-generation new town — extensive yet with considerable settlements of close living conditions which demanded that new residential areas should be lower density to give more spacious quarters for future inhabitants. Those inhabitants would not be very far in the future if Sir Frank and his board, and the new general manager, Emyr Thomas, had anything to do with it. Emyr Thomas had joined DDC in 1964 as secretary and solicitor, having been deputy town clerk of West Bromwich. He was therefore fully conversant with and involved in the day-to-day running of the 'controversial animal' that the development corporation had been called.

Relaxation of its strict control on IDCs and areas of recruitment for industry on the part of the Board of Trade (soon to be the Department of Trade and Industry), prompted TDC into another vigorous campaign. 'Come to Telford' exhibitions were mounted and leaflets distributed, which were later translated into Asian languages. Publicity among potential workers resulted in many enquiries for homes. During May 1969 there were 300 in the space of three weeks, and it was confidently expected that the dwellings in the new residential units standing empty would be occupied by the autumn. There was also what has been described as 'a surge of interest' among companies, and a number of new firms, including Eaton Yale & Towne which brought 500 jobs, relocated to Telford. And this was at a time when the country's general economic climate was deteriorating.

The establishment of the name Telford was pursued in many ways. The Telford postmark was introduced in May of that year, despite complaints from Wellington that the timing was premature. The next month the first directional road signs for main roads were erected. The Dawley Town Band that had become the Dawley New Town Band, changed its name to Telford Town Band.

Early the next year, 1970, the Telford postcode was established. Contact was made with the town of Telford in Pennsylvania, USA, which presented its namesake with a gavel. A competition was run to find a suitable name for the inhabitants of the town, and out of such possibilities as Telfordinian and Telfordonian, the name Telfordian was chosen. Wellington Town Football Club changed its name to Telford United FC, and later distinguished itself as the first Shropshire team ever to play at Wembley when it reached the finals of the FA Challenge Trophy. One little setback to the campaign to spread the name of Telford came when the latest AA handbook was published — without a mention. The local press were quick to pounce on this, with such headlines as 'Telford — the town to which no roads lead'.

TDC published the first edition of its *Telford New Town News* which went to every householder in the designated area, giving news and views, seeking to keep all Telford's citizens — reluctant, enthusiastic — informed on the trans-

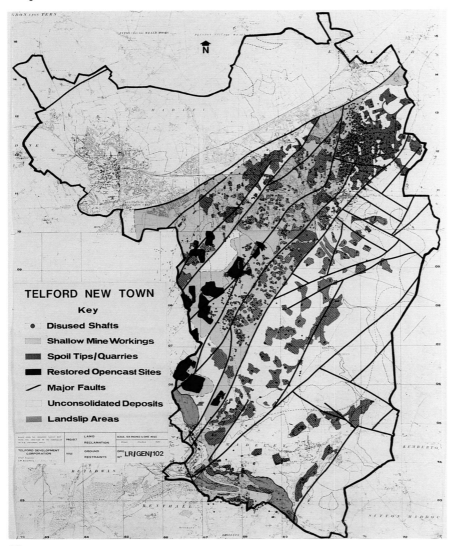

*Incorporated in this map showing the different types of derelict land that had to be tackled is the 'measles' map which Telford's engineers compiled of the many mine shafts and adits.*

TELFORD NEW TOWN

Key

• Disused Shafts

Shallow Mine Workings

Spoil Tips/Quarries

Restored Opencast Sites

Major Faults

Unconsolidated Deposits

Landslip Areas

formations that were affecting the lives of so many of them. One of these would have been the possibilities of district heating, already mooted. Unfortunately it became evident that, despite wonderful suggestions of heating a home for £30 a year mentioned by an enthusiastic press, the project could not be made viable either for a whole district or a much smaller section of housing. During the investigations the miners of Granville colliery, still going strong, made a play for their coal to be the fuel for such a heating scheme.

## Urban renewal

From the beginning, Telford Development Corporation acknowledged its strong obligation to close involvement with existing communities, to urban renewal, and the general uplifting of the whole area. Madeley town centre's first phase was completed in 1969 with the second and final phase two years later. Through traffic was taken away by the bypass and a new internal road system. The centre was pedestrianised with two squares each faced on three sides by shops, about twenty in all, including three supermarkets. Servicing was at the rear together with car parking. Refurbished buildings retained the essential character of the town built up over centuries. Also in Madeley the first and innovative education and recreation centre was built, opening in 1971. It comprised a comprehensive school and educational facilities for the general public together with recreational facilities for all. It covered fifty-six acres (twenty-three hectares) of playing fields, wooded pit mounds and open ground — almost all the complex being on reclaimed land. However, six houses had to be demolished to make way for car parking close to the buildings.

The centres of Dawley, Wellington, Oakengates and Hadley would all merit similar treatment, which in general would mean the creation of a ring road round the main shopping and commercial centre with rear access roads leading in from it, and the same progressive pedestrianisation of the main shopping streets and refurbishment of buildings and premises. There would be eight definable districts in Telford, each with approximately 24,000 people, with district centres at Madeley, Stirchley, Dawley, Wellington, Hadley, Oakengates, Donnington, and later somewhere in the Priorslee/St George's/Red Hill area. Shropshire CC unveiled plans for a comprehensive school at Stirchley as well as primary schools, and comprehensive education within two years at all the district centres in the north. As if gearing up for the new town, the Walker Technical College in Wellington planned extensions costing £0.25 million.

## Ironbridge Gorge Museum

The Severn Gorge presented the development corporation with its most obvious immediate urban renewal cause. In January 1969 TDC helped financially with the renovation of the shopping centre, the first of a long line of Ironbridge and Coalbrookdale works so financed. Derelict houses were cleared, grass sown and trees planted. The Ironbridge Gorge Museum Trust had been established with TDC backing in 1967. The trust had been formed for the purpose of securing 'the preservation, restoration, improvement, enhancement and maintenance of features and objects of historical, domestic and industrial interest'. An appeal for £1 million was now made, and Blists Hill Open Air Museum was begun on the site of collieries, brickworks and blastfurnaces formerly belonging to the Madeley Wood Company. The museum and TDC unearthed the Coalport inclined plane and winding house, and dug out a section of the canal. At Coalbrookdale the trust accepted a lease of Abraham Darby's old furnace and a museum of ironfounding established by Allied Ironfounders in 1959.

## Reclamation of the blighted land

Slowly the huge task of land reclamation was tackled. Within the Telford designated area there was a total of 5,230 acres (2,117 hectares) of derelict land. Of this 2,821 acres (1,142 hectares) were covered by spoil and waste products created largely by the two to three tons of waste per ton of coal mined, and ten tons of waste for every ton of ironstone. In general the spoil from shallow mining had been spread out in a blanket from ten to twenty feet thick (three to six metres). The deeper the mining the bigger the tips which covered from five to fifty acres (two to twenty hectares) and rose up to fifty feet (fifteen metres) in height. There were 2,957 known abandoned mineshafts or adits, and an unknown number of unrecorded shafts. A total of 833 acres (337 hectares) of disused quarries and opencast mines, 121 miles of abandoned canals, railways and mineral tramways, 3,733 acres (1,511 hectares) affected by abandoned underground shallow workings and many acres where subsidence had caused problems. Ruined and abandoned buildings, depressions, cavities, steep and sheer slopes, rock debris and flooding were problems that had to be tackled. Some of the earlier attempts at filling shafts had caused further damage and disfigurement.

*The major task of land reclamation was soon under way. Of 5,230 acres (2,117 hectares) of derelict land in Telford, some 2,821 acres (1,142 hectares) were covered by spoil and waste products.*

The spoil was often unconsolidated and of low bearing capacity unsuitable for building without treatment. There were toxic elements, and noxious gases provoking a fire risk. In other mounds were the remains of blast furnace slag not taken in earlier times, boiler and furnace ash, foundry moulding sands, ceramic shards from brick, tile, pottery and refractory fields, and domestic refuse.

Where earlier attempts at planting pit mounds had been successful and where natural regeneration had taken place with trees, shrubs and heather, the decision was made to incorporate these areas as landscape, amenity and open space. Usually only minor works were required to ensure that they were safe. Otherwise measures necessary before reuse was possible — depending on the land use envisaged — included scrub clearance, demolition of derelict buildings, recovery of reusable topsoil, drainage of waterlogged areas and removal of toxic materials. Areas were remodelled to improve topography, filled, compacted for better bearing capacity, and steep slopes stabilised. New land drainage was necessary, bearing in mind the huge overall new surface drainage schemes for both sides of the watershed in the designated area. Selective resoiling was followed by fertilisation and cultivation, grass seeding, tree and shrub planting.

*Capping a mine shaft. Over 3,000 had to be made safe. Where development was to take place, the shafts were injected with a mixture including cement before being capped with reinforced concrete.*
(John Rea Studios)

Only in 1911 were owners required by law to take safety measures when abandoning a mine or shaft. Most were 'made safe' by a timber or metal platform often only a few feet down and filled in or by building up the shaft wall ten to fifteen feet (three to four-and-a-half metres) above ground level, domed and topped with turf or spoil. Adits were usually walled up at the entrance. Many shafts before 1911 had been used as wells, cesspits, soakaways, filled with domestic and industrial refuse and effluent. Many were flooded or had caved in, leaving big craters, and there were numerous gas emissions. Some shafts had been filled in by landowners, others by local authorities and the National Coal Board. Many partially-treated shafts had disappeared under tipping and vegetation.

From the start problems were systematically assessed, then work undertaken to fit in with the gradual development of sewerage, roads, industry, schools and housing. Under the basic plan some 3,000 of the total acreage (1,214 hectares) were to be reclaimed for various uses depending on high or low ground-bearing capacity. Every effort was made to maximise the use of less badly affected areas for construction. Later a good deal of major land reclamation was undertaken by Telford Development Corporation in co-operation with the National Coal Board, both in reclaiming coal from tips, consolidating and landscaping at the same time, and in opencast mining where the land was returned to good agricultural grades.

Laurie Buckthorp came to Dawley Development Corporation in 1963 as chief engineer. He recounts how by patient reconnaissance and perusal of records, the famous 'measles' map was compiled, showing every known shaft and adit. 'Where development was to take place shafts were fully treated,' he recalls. Excavation and probe drilling preceded injection of pulverised fuel ash (flyash from power stations), sand and pea gravel, and cement grout. When properly compacted the shaft was then capped or plugged with concrete, and surrounded by permanent security fencing. The old canals and railways presented simpler problems. Some canal stretches had been filled in, others were open stagnant water or had broken banks causing bog and marshland. Disused railway embankments, cuttings, derelict bridges, tunnels, basins, wharfs, reservoirs, goods yards, engine sheds, signal boxes and stations all had to be dealt with and reintegrated into the new infrastructure. For instance, some of the sewage pipelines were laid along old railway tracks. Other old transport lines were incorporated into footpath routes. Several industrial buildings, notably the chimney of the Randlay brickworks now in the town park, were retained as reminders of Telford's grand past.

Laurie Buckthorp emphasised how the derelict land's reclamation requirements dictated where the sewerage and drainage lines were placed, which in turn influenced the search for easily developable land initially, and how the composite team of planners, engineers and landscapers was so important to the overall reclamation work at Telford. A twelve-acre (4.9 hectares) nursery was set up at Stirchley to produce annually 6,000 trees, up to 70,000 shrubs, and 120,000 ground cover plants, and was expected to be in full production by the planting season of 1976/1977. It replaced a small nursery garden at The Hem, near Halesfield.

The Gitchfield sewage works was in operation by 1970, serving Madeley, Dawley and the new housing developments at Stirchley. Drainage to the north

84

was the next urgent job to be tackled. This was to the Strine brook and there were severe gradient problems in the flat land in the extreme north of the designated area. Extensive balancing pools to reduce flows and an open drainage channel were planned. Large sewage works at Rushmoor were to serve eventually the whole of north Telford's enlarged population, but initially 45,000 people. Wellington UDC and RDC were asked to contribute £1 million to the costs, and a completion date of 1974 was set.

*TDC engineers inspecting the Coalport Sewage Purification Works at Gitchfield. These were in operation by 1970, serving Madeley, Dawley and the new developments in south Telford.*

## Plans for Telford town centre

The development corporation was always mindful of the need to pull the still separate settlements within Telford closer to an overall 'town' identity, and appreciated the central role of attractive shopping facilities. But first 186 acres (75 hectares) of mine wastes, shafts, old brickworks, mineral tracks and low-lying waterlogged and often flooded land had to be reclaimed. The hamlet of Dark Lane had to be demolished and its inhabitants housed elsewhere. As it was, the children of the hamlet walked two miles each way to school at Langley, near Dawley. Sir Frank Price promised the residents better housing not too far away, and tried to house them as a community. The first twelve families were moved to Oakengates. Their fate prompted the inhabitants of Old Park, on land planned for a later town centre phase, to wonder about their future. They recalled the days when their school had sixty children, when the chapel was full of worshippers, and when there were viable village shops, and prosperity — at least from time to time.

Phase one plans were for 268,750 square feet (24,967 square metres) of retail shopping space, including a 100,200 square feet (9,309 square metres) hypermarket, a supermarket of 55,000 square feet (5,108 square metres) and twenty-three shop units. There would be parking for 1,400 cars — no multi-storey car parks but parking on the flat. Chambers of commerce in Dawley, Oakengates and Wellington were immediately fearful that the town centre would threaten the livelihoods of traders in their centres. They asked TDC to keep the interests of the three towns closely in mind.

Students from a Brighton college on a research project concluded that the new town still lacked community spirit. They listed the reasons as the difficulty of mixing happily on the new housing estates, a lack of facilities, especially for the young, and poor transport. A year later in 1971 incidents of vandalism were reported in Sutton Hill when street lights, trees, windows and telephone kiosks were damaged. The Blists Hill adventure park and two play centres were also vandalised. TDC's chairman was prompt in deploring 'the stupidity and menace' of vandalism. In fact it was obvious that some families transferred from secure and known backgrounds into the pioneer conditions of Telford suffered from disorientation. More social workers were assigned to aid the newcomers in settling in. As if to show that Telford youth could be beneficially occupied, TDC's float at the Lord Mayor's Show in Birmingham that year had as its theme 'youth', depicting for 300,000 spectators Telford as the 'young-at-heart' town. The float was a discotheque on wheels, with music supplied by a four-strong Telford group called The Biancos, with sixteen girls dancing non-stop.

## Birmingham's change of heart

Back in March 1970 had come the first intimation that government might allow Birmingham to build homes in the conurbation, and permission was given for 11,000 houses just over the city boundary in north Worcestershire. The next year this was followed by the West Midlands Planning Council's plan to expand on a Lichfield/Tamworth/Burton and Redditch/Worcestershire axis — north-east to south-west. This was not the axis on which Telford lay, and a precarious future for the town was forecast if the plan went ahead. The council also indicated there were signs that earlier population projections were proving too high.

*Emyr Thomas, general manager, Telford Development Corporation, 1969 to 1980.*

86

Birmingham was among other large cities to call on government to reverse the national policy of dispersal from conurbations, to cease financing new towns, and to use the money to aid big cities in urban renewal.

All this took place in gradually worsening economic conditions for the country. In Telford the temporary relaxation of IDC constraints had brought some new firms to Halesfield and Tweedale — by now there were fifty-three firms employing 2,200 and occupying 1,170,000 square feet (108,693 square metres) of space — but the older metal-forming industries such as Sankey's and Lilleshall were still in decline and shedding jobs, as were some smaller manufacturers in Wellington.

However, when Sir Frank Price resigned after three years as chairman, he expressed confidence that the town was now set for a period of expansion in housing, industry and commerce, the basic plan had been approved, and better communications promised. Sir Frank regarded his achievements as a greater understanding with local authorities, with liaison committees and councillors as TDC board members, the reappraisal of the IDC approach to Telford, and the first phase of the town centre begun. He believed that he had given TDC 'a more businesslike approach'. He told the press it had been 'a rumbustuous three years' and he had enjoyed it all. There were many expressions of regret from all sides that he was leaving so soon.

*The start of Telford town centre. Phase 1 under construction, with the basement under the main shopping centre in the foreground and the superstructure of the hypermarket in the distance.*
(John Rea Studios)

## Change of chairman

John Dugdale, TDC's new chairman, came from a different background to his predecessor. He was a farmer just across the Severn from the southern boundary of Telford, with London property interests, and educated at Eton and Oxford. He was a county councillor. He pressed immediately for an early start to the M54 motorway link, already approved by government after a public enquiry. In an interview with the *Birmingham Post* he said that he was looking forward to and working towards the time when people would say with pride 'I come from Telford'. He took over not only when the basic plan was complete and approved, but Madeley district centre was almost built, and plans for the centres of Dawley, Oakengates and Wellington were made. The Mayfield development at Madeley of fifty-three houses won an award for good design. They were for those displaced by the redevelopment of Madeley town centre. House building at Brookside was proceeding with 372 completed and 428 in course of construction, and there were plans for housing at Hollinswood in close support to Telford town centre. There would be town houses, three- and four-storey blocks of flats, and a high proportion of old peoples' dwellings.

*John Dugdale, chairman, Telford Development Corporation, 1971 to 1975.*

*The Woodside residential unit from the air, showing the typical Radburn layout of a 'superblock' encircled by a perimeter road, and dwellings arranged in a series of cul-de-sacs so that pedestrian and vehicle road systems are independent of each other.* (Aerofilms Ltd)

The early Brookside housing still followed the Radburn principles of Sutton Hill and Woodside. But the thinking of TDC's architects was moving to more traditional forms of layout with lower density housing. The north side of Brookside was being planned with curved roads and narrow carriageways so that the speed of vehicles within the housing layouts was no more than fifteen miles per hour. Pedestrian and vehicular traffic could therefore co-exist, although the interests of the pedestrian were dominant. Stirchley and Randlay were to develop these layouts further. TDC policy was being developed to build not only public housing for rent but also for sale, and already the standards of public housing were being raised as far as funds allowed with the idea of eventual sale in mind. The eastern primary road, built to motorway standards, was opened, and this led to a start on site preparation and servicing of the Stafford Park industrial area to the east of the new town centre.

*HOUSING STUDY — Briarwood, Brookside.*
*TDC housing for rent, 1968/69. Designed by the development corporation's Architects' Department. Part of the first phase of Brookside, moving away from the Radburn layout of Sutton Hill and Woodside, with an experimental layout allowing slow traffic and pedestrians on the same roads. Total site 33.38 acres (13.5 hectares), 471 dwellings, fourteen to the acre (thirty-five to the hectare), 716 car spaces, 303 garages. There are five house types of two, three and four bedrooms.*

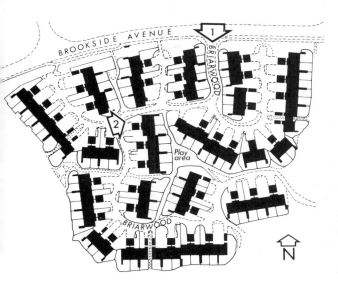

In mid-1971 the *Birmingham Post* detailed the excellent facilities now available at the heart of the 8,000-inhabitant units at Telford and praised TDC for its welcome to incoming families. By now it was obvious that Sutton Hill and Woodside were staging posts for many families, searching for more permanent 'up-market' housing in the new town. Towards the end of the year residents in the two units and in Madeley were offered the chance to buy their own homes.

A story published in the *Daily Express* perhaps indicated that the initial antagonisms between incomers and older inhabitants were beginning to lessen with time. A young wife with a six-month-old daughter lost her husband in a road accident on the day he got a job in Telford which would have qualified him for a house. He left her virtually penniless. The development corporation bent the rules and gave her a rented house. Neighbours furnished it for her. The young widow said, 'they even bought me food to stock the larder. And I've so much bed linen I don't know where to store it.' The newspaper concluded that Telford was 'a town with a heart of gold'. However, TDC's proposal for a permanent gypsy site in Oakengates was turned down by the local authority and thus began a long battle to find a suitable site.

## Landscape structure plan

During the winter of 1971/1972 the landscaping round the first two housing estates was augmented by the planting of thousands of trees and shrubs. Overall and mostly in south Telford some 42,000 trees and 65,000 shrubs went in. The anticipation was that TDC would work up to a million plants a year. To plan the years ahead of landscape work, the development corporation produced a landscape structure plan which truly laid the foundations for the 'town in a forest' that Telford was to become. TDC instigated regular surveys on housing and employment to check that they were in step with one another. In February 1972 there were 36,000 employed, including 17,000 in manufacturing industry, 18,000 in service industries and the remainder in agriculture and in mining — there was still the Granville mine operating. There were some 1,200 coloured immigrant families, of which twelve were Ugandan Asians housed by TDC and Dawley UDC. The current building rate was 1,000 houses a year, and this despite the recession from which the West Midlands was now suffering. TDC's policy of building standard factories for rent appeared to have paid off, with the smaller companies able to weather the economic storms and keep employment up. However, there were still empty houses, and efforts were made yet again to bring some kind of government aid to the town.

At the Lord Mayor of Birmingham's Show in May 1972, the theme of Telford's float was on homes to rent and buy. Two giant keys decorated it, with the slogan 'Telford — The Key to a Bright Future'. Free bus tours, first for outsiders and later for Telfordians, were laid on to show them the progress being made on all fronts in the new town. A mobile exhibitions trailer was sent out into the West Midlands in a campaign to sell the town as a place in which industry could expand and thrive. About this time, with the prospect that the temporary lifting of the strict IDC regulations might have come to an end, the idea of trying to recruit firms from abroad was first mooted. The first talk of possible changes in district council boundaries was also heard, and agitation for a larger 'Telford' local authority was begun.

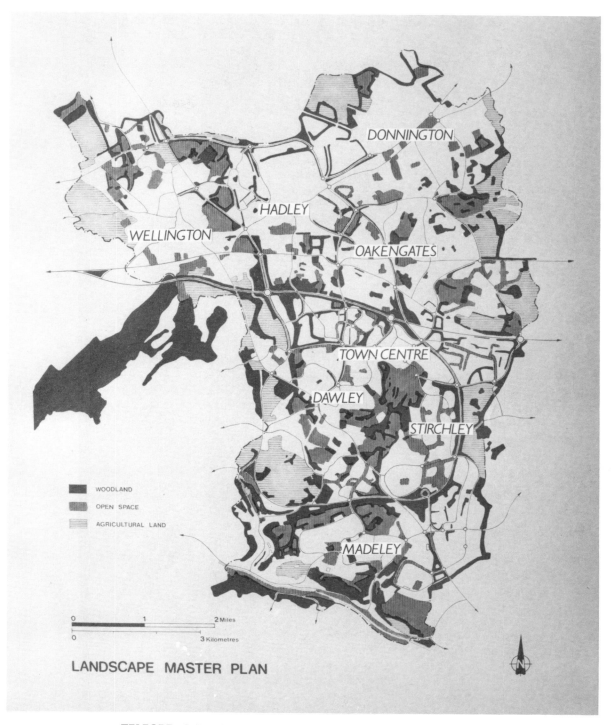

WOODLAND

OPEN SPACE

AGRICULTURAL LAND

LANDSCAPE MASTER PLAN

*TELFORD LANDSCAPE MASTER PLAN. This innovative concept married the built environment and the landscaping firmly together and began the long process of creating 'a town in a forest'.*

*An aerial view looking north, showing the town park before restoration, with tipping still in progress. A part of Dawley is to the left, with Malinslee beyond. The Ever Ready factory is at the right, and is still on the edge of the town park.* (Aerofilms Ltd)

Work started on the Wellington bypass of the A5, which the Telford optimists called the first phase of the M54. But there was no firm commitment as yet that the full 17½ miles to the M6 would be built. Indeed, there was considerable opposition to it from vested interests in the West Midlands. A Dawley bypass was proposed which would eventually become part of the Dawley/Donnington distributor road. The first families moved into Brookside in June 1972. By then Sutton Hill and Woodside were largely complete, with the new housing at Madeley being built to bring the town up to its approximate 8,000 inhabitants. The building preliminaries at Stirchley were under way — the rural inhabitants about to be invaded were happy to note that the village centre was to remain largely untouched. The Hollinswood plans were maturing as were those for housing in north-west Dawley and at Malinslee. TDC decided to restore the medieval and Elizabethan Madeley Court, once the home of Abraham Darby I, and now fallen into disrepair.

It was now the turn of Old Park, whose residents had waited sadly for the inevitable upheaval with the reclamation of the pit mounds round them and preparation for the next phase in the town centre building. Many of the villagers were rehoused together in St George's. Mrs Ethel Perrin, aged 84, who had lived at Old Park all her life, moved with her son and daughter-in-law to Ketley Bank. She took not only her possessions but the rose bushes from her garden. There was a hiccup in the application for a compulsory purchase order for 128 acres (52 hectares) at Old Park. It was turned down at first because the papers did not state precisely what each area of land would be used for and where the roads would run. Land shaping and planting of trees and shrubs began in the northern part of the town park, whose 450 acres (182 hectares) came right into the heart of the town centre.

## Tenth anniversary

The tenth anniversary of the town took place in January 1973. Sir Reginald Pearson, Sir Frank Price and John Dugdale — the three chairmen — cut the birthday cake. There was much to celebrate even if this new town had been spurned by government and the great city of Birmingham who had together, as it were, called it into being. There were better homes for those without homes, and in gradually greening surroundings. There were jobs and a trickle of new companies came because of the improving conditions. Faith in Telford that had wavered with Birmingham's defection and lack of whole-hearted government support, was still strong enough, as was the enthusiasm of the men and women who were creating it. TDC had built 4,233 houses, had another 854 being built with 554 planned. Fifty miles of road had been built with seven more under construction, and twenty-five miles of trunk sewers laid. A total of 1.5 million square feet (139,330 square metres) of factory space had been built. A total of 280 acres (113 hectares) had been reclaimed, the first phase of the town centre was well under way. TDC had spent £55 million. The town's population stood at about 87,000, an increase of 14,000. A leader in the *Shropshire Star* said, 'an upturn in the economy would now give Telford that little nudge needed to make it a success'. The *Telford Journal*, a little more fulsomely, commented, '10 years on one can hear the heart of Telford beating stronger'. The paper called on all Telfordians to make the new town work.

Certainly Shropshire County Council had played its own big part in the first ten years. Plans were now well ahead for schools to serve the residential units in Stirchley district, and another combined educational and recreational centre, as at Madeley, was planned. TDC's relations with the still fragmented local authorities were good and not so good. The gladiatorial confrontations which continued did at least keep everyone trying to do the best they could in complex and difficult situations in housing, jobs and communications, and with many sociological growing pains.

*The tenth anniversary of the new town in 1973. The three chairmen of the development corporation cut the birthday cake. The current chairman, John Dugdale, was flanked by Sir Reginald Pearson, left, and Sir Frank Price.*

In March 1973 TDC acted to help the financially-pressed Telford United FC. It bought the club's Buck's Head ground in Wellington and leased it back at a nominal rent. A viable Telford football club, even if not in the First Division, was an important part of the development corporation's strategy to bring the new town's name to a wider public. On a far bigger scale it had high hopes of the new large district council due to be established in 1974 under the government's wide-ranging realignment and reorganisation of local authorities. In the event, although four of the five councils involved in the merger voted for the new district to be Telford District Council, the Wellington UDC was implacably opposed and the compromise name of Wrekin was eventually accepted. Isaiah Jones, deputy chairman of TDC and long-time member and sometime chairman of Wellington RDC, spoke out. He was from a mining family long established at The Rock and an early convert to the worth of the new town. He pleaded in vain for Telford.

Despite deepening economic depression during the year, Telford's growth was reasonably maintained. Halesfield and Stafford Park industrial areas expanded. A major industrial area at Hadley Park was planned as were two small service industry areas at Heath Hill in Dawley and at Trench Lock. A 'Home and Jobs' campaign was launched to try and secure more skilled labour. Landscaping continued with over 70,000 trees, 66,000 whips, 122,000 shrubs and 1.25 million bulbs planted. The many bulbs already in the ground had produced that spring 'carpets of crocus and daffodil' which drew much favourable comment from the public. The planting programmes year by year were to build up Telford's reputation for floral magnificence that were later to culminate in national and international accolades. But in 1973 a 'Come to Britain' award was made to the Ironbridge Gorge Museum Trust. The exceptional qualities of Ironbridge and Coalbrookdale were, with TDC support, already becoming apparent and drawing increasing numbers of visitors.

In October the first phase of Telford town centre was opened for trading. The general manager, Emyr Thomas, said it would 'provide a visual and social focus to the town'. It began to remedy a crucial convenience shopping deficiency in a central location where people from different parts of the extended town could meet. 'And people did bump into each other', he says.

*Halesfield industrial unit showing a typical range of standard factories built by TDC with offices on the ground floor. The factories are of steel portal-frame construction with glazed gables for maximum light into working areas.*

As the year drew to a close, the *Shropshire Star*'s hope of an upturn in the economy was not fulfilled and there was every sign of a severe recession coming. Uncertainty over Birmingham's plans under the 1971 scheme was still worrying the development corporation and all who had thrown in their lot with the new town. Despite all the efforts to get the name of Telford well-known and used — many subscribers now had six-figure Telford telephone numbers — this sad little story came from London. A woman wishing to travel to Telford approached the ticket office at Euston station. 'Never heard of the place,' said the booking clerk, who should have known that he had to direct her to Oakengates or Wellington. He suggested she went to Charing Cross to pursue her enquiries there.

## TELFORD DEVELOPMENT CORPORATION 1969 to 1973

By the end of the period covered by Chapter 6, the town's statistics were:

| | |
|---|---|
| Population | 87,100 |
| Dwellings | 29,546 |
| Average number of persons per dwelling | 2.95 |
| Houses built during period | 4,767 |
| Total employment | 39,850 |
| Manufacturing | 20,210 |
| Services | 15,086 |
| Other | 4,554 |
| Residents economically active | 40,240 |
| Number living and working in Telford | 32,050 |
| Percentage of economically active living and working in Telford | 80 |
| Percentage unemployed | 3.4 |

By March 31, 1973 Telford Development Corporation had borrowed £55.6 million from government at an average rate of 8.36 per cent. From this sum £49.7 million had been spent on assets, £4.8 million to finance revenue deficits, with the remainder being used as working capital. The position was:

| | |
|---|---|
| Total spent on purchase and development of land and buildings, where development had been completed | £26.5 million |
| Total spent on 6,821 acres (2,761.5 hectares) of land awaiting development | £5.1 million |
| Total spent on the creation of assets still to be completed | £6.2 million |
| | £37.8 million |
| Construction of roads | £2.7 million |
| Construction of sewers and sewage disposal works | £7.3 million |
| Derelict land reclamation | £0.8 million |
| Landscaping of public open space | £0.4 million |
| Contributions to water authority and local authority for provision of water and sewerage | £0.6 million |
| Loans | £0.1 million |
| | £11.9 million |
| Grand total | £49.7 million |

Buildings purchased or built were:

| | Purchased | Built | Cost |
|---|---|---|---|
| Dwellings | 220 | 4,767 | £19.9 million |
| Industry in square feet (square metres) | 203,000 (18,859) | 1,063,000 (98,753) | £4.7 million |
| Commerce in square feet (square metres) | 43,000 (3,995) | 87,000 (8,082) | £1.1 million |
| Other | | | £0.8 million |
| | | | £26.5 million |

Major companies coming to Telford during the period were: Fulton TI – Bundy, steel tubing, Lang Pneumatic, pneumatic control systems, Eaton Yale & Towne, forklift trucks, Joseph Lucas, electrical lighting/wiring, Link 51, boltless racking systems, Brintons, carpets, Telford Foods, food packaging, Merlin Gerin UK, electrical components, Arnhem Engineering, brake pads, George Hill, fencing, AMF Venner, central heating controls. Also IHW Engineering, vehicle door systems, National Standard, wire cord, Coventry Hood & Seating, vehicle trim.

# 7 Some Growth at Last 1974 to 1978

In January 1974 government approved the West Midlands Planning Council's scheme to consolidate the Birmingham conurbation on an axis of development south-west to north-east, which presaged ill for Telford and as TDC general manager Emyr Thomas put it, was not a good start to the new town's third five-year period of development. Yet despite the first oil shock, when Middle East producers quadrupled the price of crude, Telford's plans escaped the worst of government spending cuts. TDC launched into a capital programme of works worth £20 million, substantially above previous years. The programme aimed to offer housing, factories, roads and employment at an accelerating rate. With rising inflation, private sector house building collapsed and the development corporation sought to raise its housing starts above the 1,000 a year envisaged.

The first office block in the business park of Telford town centre. Designed by TDC Architects' Department, it was built as a prestige office building speculatively and sold to an insurance company. Its concrete structure with mirror glazing as cladding produced a startling and bold form.

To boost employment Telford asked the minister responsible for the civil service for a major government installation under the current policy of dispersing these from London, such as the Royal Mint's move to Wales. The hope was also to attract service employment and especially externally-orientated service industries. But there was still no M54.

While plans were laid for housing in Leegomery and Shawbirch in north-west Telford, and for the development of Hadley district centre, more housing association involvement was encouraged in south Telford. In February a letter to the *Shropshire Star* from a Woodside resident set the correspondence columns buzzing. Violence, vandalism and marital infidelity in the Woodside community were the result of a lack of anything to do, so the letter went. Woodside was a 'sin city'. Replies poured in refuting the points the letter made, and listing all the activities in what was over and over again described as a thriving community. The list included a senior citizens' club, three women's clubs, a dance club, table tennis club, the New Town Singers, Scouts and Guides, a junior club, and young people's fellowship group. A south Telford man complained to TDC of inadequate cycle paths, and the chairman, John Dugdale, borrowed his son's cycle and went out on a wet February day to experience the cycle paths of Sutton Hill, Halesfield, Aqueduct and Madeley for himself. He agreed that TDC would discuss new cycle path proposals and improvements to existing paths.

The Leegomery housing plans suggested a population target of 8,100 on a total of 226 acres (91 hectares), 130 acres (53 hectares) of private development at ten dwellings an acre (twenty-five to one hectare), and TDC housing on the remainder at thirteen dwellings to the acre (thirty-two to one hectare). There would be local shopping, two primary schools and a comprehensive, and a green core in the centre to make strong use of good landscape elements. The cost would be £15 million, and TDC hoped to start in April 1975 with the first houses completed in spring 1977. Although the private house building sector was temporarily in disarray, there was evidence of growing interest in individual houses on individual plots. Suitable areas were pinpointed, mostly on land in the older settlements where reasonable infill sites were available.

## Wrekin District Council

The year 1974 saw the establishment of the new super district council. Another attempt to rename it Telford DC was made. A majority of twenty-eight to sixteen councillors voted for Telford, but this fell short of a two-thirds majority by two votes. On a second bid at the end of the year the pro-Telford councillors again failed to achieve the required majority. But in the intervening months much happened in the town which indicated both that advances were being made on many fronts, and that setbacks continued to dismay the new town's builders. A carefully selected site for a hospital, at Nedge Hill, was abandoned by the health authority. Although centrally convenient to north and south Telford, it was near Stafford Park industrial area with two doubtful environmental hazards, SCC's waste incinerator and an aluminium refinery. Some fourteen other sites were investigated, including that at Apley Castle. A proposal was made to enlarge the Wrekin Hospital in Wellington instead of building a new one, and anxiety expressed that the hospital at RAF Cosford, east of Telford, should be kept open until Telford's own was built. The Shropshire Horticultural Society laid plans for a show in Telford in 1975, while making clear that the annual Shrewsbury

Flower Show would continue. SCC turned down a £1 million plan for new sewerage in Ironbridge. There were calls for better bus services between the northern and southern parts of Telford, but Midland Red Bus Company announced a big loss on the new town's services. A dry ski slope was built at Madeley. A Telford arts festival was held with backing from TDC, the Wrekin DC and the Ironbridge Gorge Museum. More sites for a permanent gypsy camp were proposed — at Donnington Wood, Tweedale and Eyton — and turned down by the local authority.

In June, John Silkin, Minister of Planning and Local Government, officially opened Telford's 150th factory. He pledged that government would stand by the new town. By August, TDC was receiving 350 housing enquiries a month. The National Coal Board proposed a hundred-acre (forty hectares) opencast coal prospect at Dawley which would yield 400,000 tons. A coal recovery project costing £1 million associated with land reclamation at Lawley was put forward. About the same time TDC paid £20,000 for equipment to clean mud and dust off the town's roads. In November, Wrockwardine Wood school was troubled by old mineshafts. One was only yards from the deputy head's office, others were on land behind Oakengates leisure centre, scheduled for playing fields. TDC filled them in with grout and capped them. The Coalport water pollution control plant at Gitchfield was handed over to the Severn-Trent Water Authority, while the Rushmoor plant and sewerage lines for north Telford went ahead with the laying of concrete pipe sections weighing 6¾ tons each.

## Town centre phase 2

While work went ahead on Wellington's and Oakengates' ring roads and further rehabilitation in the centres, phase 2 of Telford town centre was announced. It would cost £4½ million, and would bring big stores selling durable goods, as well as the comparison shopping of the phase 1 shops. The last two phases would add commercial office accommodation, a theatre, library, art centre, cinema, swimming pool and sauna, a night club and discotheque, as well as a racquets centre. The ultimate aim was 800,000 square feet (74,320 square metres) of shopping and offices and 4,000 surface car spaces. From an early stage in the planning, TDC had decided on surface car parking which would be free. The announcement of phase 2 brought protests from the smaller centres. Wellington Chamber of Trade stressed that it was not 'anti-new town' but that phase 2 was premature. But the development corporation was confident that the increasing population of the new town would keep district centres prosperous, including the much larger Wellington and Oakengates centres.

Government sources let it be known that plans for the M54 had not been affected by the economic squeeze. Work would start in 1976, the costs were expected to be between £20 million and £25 million for the 17.6 miles of motorway. TDC officials would have been excused if they had said 'we'll believe it when we drive along it'. The Dawley/Donnington distributor road did however start under TDC auspices, and the Hadley district centre plan was on show to the public.

The relaxation of requirements for IDCs back in 1970 had allowed factories of up to 5,000 square feet (464.5 square metres) to be built and occupied without DTI approval, instead of only 3,000 square feet (278.8 square metres). In 1972 this had been raised to 15,000 square feet (1,393.5 square metres) but now in

1974 the figure was reduced back to 5,000 square feet and the policy strictly enforced. One particular factory, already established, had nowhere to go. This was a maggot factory. For over a hundred years the unsavoury smell of rotting carcases had pervaded the Oakengates air, the factory producing 800 gallons of maggots at the peak of the angling season. TDC made clear to Jack Hodson, its owner, that the 'premises were unsuitable (for maggot production) in terms of future planning', and would serve a compulsory purchase order. Unfortunately, neither it nor the county council had an alternative site to offer. Mr Hodson wrote to the press, 'once our licence has gone in this trade you could never get it back'. He argued therefore that he had to stay until a suitable site was found for him.

Miss Telford New Town, described in the press as a 'tiny explosive redhead', otherwise seventeen-year-old Tina Brown, was elected with the object of helping to organise community events, and 'talking to people and encouraging strangers to talk to each other'. For Christmas that year, TDC arranged a sky sculpture using laser beams and mirrors to project thin rods of colour into the sky to create a blue and green confection up there. Miss Telford pressed the switch and unfortunately, as the press was bound to mention, it 'opened with a whimper'. But after adjustment the sky sculpture attracted favourable comment. It lit up the town centre and could be seen from a ten-mile radius.

As costs soared with inflation, so there were in 1975 numerous protests about what were considered 'unnecessary' plans. A Staffordshire MP called yet once more for the M54 to be scrapped to help cuts in public spending. But in March, the Transport Minister again reiterated that the motorway would go ahead. Other protestors said that TDC should spend its moneys on a hospital before roads, housing and more shops in the town centre, despite the fact that the development corporation could not use its funds for the hospital. A resident of Sutton Hill wrote to the newspapers begging for better public transport. At present, he said, the old bus routes before the new town, had been 'bent' slightly to take in the new development. He proposed a modern tram system which would not follow the roads. Some form of 'own track' transport had been looked at in the days of Dawley Development Corporation, and the letter now occasioned a rash of other letters with proposals for an electric tramway, a narrow gauge steam railway and a diesel light railway, none of which proved feasible.

Following its principle of refurbishing worthwhile older buildings, the development corporation turned twenty-nine early 19th century miners' cottages at Priorslee into twelve houses for sale. It proposed to spend £0.5 million on conservation measures in the Severn Gorge. The works would include riverside walks, development of angling and canoeing, and management of woodland. New roadworks and a 'park and ride' scheme were designed to take care of traffic into the future. A new bridge across the river was again mooted. The museum won a Heritage Year award from the Civic Trust which included special commendation for landscape works already carried out, among them TDC's imaginative creation of the park on thirty-two acres (thirteen hectares) at Dale End where the Coalbrookdale valley met the river.

In July 1975 the development corporation's board was given a new deputy chairman. He was Donald Chapman, formerly and for nineteen years the Labour MP for Birmingham Northfield. He had been educated at Barnsley

Grammar School and Cambridge, where he had gained degrees in both economics and agricultural economics. He had served as a Cambridge City councillor, and had lately been a highly successful chairman of the Development Commission charged with rural regeneration.

Unemployment in the town hit 7.1 per cent, the highest of anywhere in the West Midlands. Companies closed, but others continued to raise Telford's hopes by moving in. As if to demonstrate that the last of the primary industries were still alive and kicking, Blockleys gained permission to extract clay for the next fifty years, and to extend marl extraction down to 100 feet (30.5 metres). The Granville colliery which employed 580 men and had been threatened with closure, discovered a new seam of coal.

During this bleak period in the town's fortunes, the Minister of Planning and Local Government announced a cutback in the population target. He was John Silkin who, as the son of Lewis Silkin, could only have had the welfare of the new towns close to his heart. Although the eventual target was 220,000, more immediately development should aim for 145,000 to 155,000 by 1986. As if to emphasise the slow growth in population and therefore in supporters of Telford United, the club was again in financial difficulties due largely to low gates. But all was not entirely gloomy. The Rushmoor water pollution plant was now operating and would ultimately provide its services for 155,000 people of north Telford — a figure now very far in the future. In October, government sanctioned phase 2 of the town centre. Internal roads continued to be built and opened, and work proceeded on the centres of Wellington, Oakengates and Dawley. Although TDC had tried hard for the central site of Nedge Hill for the hospital, at least the health authorities had taken a step nearer eventual realisation of the facility by choosing a site, Apley Castle in the north-west. The Telford and Wrekin arts festival for the year included the Poet Laureate John Betjeman, the BBC Welsh Symphony Orchestra, the band of the Coldstream Guards, Adrian Henri the Liverpool painter and poet, the pianist John Ogden, the English Folk Dance and Song Society, and the Rupert Bear Show.

## Change at the top

In November 1975, John Dugdale, who had earlier been appointed Lord Lieutenant of Shropshire, resigned as chairman of TDC. He had presided over Telford during difficult economic times and changing demographic circumstances, when Birmingham had finally made clear its disinterest, and a loss of faith in the new town had to be combated. Yet the groundwork for Telford's eventual success had largely been done, and under his leadership TDC had developed a momentum which was to carry the town forward to its later unparalleled growth. Donald Chapman succeeded him and was shortly made a life peer as Lord Northfield of Telford. Lord Northfield recounts how Peter Shore at Environment gave him only the briefest of instructions for his new post. 'Go and give the place some style,' he had said. The new chairman was well-connected on both sides of 'the House' at Westminster. He soon developed an abiding belief in Telford as an exceptional place to live and work, and entered into a partnership of talent with TDC's general manager, Emyr Thomas, whom Northfield credits with visionary powers and 'an unshakable conviction in Telford's ultimate success'.

*Lord Northfield of Telford, chairman, Telford Development Corporation, 1975 to 1987.*

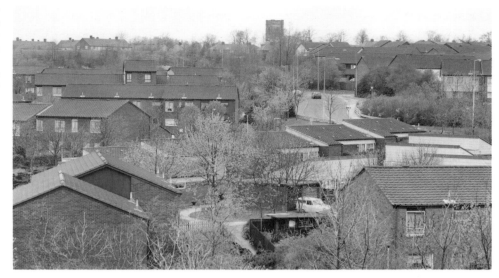

*TDC housing built for rent at Malinslee in the mid-1970s. The photograph taken from Spout Mound shows single-person patio dwellings and family housing. Malinslee church on the horizon is reputed to have been designed by Thomas Telford.*

'At the stage I took over, with inflation, rising unemployment, hindrances to industry moving to us, no motorway and no hospital, it was imperative that TDC projected to everyone absolute confidence in the future,' the new chairman said. In his first annual report, he stated that TDC's aim must be to grow by 5,000 people a year for the next ten years. In its five-year plan, TDC was again to encourage service industries of warehousing and distribution, and office employment. Now that the town was beginning to look more attractive to office development, both private and institutional capital would be sought. More social and leisure facilities were planned. The development corporation also instigated a Royal Institute of British Architects competition for the overall design of the town centre. Much closer liaison with local authorities was proposed. TDC would strive for 'a sense of intimate partnership'. Phase 3 of the town centre and the rejuvenation of the Ironbridge area were to become pet projects of the chairman, although he strove as hardily and to good effect for the three main priorities of communications, industry and a hospital. He was also to have an impact on the quality of housing design.

*The Abraham Darby comprehensive school at Madeley was built in the 1930s and greatly expanded in the 1950s and 1960s to take pupils from the new residential areas.*

On December 8 1975, the Greyhound link of the eastern primary road was opened by John Dugdale as the county's Lord Lieutenant. Three days later fog shrouded the first 4½ miles of the M54 between Ketley and Hollinswood as the section was opened for the first time. The Lord Lieutenant again officiated, saying that the opening was 'a harbinger of better things to come'. There was still no firm date for the start of the main motorway section. Towards the end of the year Telford's chairman told a reporter that 'despite the economic situation factories and homes must continue to be built in readiness for the boom to come'.

## The making of the forest

By having a landscape structure plan drawn up, TDC had acknowledged that landscaping was indeed structural and not an adjunct to development. It was as Emyr Thomas put it, 'a forest context into which development must fit'. He believed that in the years to come the developing settlements would be seen to repose naturally within a total landscaped area. Perhaps he had in mind as an aim the quotation from John Ruskin of 'that warm look of self-sufficiency and wholesome quiet with which our villages and hamlets ought to nestle among the green fields and woodlands'.

*A major policy of Telford's landscape plan was to plant green corridors on either side of all major roads. These are frequently on banks and berms to add to the noise-cutting propensities of the vegetation.*

There are today some 2,500 acres (1,012 hectares) of woodland in the designated area, of which half are newly planted. The woodlands of the Severn Gorge cover 650 acres (236 hectares). When the new town was designated these woods varied in their tree species depending on soil and slope, but in general contained oak, ash, beech, wych elm and sycamore. Alder, rowan, willow, with elder and hawthorn were common, while hornbeam, large- and small-leaved lime, and the wild service tree were also present. Hazel was the main understorey tree. Sycamore, sweet chestnut, larch, Scots pine and poplar had been introduced at various times to what was largely the vegetation of ancient woodland. So in the gorge, and in pockets elsewhere were to be found patches of semi-natural woodland.

*The forest element beginning to grow up and envelope new buildings of Stafford Park industrial estate.*

Pit mounds had been colonised, depending on the pH of the 'soil', by heather, gorse, birch, oak, hawthorn, brambles and rosebay willowherb. Oak and birch grew on the more acid materials, with hazel, hawthorn and willow on the richer and more alkaline soils. A limestone grassland at Lincoln Hill on the edge of the gorge was a geological SSSI (Site of Special Scientific Interest). Other SSSIs contained ancient woodland and marshland. At sites in the Randlay valley, at Horsehay and in the town park were a surprising number of ground plants including common spotted orchids, hybrid marsh orchids, wild carrot, mellilot, yellow rattle and soapwort. Others were centaury, meadowsweet, tansy, fleabane and a variety of aquatic plants. Southall Road wood in Dawley consisted of oak, whitebeam, birch with heather and supported a large number of butterflies of different species. These were all prime sites for nature conservation.

The landscape structure plan's first objective was to provide a wooded edge to the town. Views into and out of the town were to be considered, and less attractive areas screened. The creation of green corridors was the second objective. These would be part of the road system and would act as sound baffles. A network of open space linking the centre of the town with the surrounding countryside was the third objective, while the fourth was the landscaping within and round the residential, industrial and commercial developments. Land would be used to maximum environmental, ecological, recreational and agricultural advantage, taking into account capital and maintenance costs, revenue possibilities and management requirements. Forestry principles were applied to establish a good density of tree cover. Although opportunities for commercial forestry were limited, income from thinnings, coppicing and mature trees was envisaged.

As David Wassell, TDC's chief landscape architect explained, the decision was made to reclothe the countryside largely in the same species that had colonised it naturally in the far-off days of the Wrekin or Mount Gilbert forest. Pioneer species capable of quick growth on a wide range of acid to alkaline soils were used to create conditions for the more permanent tree and understorey cover. These were birch, varieties of black poplar, two types of alder — one for riverine sites, the other for hard open sites liable to crusting — and white, goat and crack willow. The main longer-lived plantings contained newcomers to the ancient woodland list to provide more variety in habit of growth, seasonal leaf and fruit colours. The final list included two English oaks, the common and sessile, American red and scarlet oaks, ash, hornbeam, beech, large-, small-leaved and common limes, Spanish chestnut, the gean or wild cherry, rowan, and Norway and sugar maples. Scots pine, beach pine, yew and the occasional holm oak, the evergreen *Quercus ilex*, were planted to give winter colour to the woodland. Sycamore was deliberately planted both as a pioneer and to grow into a longer-lasting woodland tree. Beside the problem of scattering its seed far and wide, the sycamore does have its beneficial side as David Wassall pointed out. It grows fast, breaks up the soil well and provides abundant leaf mound for humus.

In some areas a proper, if short-term forest crop in plantation was established. These were of western hemlock, European and Japanese larch, Scots pine and Sitka spruce. Understorey plantings within the general woodland were made in holly, yew, wild privet and viburnum. The woodland edges were planted with hazel and hawthorn, dogwood and laurel. In essence the forest plantings were made with the eventual aim of oak being the dominant long-term tree crop over at least half of Telford's new forest, backed up by beech, ash and pine.

## Mostly progress

Early in 1976 Stirchley's health centre designated for a population of 24,000 in Brookside, Randlay and Stirchley, was opened. It joined the already-established ecumenical centre there which had a church consecrated by both the Church of England and the Roman Catholic Church. Another three-quarters of a mile of the Dawley/Donnington road was in use. The Ironbridge Gorge Museum opened the Coalport china works museum and the golf course at Sutton Hill was inaugurated. Woodside residents were supplied with 106 allotments, while other allotments at Brookside were available at £8.50 a year. A boost to the employment situation was announced by COD Donnington with 750 new jobs.

*An aerial view of GKN Sankey's Castle Works with Blockleys brick-works in the distance. Before and throughout the new town's life GKN had mixed fortunes but con-tinued to be the major industrial employer in Telford.*

It was confidently expected that phase 2 of the town centre would create 1,000 jobs, mainly for women. After a temporary backing-off 'until the population had grown some more', Marks & Spencer announced its imminent arrival in the town, but this was later to be postponed for some years. Telford would one day have its own central railway station at Hollinswood, a few hundred yards from the town centre. A £1 million recreation centre for Wellington was announced, with swimming pools, squash courts, a meeting hall and rooms, a bar and restaurant. On the other hand, there was doubt about the gypsy caravan site at Lodge Road, Donnington — it was on, then off, then on and permanent, then temporary. Eventually, in 1977 TDC built a ten-pitch camp for 'settled' gypsy families at Lodge Road and gave it to WDC to run. The Telford Angling Association with 1,700 members was worried about the future with what it saw as encroachment of fishing waters by canoeists, pleasure boating and sailing, and sub-aqua activities.

Lord Northfield's close interest in architectural matters resulted in a change of attitude towards housing. New housing developments would comprise smaller groups of dwellings of different tenure — rented, owner-occupier, and co-ownership. The mix was designed to provide a housing ladder for those with the aim of owning their own homes. There would be greater informality. Design and layout would seek to add excitement and interest to home ownership. To point up the new requirements, TDC commissioned 248 houses at Aqueduct from the Eric Lyons partnership. These were designed in informal groupings around common green spaces connecting to village greens of different sizes. The range of dwellings would be from two-bedroomed flats to four-bedroomed houses. Lyons, who was president of the RIBA, was retained for a brief period as housing design layout adviser. The impact of these new housing policies was to be felt at Leegomery, and later Shawbirch and Priorslee. TDC made every effort to obtain co-operation from private developers in producing better layouts and housing designs. A home finder centre was set up to try and help the still sluggish private house market.

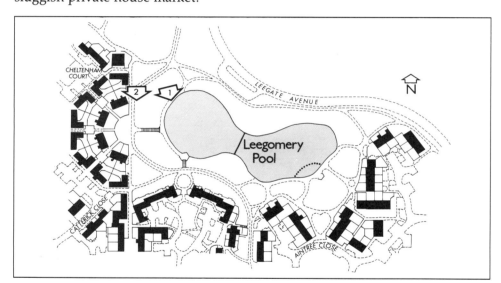

*HOUSING STUDY: Leegomery. Designed and built by TDC Architects' Department for rent, 1977. Traditional brick construction with decorative brickwork, rendering and other architectural features. Won Civic Trust award for design. Site area 19.6 acres (7.9 hectares), 321 dwellings, sixteen dwellings to the acre (forty to the hectare). Twenty different house types ranging from single storey one- and two-bedroomed dwellings to three-, four- and five-bedroomed houses.*

## Five-year plan

All this was an important part of TDC's new five-year plan initiated in 1976 to widen the range of employment opportunities and strengthen all aspects of community development and social work. Only by improving Telford's appearance and its amenities, and making it increasingly attractive to residents, companies and investors, could the town progress. All this was hampered still by the tighter IDC policies and the lack of a completed M54. On both these points Lord Northfield continued, in his own phrase, 'to pester' the relevant government ministers, while in its search for more industry, the development corporation began to look at the possibility of going overseas in order to bypass the IDC controls. Tentative feelers were put out in the United States of America, and Germany. Because companies were still hesitant to invest capital in buildings, TDC continued to build factories to meet market needs. From 1976 onwards standard factories ceased to be subject to IDC controls after ten years, so TDC began to acquire a small but increasing pool of factories through relets which were not subject to IDC control.

During this year TDC took firm steps to bring liaison with the local authorities closer still. Officers of the county council and Wrekin DC worked with TDC staff preparing the details of development schemes. There were regular meetings between TDC board members, councillors and senior officers of all three bodies. In its turn, Wrekin DC set up a joint development group to which TDC board members were formally co-opted. Finally the chief executive of the district council was invited to attend TDC board meetings on a regular basis. In Lord Northfield's view this close communication and the agreements which sprang from it were a major factor in the town's eventual success.

## Life goes on

A series of open days was held by TDC to show the world the progress of the town. There was a Made in Telford exhibition with everything from billiard cues to jewellery, clothing and automotive and electronic products on display. TDC set up its own business services unit with the express intention of fostering growth, offering advice to businesses on management, accountancy, production and marketing. After all, it was the 200 or so smaller firms on which the town depended for the bulk of its employment. The Dawley bypass was opened, and plans went ahead to 'rejuvenate and revitalise' Dawley's centre which had for years, as a press report described it, 'combined narrow streets, sharp bends and a pet herd of large lorries'. Five cottages in Princes Street, Madeley, dated 1840, were renovated by the development corporation and sold for £4,350 each. As the emphasis of new developments swung from south to north Telford, housing at Priorslee consisting of 2,600 houses on 260 acres (105 hectares) was planned for around 10,000 people. Pointing up a trend, some 190 acres (77 hectares) were earmarked for private housing, continuing efforts to attract a balanced population across the income groups.

However, there were still empty TDC houses — in August 466 out of a total of 6,763. A recruiting campaign in Birmingham resulted in 2,500 applications, and a month later 241 of the empty buildings had been let. As always there were mixed opinions about how far the community spirit of Telford was developing. Brookside Community Association circulated 2,000 homes with a notice of a special meeting. Six people turned up. But in Sutton Hill, now over a decade old, the neighbourhood association was 'a force to be reckoned with'. A report from the West Mercia Police did meanwhile suggest that Telford was the authority's worst area for crime, with sixty per cent of it committed by teenagers. Lord Northfield called for greater provision of youth activities — for which the county council was responsible. SCC, the bulk of whose education moneys for the year were being spent on schools in Telford, let it be known that TDC must provide the funds. The maggot factory at Oakengates was told, if it wanted to stay where it was, to rebuild with modern equipment and cleaning facilities so as to eliminate the smell. The design competition for the town centre was won by A. G. Sheppard Fidler and Associates. The firm's entry was an imaginative reassessment of the whole town centre which confirmed the emphasis on the importance of the human scale, and recommended the further development of an emerging town centre/town park axis.

In April 1977, James Callaghan, the Prime Minister, and the brothers John and Sam Silkin, came to open the Silkin Way, named after Lewis Silkin. This pedestrian route of sixteen miles ran from Coalport to the north-west boundary of the designated area, often using old railway tracks and linking old settlements with new communities.

*TELFORD'S SILKIN WAY AND OTHER PRINCIPAL FOOTPATHS AND CYCLEPATHS.*

*The Prime Minister, James Callaghan, opening the Silkin Way in April 1977. Beside him is Councillor Iris Butler, chairman, Wrekin District Council. Lord Northfield is behind them.*

## Population targets altered again

The results of a review of new towns and inner cities were published in July 1977 by Peter Shore, the Secretary for the Environment. Telford's population targets of 1975 were further moderated to 135,000 by the end of 1986 when induced growth would end, and rising to 150,000 within ten years of that date by natural increase. Continued growth was to be employment-led, in other words housing and facilities of all kinds were to follow industry and the availability of jobs. This confirmed Telford's status as an economic growth point rather than an overspill town. By the autumn TDC had produced a ten-year plan taking into account the new population target. It had been thrashed out in close co-operation with the county and district authorities. The plan eliminated house building foreseen in the basic plan from several areas round the town's eastern and northern edges at Wrockwardine Wood, Admaston, Bratton and in Donnington Wood. The district centre envisaged at Priorslee/St George's was deferred indefinitely. Acting on an earlier transport study there was a reduction in the town's planned road network. The western part of the primary ring road was abandoned while sections were reduced in specification as part of a more local road network. The planned 'ring' road therefore became a cross formed by the eastern primary and the M54.

The IDC policy of the DTI was further tightened, and grants became even more difficult to obtain as government attempted to slow the new town's advance factory building in view of the reduction in population targets. Telford was restricted to industrial recruitment from Birmingham and the Black Country, but Birmingham's inner city area was now excluded. High interest rates were inhibiting companies from expanding. There was evidence that the numbers of companies that wished to build factories in Telford was increasing, but the continuing lack of a motorway link remained a disincentive. TDC was concerned that office jobs were not being created as fast as there were school leavers, especially girls. Youth opportunities programmes through the Manpower Services Commission were begun, and later TDC employed a project officer and staff to aid programmes for the young. A skills centre was opened and by mid-1978 a total of 174 youngsters were being helped through TDC job-creation schemes. TDC redoubled its efforts at overseas recruitment of industry, and began the 'wooing' of Japanese businesses. The regional office of the Department of Trade and Industry did soften its attitude and conceded that new towns were a legitimate option for industries unwilling to go to development areas.

The main thrust of house building was now in Randlay, Malinslee, Hollinswood and Leegomery, and at Aqueduct. Plans for 400 houses on 100 acres (40 hectares) at The Rock were made, and a 40-acre (16 hectares) tree nursery established at The Humbers, Donnington, to help with planting material in the north. The work of rehabilitating the district centres of Wellington, Hadley and Dawley was proceeding well, while smaller centres at Hollinswood, Randlay and Malinslee had been completed and let. Bearing in mind the part the public house had played in the East Shropshire coalfield's history — and many pubs in the old settlements were still trading — TDC built at least one pub in each residential unit. In December 1977 a new pub at Holmer Lake, the Lakeside Tavern, was opened.

110

*HOUSING STUDY: Aqueduct. Commissioned by TDC as housing for rent. Designed by the Eric Lyons Partnership, 1977. Built on reclaimed land among pit mounds to a 'village green' layout with a variety of house types and materials. Site area 15.4 acres (6.2 hectares), 247 dwellings, sixteen dwellings to the acre (forty to the hectare), 247 hard-standing parking spaces (no garages). Houses provided two- to five-bedroomed accommodation, and flats with two bedrooms. Some chalet designs.*

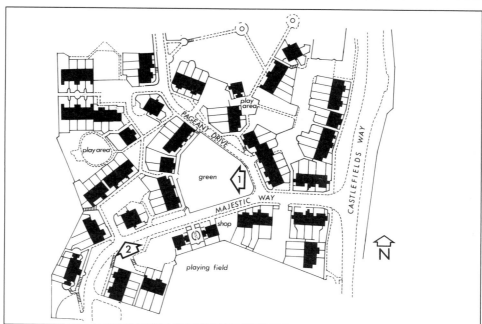

Land reclamation proceeded northwards with work beginning at Snedshill and at Priorslee, where 171 acres (69 hectares) were to be excavated and redistributed with a recreational lake created. Reclamation costing £2 million of 164 acres (66 hectares) at The Lodge, Donnington, would be for housing, and would reprieve good farmland in the north-west of the designated area. In the Severn Gorge the museum won the 1977 British Museum of the Year award and in 1978 carried off the trophy for European Museum of the Year. Visitor figures were now over 160,000 a year. Plans for Telford's hospital, although not the starting date, were announced. It would have 700 to 800 beds with a 304-bed first phase.

While all this went on, the country's economic situation deteriorated, and unemployment rose. The West Midlands, too, seemed to be moving inexorably towards recession. The employment situation in Telford from 1972 to 1978 was that 4,000 jobs had been created on the new industrial estates. This had been offset by 1,500 job losses from the older declining industries to produce a net gain of 2,500. As the TDC annual report to March 1979 pointed out, this indicated just how bleak an economic future the area would have had without the new town. At the end of 1978 the unemployment rate was about eight per cent.

By the year's end, although the momentum of growth was still upwards, there was still no news of the M54 extension to the M6. Industrial recruitment was being strangled. Only the continuing groundwork for possible recruitment of industry from the USA, continental Europe, and Japan, held out much hope to alleviate the increasingly desperate situation in which Telford found itself. Yet the reclamation and landscaping, and the good roads, the bright industrial estates, and new comfortable homes, were at last beginning to change the overall character of the area, and the image the town presented to the outside world. Of the brand new and exciting town centre, Lord Northfield in a moment of euphoria, was reported as saying that he expected that travellers on the M54 'would whistle as they saw it'. He added, 'we want to bring a sense of magic, majesty and romance to the town'.

# TELFORD DEVELOPMENT CORPORATION 1974 to 1978

By the end of the period covered by Chapter 7, the town's statistics were:

| | | | |
|---|---|---|---|
| Population | 100,300 | Residents economically active | 46,140 |
| Dwellings | 36,162 | | |
| Average number of persons per dwelling | 2.77 | Number living and working in Telford | 35,529 |
| Houses built during period | 7,276 | Percentage of economically active living and working in Telford | 77 |
| Total employment | 44,681 | Percentage unemployed | 8.5 |
| Manufacturing | 21,946 | | |
| Services | 18,003 | | |
| Other | 4,732 | | |

During this period TDC transferred its sewers and sewage disposal works to the newly-constituted Severn-Trent Water Authority. The cost of the transferred assets was £9.9 million, and the water authority was required to reimburse the loan charges incurred by TDC in borrowing to meet the capital expenditure of their construction.

Borrowing from government on March 31, 1978 was £190.5 million at an average interest rate of 12.2 per cent. From this sum £172.7 million had been spent on the creation of assets with the balance being used to meet revenue deficits and provide working capital:

| | |
|---|---|
| Total spent on purchase of land and buildings, where development had been completed | £102.6 million |
| Total spent on 7,551 acres (3,057 hectares) of land awaiting development | £9.1 million |
| Total spent on the creation of assets still to be completed | £17.2 million |
| | £128.9 million |
| Construction of roads | £15.3 million |
| Derelict land reclamation | £5.2 million |
| Landscaping of public open space (including cost of land) | £8.3 million |
| Contribution to water authority for supply of water and sewers for development | £5.0 million |
| Loans (including that to Severn-Trent Water Authority) | £10.0 million |
| | £43.8 million |
| Grand total | £172.7 million |

The built assets comprised:

| | | |
|---|---|---|
| Dwellings | 10,294 | £79.3 million |
| Industry in square feet (square metres) | 3,382,390 (356,029) | £13.5 million |
| Commerce in square feet (square metres) | 351,529 (32,657) | £5.7 million |
| Other | | £4.1 million |
| | | £102.6 million |

Major companies coming to Telford during the period were: Whitfield & Son, compounding, BKL Alloys, scrap aluminium, Lindemann (UK), reclamation machinery, British Brown Boveri/ABB Power, electrical equipment, T. H. W. Dodd, electrical contractors, UBM Amari Ltd/ Triad Windows, windows, SMP Security, safes, Hoover Ball & Bearings, automotive components, Silhouette Ltd, clothes, Unimation (Europe)/Staubli Unimation, robots.

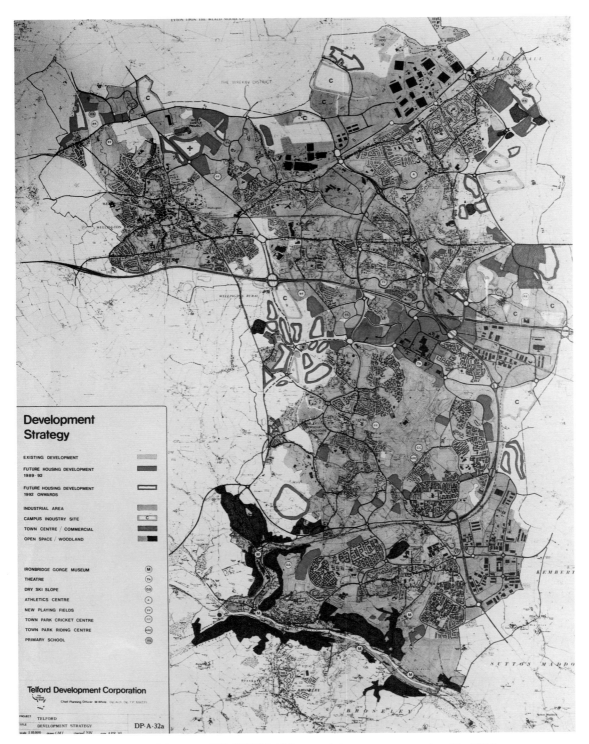

## Development Strategy

EXISTING DEVELOPMENT

FUTURE HOUSING DEVELOPMENT
1989-92

FUTURE HOUSING DEVELOPMENT
1992 ONWARDS

INDUSTRIAL AREA

CAMPUS INDUSTRY SITE

TOWN CENTRE / COMMERCIAL

OPEN SPACE / WOODLAND

IRONBRIDGE GORGE MUSEUM ⓜ

THEATRE ⓣⓗ

DRY SKI SLOPE ⓓⓢ

ATHLETICS CENTRE ⓐ

NEW PLAYING FIELDS ⓟⓕ

TOWN PARK CRICKET CENTRE ⓒⓒ

TOWN PARK RIDING CENTRE ⓡⓒ

PRIMARY SCHOOL ⓟⓢ

**Telford Development Corporation**

Chief Planning Officer M.White.  Dep.Arch. Dep. T.P. MINERS

PROJECT   TELFORD
TITLE      DEVELOPMENT STRATEGY       DP·A·32a
scale 1:10,000   drawn GMT   checked SW   date APR 90

*TELFORD'S 1977 DEVELOPMENT STRATEGY. This amended strategy was produced by TDC
in response to a government reduction in target population to 135,000 by the end of 1986.*

114

*Super Saturday in Telford's town park in 1978 attracted thousands of Telfordians of all ages and backgrounds.*

# 8 Recession and High Unemployment 1979 to 1982

*A group of old people's dwellings in Madeley, designed by TDC Architects' Department.*

With a population of 103,000, Telford now contained a third of Shropshire's people. It already had its hinterland for whose villages it was becoming a shopping centre and a source of employment. Yet the new town was some way short of establishing its identity as a single town. To many the impression was still of a scattered urban complex made up of five small towns and a number of villages. While this would only be remedied by time, Telford Development Corporation aimed in the next ten years to complete the urban structure and establish the town as a higher-status service centre. There would be a better balance in terms of employment, public and private housing, income groups, and social and leisure facilities. The threshold of maturity was seen as a population of 130,000. By the end of the 1970s the housing stock had increased by 16,000, including 10,500 rented TDC dwellings. Factory space was nearly five millon square feet (464,500 square metres). About sixty miles of roads and 100 miles of trunk sewers had been built, with 2,000 acres of derelict land reclaimed and 1,000 mine shafts treated.

Although the jobs in service industries that Telford was so keen to attract had increased by 665 during 1979, the net loss of jobs which included nearly 600 from primary industry and over 400 from manufacturing, was 527. During this year the Granville mine closed with a loss of 512 jobs. Those nearing retirement were made redundant, many others were offered and accepted jobs in pits at Cannock. In a brave attempt to modernise, John Maddock of Oakengates, founded in 1869 as nailmakers and now producing castings for wide-ranging industrial use, installed a new heat-treatment furnace producing 300 tons of castings a month. But within a year or two it was trying to sell its foundry and axing jobs.

## Industrial restriction loosened

The worsening economic conditions brought in March 1979 a loosening of the industrial restrictions, and Telford was allowed to recruit from the entire West Midlands, now including the counties of Staffordshire, Warwickshire, Shropshire, Worcestershire and Herefordshire, except for the inner city area of Birmingham and the Oswestry assisted area further north in Shropshire. While welcoming this, Lord Northfield made clear that in order to counter the decline in the old traditional industries, Telford must be able to recruit industry on a worldwide basis and to rebuild its economy on the foundations of advanced technology. Already on TDC estates were companies manufacturing industrial robots, electronic components and miniature electric circuit breakers. Many more such firms were needed.

Government gave permission for the first phase of 500 houses in the large Priorslee development, and village-type public sector housing at Leegomery proceeded, with some homes specially designed for the physically handicapped. But all was evidently not well with some of the first TDC houses to be built. The press had photographs of an elderly housewife with a disabled husband, holding up a bucket to catch the rainwater coming through the roof of their Sutton Hill house. A TDC spokesman was quoted as saying that specialist repairs were not possible during bad weather but would be carried out as soon as practicable. No mention was made of any attempt temporarily to stop the rain coming in. This may or may not have been a case where TDC was guilty of not taking prompt action. But there undoubtedly were cases where complaints of Telford residents generally and TDC tenants in particular were first answered by letters. The chairman stopped the letter writing, insisting that complaints were immediately investigated in person by TDC officials. He himself looked into numbers of cases personally. 'I also insisted that if TDC had made a mistake, this was admitted and an apology sent straight away. It was vital to build up a reputation for not only caring about Telford's people but also for prompt action on their behalf.' The state of some of the earlier housing, as to sound-proofing of windows and poor central heating systems, were to be dealt with progressively, as was the refurbishment of others for sale. The swing to building more private housing and fewer TDC dwellings for rent continued.

The development corporation renovated Admaston Spa, a group of late 18th century buildings, into three executive-type houses, and planned this as a nucleus of such housing. An application to build these houses was initially turned down by the district council, but was eventually resolved. In general most of TDC's building applications were supported by the local authority first time, due to close liaison at the planning stage. Where objections were lodged or applications turned down, normally TDC obtained final Department of the Environment permission with amendments made to satisfy the district council. Examples of close collaboration and thoughtful assessment of each other's views were to become more obvious. In some matters both TDC and Wrekin DC put funds towards the solving of problems. The vexed question of bus services in the town was one. Telford buses, despite the introduction of the Tellus system of small buses, continued to run 'in the red'. A Tellus four-weekly ticket scheme had proved expensive to administer and unpopular with passengers. TDC and Wrekin DC were obliged to continue to subsidise the service.

## M54 support

During 1979 quite significantly, groups of people who had not previously been engaged in the M54 controversies, signed petitions to speed up the arrival of the motorway. An M54 support group that included long-time protagonists like the CBI, trades unions and commercial interests, was joined by farmers and country people in signing a 3,000-name petition to the Minister of Transport, avowing that the motorway would benefit not only Telford but all East Shropshire.

*The A5 Wellington bypass, later to become the M54, being built at Ketley Bank.* (Shropshire Star)

A thousand people in Newport, the small town seven miles to the north-east, also sent a petition calling for the 'earliest construction' of the M54. Two sporting events put Telford's name about in circles where normal media methods did not reach. Telford Boxing Club held a tournament in the Anstice Hall in Madeley, sponsored by the development corporation, with boxers from many parts of the country taking part. A month or two later a youth international football festival took place — 'a mini World Cup soccer tournament' as it was dubbed by the press — with youngsters from the USA, France, Germany, Switzerland and Ireland. TDC also backed a national professional cycling championship scheduled for June 1980 in the town. Another example of this reaching out beyond the confines of the West Midlands was the fact that four Telford companies took stands at the Hanover Trade Fair in Germany. In a number of ways therefore, Telford was preparing itself for the international role it was to assume in the 1980s.

118

Despite TDC's efforts the Telford town centre still lacked social activities such as a cinema, theatre and restaurants. However, the development corporation's board had long discussed what form the major capital expense in the field of recreation that they were allowed by government, should take. The decision was made to build an ice rink in the town centre. Designing also went ahead for the bus station which would abut the main shopping centre, and for further town centre phases. In the commercial business park, Darby House, an office block, was undertaken by TDC in partnership with the Liverpool Victoria Insurance Company. The Great Hay leisure complex just by Sutton Hill, to be built in conjunction with a private enterprise, was begun. There would be a sixty-bed hotel. Down at Ironbridge the bicentenary of the Iron Bridge was held in July. A procession of 700 local schoolchildren dressed in 18th century costume, depicted aspects of life there 200 years before. The Prince of Wales opened the new Museum of Iron. The museum complex was enhanced by the arrival of the Elton collection of industrial artefacts, paintings and drawings which were entrusted to TDC and in the museum trust's curatorship. Ironbridge was still growing as a tourist attraction of great pulling power, and property values were rising. TDC was at pains to enhance the town's residential role and planned small-scale building and more old people's housing. Meanwhile, the town's residents complained of the 'eternal roadworks' caused by road widening, and sewerage works, at last approved, which were designed to serve Ironbridge and Coalbrookdale more than adequately for many years to come. Indeed traffic problems from lorries were already becoming serious.

*Typical TDC advance factories at Hortonwood, built speculatively and offered for rent. Construction was portal frame with coloured steel cladding, mostly in browns to be in sympathy with the landscaping.*

## Jockey Bank

Jockey Bank, a part of Madeley Wood, overlooking the gorge, best represents TDC's long-term efforts to rehabilitate and reinvigorate older areas everywhere in the designated area. It had become a depressing, uninspiring hamlet with little hope in a future. At the start of the 1970s a report had been written for the development corporation. The area covered fifty acres (twenty hectares) and had a population of 150. A major landslip from pit mounds of Styches colliery had cut through the hamlet and blocked one of its roads, all of which were in a poor state of repair. There were sixty-three occupied dwellings and twenty-three empty ones. Of the sixty-three with people in them, forty-two were owner-occupied and twenty-one tenanted. There were four pubs, one of which, the Golden Ball, was reputed to be the oldest in Telford. There were two general stores, one of them closed, and two school buildings, both closed. The Bedlam furnace ruins lay at the base of the Jockey Bank area.

*Jockey Bank in the 1930s, showing how the Styches colliery pit mound had cut the settlement in two. By the 1970s Jockey Bank was run-down and decayed and in great need of the development corporation's care.*

Drainage was by septic tanks, all in poor condition. Electricity was supplied by unsightly overhead cables, while gas was connected and water was adequately supplied from the mains. The landslip had happened thirty-five years before and was now overgrown and wild. Old cars had been dumped there, the empty houses had been used as repositories of household refuse. There were cheap temporary and now very shoddy buildings which had seen little or no maintenance. In these depressing surroundings the inhabitants were mostly of very long standing, born and bred there, and often now retired. There was little work available, the young had fled. Despite a sense of frustration and despair, the Jockey Bank people wanted to stay on their 'native heath', and there was a strong sense of neighbourliness.

*Reputedly the oldest pub in Telford, The Golden Ball and a row of 19th century cottages alongside, which were refurbished by TDC as part of its Jockey Bank rehabilitation scheme.*

*Infill housing at Jockey Bank on the site of cottages too dilapidated to be saved. TDC's brief to the private developer was that the houses should reflect the local vernacular in the choice of brick, gable and window treatment.*

TDC had three options, the first of which, given the development corporation's often expressed views, was really not considered at all. It was to leave Jockey Bank alone in its obsolescence and ugliness and concentrate on more immediately worthwhile projects of regeneration. The second was to 'clear fell' as it were, and start afresh. But this would have meant disruption of people's lives and a loss of historical links. The third was to clear away the temporary huts, reclaim the pit mounds and stabilise them, and to rebuild and refurbish every building that could be saved, constructing new dwellings in keeping with the older houses. At the same time it would be TDC's task to generate a new outlook among the people, encourage improvements, restore confidence in the future, and attract younger people with families back into the settlement. And that is what happened to Jockey Bank over the years of the 1970s and early 1980s.

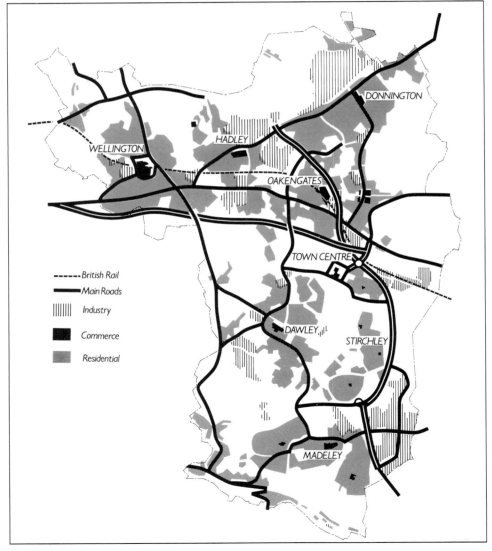

*TELFORD — GROWTH OF DEVELOPMENT, 1980*
*Compare the spread of industry, commerce, housing and main roads with the maps on pages 61 and 167, representing the years 1963 and 1990 respectively.*

## Still a growth point

In a curious way, with the United Kingdom sliding deeper and deeper into recession, the singular and sustained efforts to bring employment to Telford in the 1970s meant that the town was considered the West Midlands growth point. Probably only by comparison with other areas was this now still considered to be so. For at the start of the new decade a then staggering 9.4 per cent of Telford's workforce was out of work. Much worse was to come, and quite rapidly. The worst effects of the recession were felt in the old industries of metal founding, mechanical engineering and vehicles.

During 1980 the Manpower Services Commission was forced to close its skill centre at Halesfield. TDC with the county and district councils took financial steps to support the centre, and in the following year it was reopened as the Telford Opportunities Centre. A centre for the unemployed in south Telford was also opened, while in collaboration with the Walker Technical College in Wellington, TDC encouraged short business courses for skilled but unemployed people to start up on their own. A sum of £11,000 also went to the college for new electronic teaching aids. The Business Services Unit now had over thirty-five firms receiving its advice and assistance. A curious paradox arose on employment. Telford firms found themselves short of certain specific craftsmen, with none available from the local unemployed. TDC organised a 'flying squad' to go to places where major shutdowns had occurred in the hopes of recruiting these craftsmen, with a guaranteed good-quality house at a reasonable rent. The search was later extended to the then Rhodesia-Zimbabwe and the Republic of South Africa. Some multi-spindle auto-setters were recruited from Africa. Youth Opportunities programmes were expanded, new adult employment programmes were begun, and 140 places were available in the Telford Youth Task Force which had a variety of worthwhile projects to help youngsters mark time constructively until more jobs became available. Both GKN and COD decided that they could no longer run apprentice schemes. Staff cuts at TDC were also made because of cutbacks in government funding.

*Family housing at Leegomery. Telford Development Corporation built these for rent. Of two-storey traditional construction with a pleasant mixture of cladding materials, brickwork and rendering, they are three- and four-bedroomed dwellings. Tenants were happy to rent them and later to buy them.*

Also in 1980 Telford applied both for assisted area status and for one of the new enterprise zones which gave companies coming to them considerable rates and other advantages. Neither was successful. But earlier representations for a significant government department to be moved to Telford bore fruit with the announcement that the Inland Revenue would locate its National Development Centre for computerising PAYE systems in the town centre. The divisional police headquarters and central magistrates' courts were given the go-ahead to be built. A Post Office telecommunications engineering services centre employing 130 people was proposed for Telford, operative by 1982. The last phase of Dawley centre was begun, and the final 1½ miles stage of the eastern primary at a cost of £7.5 million. A new fire station for Telford cost £1 million.

Developments on the industrial estates did continue despite the severe economic conditions. TDC started building thirty-three factory units at Hortonwood, while workshop units at district centres also continued to be constructed and occupied. A German firm producing plastic packaging materials came to Telford. It bought the freehold of a 21,500 square feet (1,997 square metres) factory on a three-quarter acre site (0.3 hectares) at Hortonwood, bringing forty new jobs, and possibilities of expansion. American, continental and Japanese firms were showing interest in moving to Telford. On the downside, the hypermarket Carrefour that had spearheaded Telford town centre's phase 1, found itself in trouble and axed some jobs. The poor economic times were hitting all traders in the town centre and the district centres, although the TDC chairman did claim that the increase in population had put over £1 million worth of business into Wellington shops.

## The coal mine that never was

Indicative of how far the inhabitants of Telford had travelled from the coalfield days when housing lay cheek-by-jowl with pits and slag heaps, is the story of the Cockshutt coal mine that never was. At a time of high unemployment, a young mining engineer and surveyor applied to open a short-term (probably seven to ten years) drift mine under woodland and open space at The Cockshutt near Oakengates, and employ up to six men. The land surface would not be disturbed but access would be through a small residential area and involve two lorries a day carrying twenty tons of coal. The residents opposed the application as an abuse of the environment, and 'were dismayed and disgusted that proposals for a mine in the area should even be considered'. Over the next two years, as unemployment rose, the engineer persevered in trying to gain access from two other directions. Wrekin DC approved one of these, but the county council turned the application down. An appeal against the decision was dismissed.

Early in 1980 government decreed that £220 million worth of assets in new towns must be sold. But Telford would be let off lightly as the more important assets had not yet reached their full value. TDC stepped up the sales of its houses to tenants. This began in March with Sutton Hill dwellings, and continued with houses, flats and maisonettes in Woodside and Brookside. The active campaign to sell off houses would continue into the following year, 1981. TDC's chairman, despite his political background, was an ardent believer in a property-owning democracy and led the development corporation at a brisk pace along this road. Mindful, too, of the historic buildings in its charge, TDC put up cast-iron plaques on Telford's ironmasters' houses, listed dwellings and rows of company houses, on canal locks, public houses, coaching inns, warehouses, factories, shops and barns. These plaques were intended to give the people of Telford a ready pointer to the history that was all about them.

On many of those important social aspects which indicated a maturing, integrating, and balanced society, Telford continued to advance quite steadily. There was a spring open golf tournament sponsored by TDC, Telford Pipe Band was re-formed and called for pipers and drummers to join. The Royal Shakespeare Company brought Henry VI, Parts I and II, to Stirchley recreation centre, while an Elizabethan pageant was held at the open-air town park theatre including the play *Vivat Vivat Regina*. The Telford Super Saturdays, which began modestly in 1976, had by 1980 reached considerable proportions with a wide variety of events which included the Wrekin horticultural show. There was something for all tastes and a carnival atmosphere that, according to the local press, 'strengthens the town spirit'. In May some fifty cyclists, both amateur and professional, and including the British Olympic team, took part in the town's second road race. A Telford horse show was held.

At the old Horsehay railway sheds the Telford Horsehay Steam Trust was established with two locomotives. Live steam came to the town park with the inauguration of a narrow-gauge tramway. A sixteen-seater open coach with an end balcony was pulled by a four-wheeled vertical steam-boilered tram locomotive, one of the Sentinel engines evolved in Shrewsbury but with links to Horsehay at the turn of the century. Less attractive activities were also reported in the town park, where 'amateur' snipers were found with air rifles and even shotguns and crossbows, after all manner of quarry. The town park also appeared to be a dumping ground for unwanted pets. The latest reported by the wardens was a cat and her kittens found in a cardboard box. But on the plus side for Telford wildlife, nightingales were heard in coppiced woodland in the gorge for the first time for several years.

Towards the end of 1980, in October, the M54 motorway received final approval, followed immediately by some second thoughts among some ministers but not Michael Heseltine, the Environment Secretary, who gave a 'final final' go-ahead in November. He had earlier in the year visited Telford and, according to Lord Northfield, been visibly impressed with what had been achieved. At the end of the year Emyr Thomas retired. He had been with Dawley and Telford Development Corporations for seventeen years, eleven and a half of them as general manager. There were many tributes to him and to the qualities of vision and steely determination he had brought to the job, not least the award of the CBE. Suffice here to quote the *Telford Journal* which had chronicled most of the difficulties that the general manager had had to cope with. 'Despite all the problems . . . Emyr Thomas never gave the slighest indication that Telford was going to be anything but a success.' His place was taken by Joseph Boyce who had since 1976 been deputy general manager. A surveyor by profession, Joe Boyce joined Dawley DC in 1964 as chief quantity surveyor and became technical director in 1971. He was therefore well-versed in the organisation and running of the development corporation and in building a new town.

*Joseph Boyce, general manager, Telford Development Corporation, 1980 to 1986.*

125

Lord Northfield defended TDC's record on job creation in the dismal economic times which prevailed. In the last year nearly 1,200 new jobs had been achieved on the new industrial estates, and seventy-six factories built. The Great Hay leisure complex, phase 2 of the town centre and the hospital, were all potential job providers in the near future. He talked about the development corporation's campaigns abroad to bring overseas companies to Telford, and he forecast that there would be 2,000 new jobs in 1981. Unemployment stood at fifteen per cent of Telford's workforce.

## Home ownership encouraged

Early in 1981 the West Midlands Planning Council published plans for considerable industrial growth in south Staffordshire, which prompted not only TDC but also Shropshire CC to protest that this was a serious threat to Telford's future. The local authorities were urged to 'fight Telford's corner'. Meanwhile, to boost sales of public housing, TDC offered fifty houses at Woodside, with three and four bedrooms, for sale at prices well below market value. There were 300 calls on the first day and within an hour all had been sold. Prices ranged from £5,000 to £7,000. A year later there was another bumper sale of houses between £6,000 and £7,000 at Brookside, Woodside and Sutton Hill. The saga of finding a suitable place for a gypsy encampment continued with a site at Donnington Wood proposed by Wrekin DC, but quite soon withdrawn after complaints.

*Under threat of demolition, thes 1850s cottages with cast-iro windows were bought by TDC an renovated. The six cottages, buil by the Lilleshall Company, wer turned into three houses.*

With the country now deep in economic recession, government made it plain to new towns that they must in future rely on private investment, and called a virtual halt to large-scale public investment in them. The Town and Country Planning Association slammed this decision, particularly with regard to the large third-generation new towns of Telford and Milton Keynes, which it argued were at a crucial point in development. The county council added to the uncertainty by producing estimates that lowered Telford's population target of 150,000 by 1996. The estimates were based on much slower growth trends and argued a final population of 121,000. TDC countered by saying that the slow growth was due to the general economic situation which could change radically.

It was of course holding out hope of a partial rescue from overseas in alleviating the job situation. There was plenty of room on the industrial estates. At the 500-acre (202 hectares) Stafford Park, for instance, sites were available from half an acre to fifty acres (up to twenty hectares).

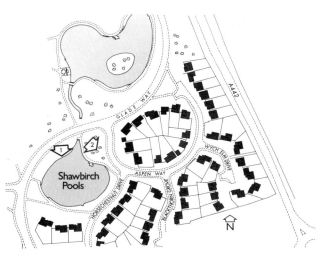

*HOUSING STUDY: Oakfield Grange, Shawbirch. A private scheme for sale by Broseley Estates Ltd, 1985/86. Neo-Tudor designs spaciously grouped with ornamental lakes. Site area 9.3 acres (3.8 hectares), sixty-eight dwellings, 7.3 to the acre (17.9 to the hectare). The scheme consists of detached three- and four-bedroomed houses with double garages, and seven single-storey dwellings.*

The agonies of the primary industries continued, with GKN Sankey's 4,000 employees on short-time and a further 1,250 jobs in jeopardy in addition to the 1,000 or more lost the year before. Glynwed Foundries' Coalbrookdale works axed sixty-four jobs, while Lilleshall Steel also had to make people redundant. On a more modern note, BKL Alloys, whose aluminium smelter at Stafford Park had been one of the two reasons for the central Nedge Hill hospital site to be turned down, shut down with the loss of 118 jobs. However, at the height of the cult for wood as heating fuel, a small foundry at Tweedale produced a new design of wood-burning stove with a normal depth but minimum projection into the room. This gallant rearguard action on the part of the foundries was named 'The Telford'. The new town tried unsuccessfully for the Nissan car factory, which went to a smaller new town in the north-east.

The development corporation proposed to turn disused buildings at the Granville colliery into a light industrial site which would complement not jeopardise the industrial estates, but this was turned down by the district council. The maggot factory asked to move there. It would build an up-to-date deodorising plant and would be happy to be regularly inspected. The residents of St George's protested, although the factory would be a half mile further from the village than its present site. One supporter of the move wrote to the press that 'they (the residents) are letting their prejudice against maggots interfere with their true judgment of the facts'.

Another major shake-up of the bus services was carried out, which involved cuts in the frequency of buses and in fare rises. A scheme for cheap tickets for the unemployed had been poorly supported. At its height unemployment was running at 22.4 per cent among men and sixteen per cent among women.

HOUSING STUDY: Water's Edge, Priorslee. Built for sale by Whelmer (Chester) Ltd, 1985/86. The scheme is on the edge of The Flash at Priorslee, with a waterfront and iron railings and period lamp posts. It has houses, flats and maisonettes built in vernacular styles. Site area 12 acres (4.85 hectares), eighty-five dwellings, seven dwellings to the acre (17.5 to the hectare). There are two-, three- and four-bedroomed dwellings, some with one garage and one parking space, others with two of each.

Life in the new town went on. In May 1981, the Telford marathon attracted 760 runners and made £15,000 for charity. Next month the first Telford and Darby brass band festival was held in the town park with a trophy donated by TDC. The Telford horse show was also held there and similarly supported. The Telford Town Park Theatre Company put on the play *Lock Up Your Daughters*, which was well attended. The town's Super Saturday in September featured a dog show, a pop concert and a darts competition. Music was supplied by local bands and choirs and the Royal Regiment of Wales. There were exhibitions of arts and crafts, displays by dance troupes, clowns, gymnasts and a motorcycle team. The Flying Bugles, a freefall parachute team, fell out of the sky into the town park. There was also that curiosity, an escapologist, who drew the admiration of the crowds, but was unable to help Telford wriggle its way out of its dire unemployment situation. Lord Northfield, fighting hard to present a brave face to the town, was reported to have admitted at a meeting that 'things are looking bad'. This prompted a cartoon in the *Telford Journal* with the caption — 'It seems like he's lost his rose-coloured specs'. Telford was twinned by Wrekin DC to the French new town of St Quentin-en-Yvelines, begun at about the same time.

On the development front, the policy of refurbishing the older estates, particularly with regard to insulation and heating, was continued. A section of the north-east primary road was opened, and there were now nine courses varying from thirteen to fifty-two weeks, with a total of 135 places at the Telford Opportunities Centre. There were also workshops for the disabled, and low-cost starter accommodation for new businesses. By now the Business Services Unit

had given practical assistance to 230 firms considering establishing businesses in Telford, and to 225 existing firms. Complementary to the BSU, TDC set up a research and development unit to help with the development of new ideas.

In November 1981, the Queen came to Telford again, this time to open phase 2 of the town centre. Both the visit and the opening of a major addition to the town's shopping gave a much needed boost to flagging morale in the town. The completed southern section of the north-east primary road was named Queensway as a reminder of an occasion that had 'lifted the gloom' as the local press were quick to point out. Where the motorway cut through the side of The Nabb, one of Telford's most impressive outdoor decorations was created on the retaining wall. A mural in mosaic tiles is on the theme of the faulted rock strata of the East Shropshire coalfield, showing coal, ironstone, sand, shale and others in rich brown, grey, ochre, black and white.

*The Queen opened phase 2 of Telford town centre in November 1981.*

## 'Its own town'

If adversity brings people closer together, then the start of 1982 may well have been the moment when Telford began to be 'its own town'. Another application for assisted area status was turned down. TDC's chairman went on record that he estimated one family in five in Telford was struggling and waiting for things to improve. He believed that the year just passed had seen 'the final welding of disparate individual settlements into Telford, a town in its own right'. News that the start of the hospital had been delayed was countered by another successful sale of TDC housing at reduced prices. A £0.5 million extension to Oakengates Town Hall was to make it a first-rate venue for cultural events. Two construction workers on the M54 at Priorslee found a hoard of silver coins dated from the reign of Queen Mary, 1554, to Charles I, 1646, thought to have been hidden during the Civil War.

In May, TDC and a private developer put together a scheme to make home-buying easier with a shared ownership. The houses would be built at Shawbirch and an occupier would make a part-payment to the developers, with the remainder taken up by TDC to whom rent would be paid. Although sales of public housing had been well received, in that month over 1,000 houses, waiting for skilled labour from outside, were standing empty. There was a Keep Telford

Tidy campaign aimed at litter louts. Although it was the local authority's responsibility to keep the town clean, TDC supplemented the workers with its own force. Lord Northfield was emphatic that the town should be tidy. 'The influence of example is very strong. If a place is clean, a great majority will leave it so.' He insisted that all graffiti — and these were sprayed on walls in the residential units as well as the town centre — should be removed immediately.

The Inland Revenue's PAYE office opened in July 1982. A majority of its first employees came from other tax offices in the country, but it was nevertheless a welcome addition, and held out future job prospects for young Telfordians. The proposed gypsy site at Donnington was abandoned, leaving no other possibilities for the time being. In July galloping horses and motorcyclists disturbed the peace and cut up the turf in the northern part of the town park close to the town centre. TDC's view was that all sports should where possible be accommodated. Bridle paths for riders were planned further south in the park, and a suitable quarry site for scramblers sought.

Traffic in the Severn Gorge had over the past few years grown and become a nightmare for the inhabitants of Ironbridge and Coalbrookdale. Fifty per cent of the heavy lorries using the gorge delivered coal to the Buildwas power station, others serviced quarries and industry. Plans for an Ironbridge bypass had been on the stocks for some years. Residents had called again and again for it to be implemented. Then a lorry careered out of control down Madeley Hill, killing four people, adding desperate poignancy to their appeal.

## The enterprise zone

A second application by Wrekin DC for an enterprise zone on 279 acres of TDC land at Stafford Park had been made. The land was serviced and ready for the development of commercial, hotel, manufacturing and warehousing businesses. The buildings of the aluminium refinery that had closed had been refurbished by the development corporation. In November 1982 government announced that Telford's application had been successful. Those of Birmingham, Coventry, Walsall and Cannock had been refused. The Stafford Park enterprise zone would be designated in the summer of 1983, and was set to attract small high-technology factories and commercial and hotel interests, all of which would employ quite large numbers of women.

Firms moving to the zone were entitled to 100 per cent allowances against corporation and income tax for capital spending and a ten-year exemption from rates. They were also exempt from Development Land Tax and property taxes. Simplified planning procedures, exemption from the IDC restrictions and from industrial training board requirements, and much faster customs facilities were also part of the generous package. Some councillors voiced criticism of the scheme, predicting that firms would 'hedge-hop' — move from an area close by. But most believed the EZ could be the turn of the economic tide for Telford. Towards the end of the year the number of unemployed did in fact dip by about 300, although the Ever Ready company shed more than 100 jobs to add to its 170 already lost, the Court Works iron foundry at Madeley made twenty-four redundant and Maddock's operated a three-day week. One of the small businesses set up in a Youth Opportunities workshop, assisted by TDC, designed and built a new bobsleigh, aiming for greater speed through aerodynamic design and a suspension system to give better control and improved steering.

By the end of the fourth year of economic troubles, Telford did seem poised on the threshold of better times. The M54 was being built, the EZ was coming, and TDC officials believed that their first Japanese company was imminent. There was new investment in industry, and new buildings going up in the town centre. Although the rented house-building programmes were virtually complete, 380 private houses had been constructed in 1982 and a further 536 TDC houses sold to give a total so far of 1,454, creating a better balance between rented and owner-occupied housing. Road works within the designated area, especially to complement the M54, were progressing, and design work for the Ironbridge bypass completed and ready. Land reclamation and landscaping had continued.

The Christmas shopping rush began early, four weeks before the day. Telford's decorations were the talk of the town, and the goods on display ranged widely over toys, home computers, fashion accessories and cosmetics. Winter clothes for the current cold spell drew the shoppers, too. In a spirit of benevolent rivalry worthy of the season of goodwill, traders in Oakengates, Madeley and Ironbridge mounted a campaign telling Telfordians to 'cut out the hustle and bustle of Christmas shopping' (presumably at Telford town centre) and visit them. Wellington advertised itself as 'brightest and best . . . warm and welcoming Wellington'. Dawley, which had after all started the whole great adventure of the new town nearly twenty years before, suggested 'shop in comfort in Dawley's traffic-free centre'.

*The mural in mosaic tiles on the side of The Nabb depicts the faulted rock strata of the East Shropshire coalfield, showing coal, ironstone, sandstone, shale and others.*

# TELFORD DEVELOPMENT CORPORATION 1979 to 1982

By the end of the period covered by Chapter 8, the town's statistics were:

| | | | | |
|---|---|---|---|---|
| Population | 106,600 | | Residents economically active | 47,437 |
| Dwellings | 40,513 | | | |
| Average number of persons per dwelling | 2.63 | | Number living and working in Telford | 31,516 |
| Houses built during period | 4,149 | | Percentage of economically active living and working in Telford | 66 |
| Total employment | 38,852 | | | |
| Manufacturing | 16,688 | | Percentage unemployed | 19.8* |
| Services | 19,219 | | (* This represented around 11,000 people) | |
| Other | 2,945 | | | |

At March 31, 1982, TDC had borrowed £390.4 million from government, of which £299.3 million had been used for the creation of assets, and £103.1 million to fund revenue deficits, the balance of £12 million being generated by disposals income and a favourable balance of working capital.

Although average interest rates for the four-year period increased only from 12.2 per cent to 13.1 per cent, the full effect of the high interest rates of the 1970s, together with a greater level of activity, had the result of increasing TDC's revenue deficit by approximately £80 million.

| | | | | |
|---|---|---|---|---|
| Total spent on purchase of land and buildings, where development had been completed | £175.3 million | | The net cost of the built assets reflects the fact that in this period TDC began to sell its rented housing stock in substantial numbers: | |
| Total spent on 4,122 acres (1,669 hectares) of land awaiting development | £7.5 million | | Dwellings | 10,710 | £119.0 million |
| Total spent on the creation of assets still to be completed | £16.6 million | | Industry in square feet (square metres) | 4,698,159 (436,459) | £25.3 million |
| | £199.4 million | | Commerce in square feet (square metres) | 523,455 (48,629) | £23.3 million |
| Construction of roads | £40.6 million | | Other | | £7.7 million |
| Derelict land reclamation | £11.4 million | | | | |
| Landscaping of public open space (including cost of land) | £17.5 million | | | | £175.3 million |
| Contributions to water authority for provision of water supply and sewers for development | £15.4 million | | | | |
| Contribution towards provision of leisure amenities | £0.5 million | | | | |
| Loans | £14.5 million | | | | |
| | £99.9 million | | | | |
| Grand total | £299.3 million | | | | |

By March 31, 1982, TDC had sold 970 dwellings which it had constructed, from a total stock of 11,347. It owned 333 dwellings which it had purchased.

Major companies coming to Telford during the period were: VG Instruments, stainless steel components, Chequer Foods, food packaging, Colourtrend/Nashua Photo, film processing, Bischof & Klein, plastic packaging, Central Circuits, electrical circuits, Tesa Metrology, measuring instruments, Ablex Tools/Ablex Audio Visual, cassettes and floppy discs, IIC/Hestair Intercraft, picture frames.

Owing to restrictions on recruitment areas, nearly all companies which were 'early movers' came from the West Midlands. A study in October 1979 showed that out of 240 companies on TDC's industrial estates, 63 per cent originated from the West Midlands (including Telford and Shropshire). Some 20 per cent were new companies, and only 17 per cent were from other UK regions or from overseas.

Many of the early movers were related to the car industry. The plastics industry firms began with small companies employing less than ten people, and by 1980 there was a total of 32 firms employing 1,022 people. The electronics industry began to develop from about 1970 with a handful of companies. During the period 1974 to 1978 there was little development owing to tight recruiting controls. By the end of 1982, with relaxation of controls, numbers of electrical and electronic engineering companies came, and employment went beyond the 2,000 mark.

# 9 Better Times Ahead
## 1983 to 1986

In the bitter January weather of 1983 there was still well over twenty per cent of Telford's workforce unemployed. Yet the prospects for the town appeared to many to be brighter and closer with the building of the M54 and the granting of an enterprise zone. The *Shropshire Star* interviewed businessmen who praised the efforts of TDC and the local authorities in providing first-rate conditions for industry and commerce. They expressed their optimism that when the upturn in the UK's economy came, Telford would be 'in the vanguard'.

There were, however, critics of TDC priorities, specifically for building leisure facilities when so many were unemployed. Lord Northfield replied that the development corporation had to provide 'a whole town' rather than just industrial and commercial estates and residential units. The whole town therefore included an ice rink, tennis centre, a new auditorium at Oakengates Town Hall, children's playgrounds, and a new swimming pool in Wellington, with everywhere the essential landscaping work. He pointed out that all facilities were for everybody, including those presently without work. 'Companies will not come to Telford unless it is a complete town.' TDC's publicity in Britain and overseas stressed that it was creating 'a total town where everyone (across the income brackets) wants to live'.

During February the first Japanese company came to Telford. Hitachi-Maxell announced it would built a factory of 120,000 square feet (11,148 square metres) on a sixty-acre (24 hectares) site at Apley Castle, initially employing 170 with a further 250 at a later stage, and manufacturing video tapes. There were 3,000 applications for the first 100 jobs offered. At the other end of the scale, Britain's only electric car manufacturer moved its operations to Telford with TDC help. Later the Telford Mini Electric Car, powered by a tractor engine and twelve six-volt batteries giving thirty-five to seventy miles, was on show at the town centre. Also with support from the development corporation, two women from Aqueduct set up their own business in a disued chapel in Oakengates, making toy clowns.

More news of Telford hospital came, bad news in that while the capital sum of £27 million for building it was available, the moneys to run it — about £9 million a year — were proving difficult to find. The Shropshire Health Authority could only scrape together £4 million. This was the beginning of a long and contentious affair which involved the West Midlands Regional Health Authority, the Minister of Health, Kenneth Clarke, Shropshire's medical fraternity and many ordinary citizens. For soon came the announcement that in order to service the new hospital, five smaller county hospitals faced being closed down or having departments or wards axed. Although some of the work of these hospitals would be taken over by the big new hospital, it seemed likely that medical care in other parts of Shropshire would suffer. More government money was demanded, plans drawn up to reduce the size of Telford's hospital, or to mothball part of it as soon as built, or to delay the second phase. A plan to close the health care centre in the town centre and shift its responsibilities to the district centres was opposed by residents until the hospital would be built.

A second Japanese company announced its intention of coming to Telford. Nikon would at first have a distribution centre for its microscopes and ophthalmic equipment. The *Shropshire Star* was moved to describe 'working the Japanese way' for potential British employees. Apparently this would include 'morning assembly, consultation, security, equality, one union, no smoking or drinking — and sweep your own floorspace'.

*The Lightmoor community was dubbed 'the Good Life village' by the media. The community built its own houses, put in roads, drains and sewerage. Several craft and other businesses are run there. One family keeps a smallholding, many grow their own fruit and vegetables.*

## A community at Lightmoor

In March 1983 discussion was invited by TDC and the Town and Country Planning Association on a proposal to set up a community on 220 acres (89 hectares) at Lightmoor. Without being an isolated community striving for an unrealistic level of self-sufficiency, it would have self-sufficiency and energy conservation as major facets, with village-type housing and with land for agricultural, horticultural, employment and recreation facilities. It would be an innovatory mix of people and skills, 'offering new solutions to current problems of unemployment . . .'. As the project was taken up by the press and public it was emphasised that it would be 'no hippy-type commune for dropouts', but a largely self-contained community with 'neighbourhood living', self-help, work-shops, market gardens and smallholdings. The land would be given by TDC and held in trust for the members of the community which would benefit as a whole from the increase in land values that its members' efforts produced. The community 'hoped to create livelihoods without destroying the countryside in the process'. Enthusiasts from Telford and further afield applied to find out more about the TCPA-run project, which had in it elements of Sir Ebenezer Howard's new community ideals embodied in his garden cities. Some twelve families proposed themselves as the pioneers. They included a nurse, teachers, a bricklayer, a mechanical engineer, the owner of a computer software shop, a computer programmer and a cabinet maker. Microprocessors, sewage ingesters, solar panels and heat pumps, and sheep, goats, cattle and poultry, fish farming and coppicing woodland for fuel, were all on the community's agenda. Lightmoor was dubbed 'the Good Life village' by the media.

135

The closure of the cinema in Wellington, and the subsequent fight to keep a part of it as a cinema, highlighted the fact that Telford town centre as yet did not have one, as TDC searched for commercial interests to provide the facility.

*An aerial view showing the enterprise zone of Stafford Park with the eastern primary road Queensway. The massive tree planting carried out to create the forest element is clearly seen.*

However, a nightclub and disco with a public house, close to the shopping centre, were planned. The indoor tennis and squash centre was being built and it was hoped a tennis star would open it. According to *Which? Heritage Guide*, the Ironbridge Gorge Museum was one of twelve top places for all-family, all-day heritage entertainment. The museum was diligent in adding to its industrial treasures. For £1 it bought the last of the Severn trows which had in years gone by worked downstream in the lower Severn estuary. *The Spry* was rescued from the mud of Worcester docks. Built of oak in 1894, the vessel was seventy-one feet (21.6 metres) long and weighed sixty tons. She would cost £11,400 (later this sum was to escalate to £100,000 and more) to restore and re-rig in her original single-mast sloop rig. The museum also bought the Jackfield tile factory and planned to open it to tile making within a youth training scheme and as a tile museum. The Telford and Wrekin Festival in 1983 began with the comedian Ken Dodd and ended with a recital by the 'cellist Paul Tortelier. There were more than fifty events, some with well-known names from outside such as the singers Instant Sunshine and the organist Gillian Weir, but many by local groups which indicated the growing strength of local cultural life. Among these were the Telford Amateur Dramatic and Light Operatic Society, the Donnington Garrison Drama Group, and Telford Chamber Orchestra. In July, TDC and Wrekin District Council sponsored a new Telford sport, a quadrathon involving twenty miles of cycling, a fourteen-mile run, eleven miles downriver canoeing, and five miles orienteering.

## The minutiae of TDC's work

While the sporting, cultural and recreational life of the town continued to expand and become richer, TDC was still struggling not only to bring more jobs to Telford, but also with the minutiae of keeping what it had built in repair, its residents happy and their belief in the new town, if not intact then at least not badly battered. This list of 1983 is typical for any year. Trees at Woodside had grown too big for their sites, overshadowing gardens and buildings. TDC tree surgeons thinned, lopped and pruned, and occasioned a rash of letters to the press accusing the development corporation of vandalising the landscape. Other letters told of TDC painters working on the refurbishment of dwellings, arriving to paint front doors when occupants were out at work, and painting nevertheless so that a half inch on the two sides and at the top remained unpainted. Sarcasm was used to suggest that there was no truth in the rumour that TDC would be painting the halls with long-handled brushes — through the letterboxes. Refuse piled up at the back of Madeley shopping malls, and TDC gave permission for the local authority to use an area of its property for storage prior to removal. A kick-about area at Randlay had been long-awaited. When it was inaugurated residents complained. Youngsters at St George's were found using a carefully landscaped and planted piece of reclaimed land as a motorcycle track. A badly-drained path in Woodside, subject to flooding in heavy rains, had not responded to first efforts to cure the problem and would need major works. TDC had to threaten 'help-yourself' gardeners with prosecution as bulbs and shrubs were grubbed up from its landscaping work and taken to private gardens.

In June, Telford suffered a great fire when one of the Central Ordnance Depot's warehouses went up in flames. It was a ten-acre (four hectares) building containing textiles and technical equipment. A total of twenty-four civilian fire engines helped the Army's own fire-fighting machines fight the blaze for six hours. A pall of smoke up to 1,000 feet (305 metres) high carried fall-out over the town, and this was found to contain traces of asbestos. TDC aided Wrekin DC and the county council in making the town safe. The damage to the warehouse was estimated at £150 million.

## Industrial losses and successes

On the industrial front there were further losses among the older industries. Ever Ready axed another 200 jobs. About 130 jobs were lost at Glynwed Foundries in Ketley. But Blockleys, the brickmaker, took on sixty more staff, and Lilleshall invested in a flowline production system making steel safety and security fencing and power transmission steelwork. On a bigger scale, GKN announced it would invest £6.5 million in a new plant at its Hadley Castle works to produce plastic vehicle springs. The engineer who had asked to open a mine under The Cockshutt now applied to do the same under Albion Bank in St George's, and eventually received the same answer as before. A survey was announced to check the Lightmoor area for coal, but any idea of mining there was dropped, out of concern to preserve its landscape character.

In its bid to become a seat of high-technology industry, Telford had another two successes in this 'turn-about' year. The Taiwanese firm, Tatung, decided to come from Bridgnorth, much to that town's disgust. And a third Japanese company, Ricoh, a leading photocopier manufacturer, announced its intention of setting up a factory. High-tech industrial sites were now envisaged at Apley Castle, Priorslee and Hadley Park. A little later than stated, the enterprise zone was finally announced in August 1983 as being fully operative by January 1984. Michael Morgan, TDC's commercial director, was appointed zone manager. There were five sites, four owned by the development corporation in Stafford Park and the town centre, and one at Priorslee belonging to the Lilleshall Company. Despite the Labour Party being against the zones, Labour-led Wrekin DC made every effort to support Telford's zone. TDC was soon inundated with enquiries, a satisfying number of which turned rapidly into firm applications.

September 1983 saw TDC holding a reception in the town centre to thank all voluntary workers in Telford's community work. Lord Northfield paid them tribute. 'You can only build a whole town if you have activities, clubs and societies organised by the people themselves,' he told them. Mindful of the continuing requirement to look after gypsies, a site was proposed in Bratton on the north-west boundary of the town. It was chosen out of twenty-seven possible sites, and was later abandoned after protests, particularly from farmers.

With a tentative date for the demise of TDC towards the end of the decade, Wrekin DC already talked of taking over the development corporation's assets. These would be industrial, commercial, housing and community-related. The latter included the town park, some car parks, sports pitches, open spaces by roads, water areas, reclaimed land now woodland and heath, some pubs and shops, community halls and clubs. Suitable properties would be offered to lease-holders first. Later a date for TDC's housing stock to be handed over in 1987 was tentatively made with other assets a year later. The development corporation itself maintained silence. There was evidently a great deal to do in completing the infrastructure, housing, and industrial and commercial building to be able to hand over that 'complete town' which was TDC's objective and obligation.

## The M54 opened

At last Telford was connected meaningfully with the outside world. The Minister of Transport, Nicholas Ridley, opened the M54 in November 1983. What was called 'the hidden motorway' had been designed with many cuttings so that traffic would not often be seen and noise cut to a minimum. The first eager travellers reported bridges with waving crowds, some open country to be seen but few houses. Already 250,000 trees and shrubs had been planted along it. Extra traffic police were drafted in. Mindful of the huge delays to the motorway, Joe Boyce, TDC's general manager, commented wryly to the *Financial Times*, that had the road been built ten years ago when it should have been, or fifteen years ago when it might have been, the story of Telford would have been very different. Originally, government had proposed only two interchanges, Castle Farm and Ketley Dingle. TDC insisted on a third, the Forge, opposite the town centre, and paid £3 million for it. Immediately the motorway added immensely to the town's attractiveness to industry. It increased the number of people using the town centre, and a blessed calm fell on the A5, once congested and accident-prone. People found themselves starting for work at the usual time and arriving much earlier than they expected.

*In October 1983 Telford was at last connected meaningfully with the outside world. Nicholas Ridley, then Minister of Transport, opened the M54 connection with the M6.*

TDC's chairman could look back in his annual report on a significant year. He wrote that Telford was 'a place which investors in the most advanced technology now automatically place high on their list of locations'. Patient work overseas was now paying dividends with further Japanese companies considering Telford, and German, Dutch and US firms already establishing themselves. The overseas newcomers' products were varied and included cooling plant for transformers, roofing materials, garden and leisure furniture, clothing, machine tools, electronic filing systems, and industrial fasteners. From Britain there were factories manufacturing electronic cash handling systems, printed circuit boards, and at the heavier end, special chassis for bus and coach builders. More small workshop and factory units had been built and TDC now sponsored or provided 262 units up to 2,000 square feet (186 square metres). Significantly, some larger units that had earlier proved difficult to let, had been successfully sub-divided. There was now strong demand for factories of all sizes.

A total of 457 private dwellings had been built, including lakeside housing at Priorslee that had been an immediate success with home owners. Later it became a favourite location for Japanese house buyers. Close co-operation with developers had achieved site layouts and housing styles of special identity. Another 440 TDC dwellings had been sold to tenants, making a total of about 2,000. New sections of the major road network in north Telford had been completed and contributed to the increasing ease and efficiency of movement through the town.

The one big fly in Telford's ointment was unemployment, still stubbornly and persistently over twenty per cent. The year showed a net increase in jobs of 185, but losses from the old industries continued to dominate the situation. Some 800 firms had now made use of TDC's advisory services. The development corporation was managing agent for youth training schemes with 425 places. Community programmes, Britain's first adult information technology centre — an extension of the successful technology centre opened two years earlier — and a travelling exhibition on computer-aided design and manufacture, were either supported or initiated by TDC. The latter was a clear reflection of the importance given by the development corporation to creative training for employers and employees alike.

## Urban landscaping

The tree and shrub varieties planted in the town centre, district centres, in housing estates, and round offices and factories, and in the part of the town park close to the town centre, all indicated that the 'wildwood' of largely native species had been left behind. By their more exotic shapes, leaf colours and fruits, and their more formal planting patterns — in windbreaks, on banks, in car parks, squares, and along streets — they showed that places of organised life-styles had been reached. TDC insisted on suitable landscaping schemes for private factory sites which would accord with its own scale-giving plantings on industrial sites.

Maples, including the autumn-colourful Norway maple, are common. There are varieties of mountain ash and whitebeam, limes, including the American lime, ornamental willows, American red oaks, hardy ornamental cherries, including the Korean hill cherry, and golden acacias. Evergreens include the ilex, Lawson's cypress, various pines, such as Scots and umbrella pines, western red cedars, deodars and cedars of Lebanon, and monkey puzzles. Some varieties of poplar and alder which are used in the more extensive landscapes also find themselves in industrial and urban contexts. Balsam poplar, tulip trees, walnuts and Turkey oaks add to the variety of scent, leaf shape, and colour of bark which distinguishes the range of planting. Some comparative rarities are to be found, such as black-leaved oaks, swamp cypresses, elms thought to be resistant to Dutch elm disease, and catalpas.

Roundabouts, formal beds and roadsides leading into major centres all have a wide range of shrubs to give variety. There are numbers of berberis, ceanothus, and prunus varieties, and cotoneaster. Willows, dogwoods, lavender, ivy, rugosa roses and the dwarf pine, *Pinus mugo pumilio*, are some of the ground cover plants used. To give long-lasting colour there are thousands of beds of roses, and millions of daffodil, narcissi, crocuses, snowdrops, scillas, aconites, grape hyacinths and tulips have been set to give great blocks of colour in their seasons. With perhaps fifty small ponds and lakes from old clay quarries, furnace pools and canal reservoirs, and fifteen larger sheets of water, TDC's landscaping team has carefully planted reed mace and sedges, water lilies, and red-barked willows, thorns and dogwoods as waterside trees. Within a few years the smaller areas of water are rich in other aquatic plants that have come in naturally.

The thoughtful and inspired landscaping of Telford with its contrasting semi-wild and civilised ordered landscapes, and the attention paid to mass colours and the seasons, were by now contributing to the strong visual appeal of the town — to residents, to would-be Telfordians, and to the managements of prospective companies.

## The town park

By 1984 the town park with its 450 acres (182 hectares) sending a thick green swathe directly into the town centre, was shaping up as an exceptional public

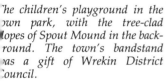

*The children's playground in the own park, with the tree-clad lopes of Spout Mound in the backround. The town's bandstand as a gift of Wrekin District Council.*

facility. To give varied landforms and landscapes 1.31 million cubic yards (one million cubic metres) of earth had been moved, and forty-eight mine shafts capped. Spout Mound, on the very edge of the town centre, from which there are views for nearly 360 degrees, is 630 feet (192 metres) above sea level. The southern portion was open space with some sports fields, and the central portion was being developed for casual pursuits and nature study, embracing grassland and woodland. Several pools and small lakes added to the landscape, and there were diverse habitats for flora and fauna.

The northern portion contained the amphitheatre overlooking Randlay pool, and several smaller bodies of water. There was a private sports club where Telford's rugby and hockey teams had their home. Award-winning gardens, a big children's play area, and a children's wonderland based on nursery rhymes and fairy tales were also there. In the latter were the old woman who lived in a shoe, the crooked house, a fairy grotto, Snow White's house, the Mad Hatter's tea party, the gingerbread house, and an animated tableau from Wind in the Willows. Much of this new recreational place was built into the contours of old pit mounds and quarries. Some of the older inhabitants were heard to sigh nostalgically that their old courting 'lanes' were now unrecognisable. The first phase of the steam train was already operative, and at the end of the previous year the West Midlands Tennis Centre, standing on the edge of the park, had been officially opened by the American tennis star John McEnroe.

## Jobs and the hospital

The year 1984 was dominated by two subjects — jobs and the hospital. The Environment Secretary, Patrick Jenkin, inaugurated the enterprise zone. Already its success was assured by a flood of applications for sites, and every purpose-built factory had been let. The Inland Revenue announced an expansion of its Telford operation. There were plans to develop the Madeley Court Works site of seven acres (2.8 hectares) as an industrial park where 150 jobs would be created. A small modern foundry was proposed, although fears of pollution from this were immediately voiced by Brookside residents. AB Cranes of Horsehay obtained a £0.75 million order from naval dockyards, while GKN won a £200 million order for military vehicles which would create 400 jobs at Hadley Castle. In contrast, Lilleshall sold the last of its manufacturing and engineering subsidiaries in the town and moved its headquarters to Gloucester, with the loss of ten Telford jobs, bringing to an end over 220 years of manufacturing activity on the coalfield.

As to the hospital, ministerial approval for it was given, but talks on its running costs and their provenance continued. Kenneth Clarke, the minister, indicated that extra funding was possible, but asked for 'a sensible rationalisation of other Shropshire services'. With extra moneys later promised, the regional health authority accepted responsibility for the running costs. At the same time the cuts envisaged in other Shropshire medical services were 'put on ice' for up to two years, and later came a plan to drop phase 2 of the hospital involving psychiatric and obstetric beds.

Meanwhile there came a rumour that TDC was planning to build a huge leisure park and housing in the town park. Telfordians banded themselves into an angry group called Hands Off Our Park or HOOP. The development corporation retorted that the plans were only at discussion stage, and that having spent £2½ million of public money on the park, it was not likely to go and ruin it. Under pressure, Lord Northfield was more specific. The plans were for a few acres of housing on the edge of the park at Stirchley, and seven acres (2.8 hectares) backing on to Spout Mound close to the town centre and to the area which TDC hoped to develop with a theatre, cafes, pubs and restaurants to prevent the town centre being emptied of life and people when the shops shut. There was also the possibility of a leisure park run by commercial enterprise. From somewhere HOOP obtained a figure of eighty acres (thirty-two hectares) for the leisure park, and was to continue its activities and protests. With changes in priorities, TDC eventually dropped the projects. The walls of a ruined Norman chapel at Malinslee, built circa 1180, were dismantled before reclamation work there, and re-erected in the town park. The West Midlands Tennis and Racquets Centre announced debts of £600,000 and was closed, later to be reopened under new management and name.

*The ice rink photographed from Spout Mound, across the Maxell cherry garden and boating lake on the edge of the town park closest to the town centre. The rink was designed by TDC Architects' Department.*

In October, Telford's ice rink, designed and built by TDC, was opened officially by Princess Anne. There were no joining fees or membership subscriptions and the rink could be used for other large-scale entertainment. In the first two weeks 36,000 people used it. With this addition to the town centre's attractions, a six-month experiment to increase the frequency of evening buses was made. News of the Ironbridge bypass had been scanty since a four-year-old boy had been killed on the narrow road through Coalbrookdale. It would cost £7 million and after an initial hold-up when farming interests challenged a compulsory purchase order and a conservation group objected to part of the route, the go-ahead eventually came towards the end of 1984. Meanwhile, with the miners' strike in full swing and sympathy action by the railway unions, coal for the power station all came by road, much of it through Ironbridge and Coalbrookdale.

Telford's Super Saturday organisation was taken over from TDC by the newly-formed Telford Society. During the year several conservation stories highlighted the development corporation's long interest and concern in this field. Planting on the roundabouts leading to the M54 was specially contrived to provide food for wildlife. A tipping site for the county council at Stoney Hill was found to be the home of orchids and other rare plants. These were carefully removed to other clay-rich sites. To help halt the decline in barn owls, TDC supported the placing of nesting boxes in isolated places in the town. Stirchley Grange Environmental Interpretation Centre, aided by TDC, aimed to link urban nature conservation and countryside studies, to generate interest in both the rural and urban aspects of the new town. Good landscaping was obviously appreciated by many in Telford. Hitachi-Maxell presented 1,000 cherry trees to the town, later incorporated into a garden in the town park. Another group that showed its faith in Telford — perhaps remembering the old mining settlements dotted with public houses — were the brewers. Many pubs, for instance in Wellington, Wrockwardine Wood and Ironbridge, were upgraded. New pubs included The Wrekin View at Lawley Bank, and Quenchers in the town centre.

*HOUSING STUDY: Holmer Lak[e] A private scheme by Tarm[ac] Homes, for sale, built 1987/8[8]. The scheme features stone, bri[ck] and rendered walls with vernacul[ar] architecture and good stone wal[l]ing. Site area 2.8 acres (1.1 hectares), fifteen dwellings, 5.3 [to] the acre (13.2 to the hectare). T[he] housing consists of five thre[e] bedroomed and ten four-bedroom[ed] houses. Two dwellings have on[e] garage and one parking space, t[he] remainder two garages and tw[o] parking spaces.*

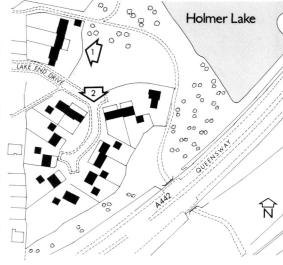

Holmer Lake

LAKE END DRIVE

QUEENSWAY

A442

N

## Intermediate assisted area status

A further application for assisted area status was rewarded with the intermediate category. There was disappointment that full status had not been given, but under intermediate status, companies were able to apply for development funds from government and the European Community. A sum of £2,500 per job created was available together with various capital, R & D, and in-plant training costs, and there were loans at low interest rates and taxation relief. The Inland Revenue's new tax centre, now expected to bring up to 700 jobs, was the subject of Hollinswood residents' anger. It would be built on land very close to housing and would include a large car park. In the event, the building, designed most sympathetically by the Property Services Agency, with its landscaping by TDC, produced a complex which has given little cause for any further concern by the residents. With one curious exception. The open-ended pipework in the design would in certain wind conditions produce a wailing sound of Wagnerian

Addenbrooke House in the business centre was built by Telford Development Corporation and sold on. Steel-framed and clad with a glazed entrance feature, the office block has an atrium through four floors.

*The shopping centre in phase 3 of Telford town centre, where a crossing of pedestrian ways is marked by a glazed lantern feature.*

dimensions. The problem was solved by closing the ends of the pipes. During 1984 the police station was opened, the central railway station and the 100-bed hotel begun. Lettings of industrial floor space were at a record level, and by no means limited to the enterprise zone. Private housing continued to be built apace, from small 'starter' homes to deluxe residences, mostly sponsored by TDC and on its land. A total of 2,240 TDC dwellings had been sold to tenants, representing twenty per cent of its housing stock. There were by now numbers of Japanese families in Telford, and TDC started a Saturday school to keep children in touch with their language and culture.

## Unemployment still high

While it fluctuated slightly, unemployment was still above twenty per cent at the start of 1985, yet there were 41,000 jobs in Telford, up three per cent on last year. As programmes and projects were completed it was the turn of TDC itself to shed some staff. The Lilleshall Company put up a scheme to develop its twenty acres (eight hectares) in the enterprise zone on the north side of the motorway, largely as a retail park. This was turned down by Wrekin DC as its operations would be bound to damage Oakengates district centre and the town centre. The company appealed, and bitterness arose when TDC later announced its intention of building a retail park on the Old Park side of the town centre. Wrekin DC decided this site was the correct one and passed it. Eventually the Lilleshall site was used for office and commercial development.

During 1985 a steady stream of new investment in industry and commerce came. The Plastics Processing ITB opened its training centre, GKN's new plastic spring and other products needed 150 skilled engineers, and an all-British industrial robot was unveiled by Unimation. A project for the development of the Granville colliery site included coal recovery with the land reclamation — some 200,000 tons of coal — of 235 acres (95 hectares), and a refuse tip for the county council, a golf course, housing, a gypsy site, industry and open space — and the maggot factory. Eventually 150 mine shafts were treated, the refuse tip was surrounded by high banks and had a capacity of 2.3 million cubic yards (1.8 million cubic metres) — enough to last Telford for twenty years. Sadly the crane company at Horsehay closed with the loss of 300 jobs. Despite its new products, GKN also sacked the same number from its older obsolescent operations.

In the year a total of 0.5 million square feet (46,450 square metres) of factory space was completed, but as yet only a third of it by private enterprise, and the conclusion was that the private sector was still holding back. A report by the county council highlighted the need, not only to plan for the last years of TDC's life — the date of April 1989 for its demise was still current — but also to ensure there would be sufficient government moneys to finish the job satisfactorily. The report suggested that for a population of 130,000, a further 11,000 dwellings, 27,000 jobs, roads, and greater development of the land straddling the M54, would be necessary. So far the enterprise zone had created 2,326 jobs and all but seventy-five acres (thirty hectares) had been developed or committed. The district council supported by TDC applied for an extension, which was not favourably received by government. All told there were now 43,500 jobs in Telford, still below the peak level of 44,681 back in 1978 before the accelerated decline of the old industries. On the bright side, the European Regional Development Fund allocated £7.3 million for infrastructure projects in the town. More companies came from the USA,

Taiwan, Belgium, Switzerland, Sweden and Japan, and there were now nearly sixty overseas firms employing 8.6 per cent of the workforce.

TDC continued its initiatives in conjunction with the local authorities to try and alleviate the persistent high level of unemployment, and was as active as ever in sports, arts, recreation and adult education services. A half-marathon was added to the Telford Marathon event. The first round of the Davis Cup series between England and Spain was held at the renamed Telford Tennis and Racquets Centre, which was also chosen as its national centre by the Squash Racquets Association. The Telford Society renamed the Super Saturday event the Telford Show. TDC made land available at Woodside for a cottage and rural enterprises village where mentally handicapped people could live and work normally. The craft centre in the old tile works at Jackfield now had workshop accommodation for thirty small businesses and twelve families in maisonettes in a TDC development.

## The Task Ahead

With an eye to its own demise, TDC took the initiative of consulting with the county and district councils in producing a document for government entitled 'The Task Ahead'. This planned the programme of work to give form and coherence to the town before the development corporation was wound up, in completing the main road systems, providing housing and commercial and industrial development. The job situation would have to be carefully reviewed according to demographic changes in the population, now over 110,000. There was a continued reduction in the number of children of school age, but a rapid increase in children of pre-school age. The working population and the number of employed residents continued to rise, and there was still growth — although somewhat reduced — in the number of Telfordians of retirement age. There were more and more single-parent families.

Despite the obstinately high unemployment rate, Lord Northfield could say that 1985 had been 'the best year yet'. The following year saw the growth of optimism in the future. There was such a rush for industrial floor space that TDC was short of suitable accommodation, and there was similarly a queue of potential tenants for offices. But the private sector still held back outside the enterprise zone. Provision of new speculative floor space was considered essential if continuing expansion and growth was to take place. Wrekin DC, backed by TDC, made a further application for an extension to the enterprise zone. Phase 3 of the town centre shopping area brought in the long-awaited Marks & Spencer. The relocation to Telford of Windsor Life Assurance suggested a growing perception of the town, long fostered by TDC, as a service centre. Two more Japanese firms arrived, ultimately intending to employ 1,700 people. There was progress on other fronts. In May, Telford Central railway station was opened by Lord Murray of the TUC, formerly Len Murray, who had been born and bred in Hadley. It was reached on foot by a covered bridge across the motorway, and had parking for 250 cars. More car parks were begun in the town centre to service the Telford Square developments which included the courts and office blocks, one of which TDC would move into from Priorslee Hall. Ironbridge Gorge was declared a World Heritage Site, and would, with luck, be largely free of heavy lorries before too long. For at last the 3½-mile bypass was begun, through terrain that was acknowledged to be difficult topographically and sometimes geologically unstable.

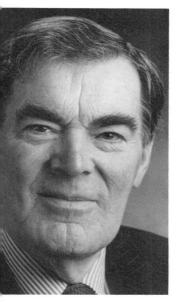

*Frank Jones, chairman, Telford Development Corporation, 1987 to 1991.*

*Michael Morgan, general manager, Telford Development Corporation, 1986 to 1991.*

## Changes at the top

Frank Jones, who was a successful Telford businessman and had been chairman of the Shropshire Health Authority during its long agony over Telford hospital, became deputy chairman of TDC's board. Joe Boyce retired as general manager. Apart from leading TDC through the worst of the depression, he had master-minded the overseas operations and established a particularly special relationship with the Japanese. His place was taken by Michael Morgan, also a surveyor, who had worked for Sheffield City Council and Derby Borough Council before joining TDC in 1970 in the commercial department. As commercial director Mike Morgan had set up the enterprise zone and had the knowledge and experience to guide TDC as it completed its task and disposed of its assets. TDC was already looking at methods of handing over its housing and exploring the possibility of tenants having a say in the matter — as between a housing association and the local authority. However, the Department of the Environment had advised it to hold fire on that issue. In fact, through the summer and autumn of 1986 TDC's operations were overshadowed by the long wait for a decision from government — having received The Task Ahead submitted by TDC and the county and district councils — on what the development corporation should try and achieve, and how long it would have.

In December approval was given both to the strategy and the date of September 1991 for the winding up of TDC. The development corporation was to become a 'facilitating agency' with a run-down in staff numbers. Professional and technical staff would be made redundant and privatise their work through the establishment of consultancies. These were seen as of long-term benefit to Telford as well as providing continuity of technical advice to the diminishing TDC.

By March 1987 there were 4,250 jobs in the enterprise zone, and 4,727 in the town centre — excluding construction jobs — of which 2,703 were occupied by women. The total number of jobs in Telford stood at 46,099, the highest number ever, and at last the unemployment percentage was on the way down, although kept up by the numbers of long-term unemployed, stabilised but not yet decreasing.

TDC could look with some satisfaction at a total of 529 private dwellings built in the year. Its own direct contribution had been two sheltered housing schemes at Ketley Grange and Dawley. A further 296 TDC houses had been sold to tenants, making 2,768, twenty-four per cent of the original stock. Apart from the Ironbridge bypass, the eastern district road was progressing northwards from the M54. Lord Northfield could write in his annual report, 'In terms of domestic and overseas investment in the town, in retail and commercial growth, in housing completions and sales . . . these are the best ever results'. He promised more and better to come — always provided TDC would receive adequate funds to achieve its aims as approved by government.

# TELFORD DEVELOPMENT CORPORATION 1983 to 1986

By the end of the period covered by Chapter 9, the town's statistics were:

| | | | | |
|---|---|---|---|---|
| Population | 110,950 | | Residents economically active | 49,474 |
| Dwellings | 43,040 | | Number living and working in Telford | 36,540 |
| Average number of persons per dwelling | 2.58 | | Percentage of economically active living and working in Telford | 74 |
| Houses built during period | 2,526 | | | |
| Total employment | 45,990 | | Percentage unemployed (Still about 11,000) | 21.7 (Feb 1985) |
| Manufacturing | 19,289 | | | 20.1 (June 1986) |
| Services | 22,970 | | | |
| Other | 3,731 | | | |

By March 31, 1986 TDC had borrowed £566.9 million from government, of which £341.5 million had been spent on assets, and £231.3 million on financing revenue deficits. There was a small favourable working balance of £6.9 million. The average borrowing rate was 12.37 per cent, a slight reduction on the 1982 figure:

| | | | | | |
|---|---|---|---|---|---|
| Total spent on purchase of land and buildings, where development had been completed | £200.3 million | | The net cost of the built assets was: | | |
| | | | Dwellings | 9,273 | £121.2 million |
| Total spent of 3,806 acres (1,541 hectares) of land awaiting development | £6.8 million | | Industry in square feet (square metres) | 3,836,448 (356,406) | £33.9 million |
| Total spent on creation of assets still to be completed | £7.7 million | | Commerce in square feet (square metres) | 527,460 (49,001) | £33.3 million |
| | £214.8 million | | Other | | £11.9 million |
| Construction of roads | £61.0 million | | | | £200.3 million |
| Derelict land reclamation | £13.2 million | | | | |
| Landscaping of public open space (including cost of land) | £21.0 million | | | | |
| Contribution to water authority for provision of water supply and sewers | £15.6 million | | | | |
| Contribution to provision of leisure amenities | £3.5 million | | | | |
| Loans | £12.4 million | | | | |
| | £126.7 million | | | | |
| Grand total | £341.5 million | | | | |

By March 31, 1986 2,394 dwellings from a total of 11,521 built by TDC had been sold. TDC still owned 146 dwellings it had purchased. In addition the development corporation had begun a significant programme of sales of its industrial assets.

This period saw a decided change in Telford's economic structure as the promotional efforts overseas were rewarded with numbers of high-tech firms coming to the town. Hitachi-Maxell of Japan came with a £30 million investment in a highly-automated video cassette plant on a 60-acre (24 hectares) site. Memcom (USA) came in 1983. Tatung (Taiwan), Ricoh (Japan), Wynn Electronics (UK) and Plastic Omnium (France) arrived in 1984. Frigon (New Zealand) came in 1986. Numbers of smaller companies in electronics, robotics and precision engineering set up in Telford, and by 1985 employment in the sector was over 3,000. The Inland Revenue's National Computer Development Centre, for computerisation of the country's main taxation systems proved Telford's credentials as an attractive location for technology-based operations.

# 10  Boom and Bloom
## 1987 to 1989

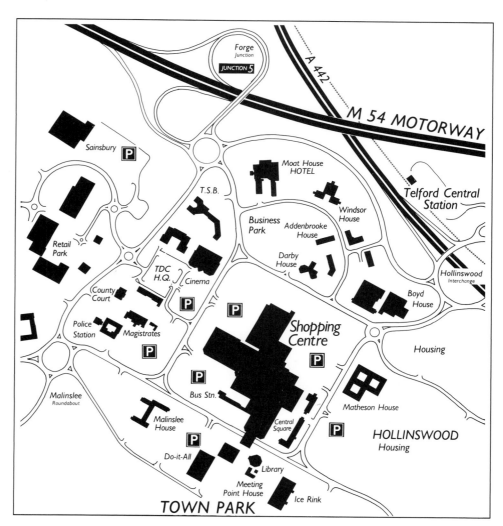

*TELFORD TOWN CENTRE.*

The first significant event of a period which was to see Telford's final emergence as a West Midlands force and a success, was the government's decision to write off £440 million of TDC's current debt of £567 million. It was expected that sales of its housing, industrial and commercial assets between 1987 and 1991 would more than adequately pay back the remainder of the debt. January 1987 saw unemployment around nineteen per cent, still disappointingly high, although quite apart from British private investment in the town, there had been substantial overseas investment as well. US firms had created 1,000 jobs, as had Taiwan. Recent Japanese companies had brought 400 more jobs, while French and German investment had resulted in 690 and 290 jobs respectively. One French company, Peaudouce, had acquired 180,000 square feet (16,722 square metres) of factory space at Halesfield to make babies' nappies. Kuwaiti investment had created 120 jobs as well. The pace of industrial expansion and commercial growth would accelerate and bring down unemployment quite sharply. Even the maggot factory was accommodated at last, with permission to build a modern factory up against the border of the designated area in the northwest on the old Granville colliery site.

That other unresolved problem remained — the gypsies fared less well. There was still only the Lodge Road, Donnington site, built by TDC in 1977 for permanent gypsy residents and run by the district council. But itinerants were always arriving, and camping in all manner of places liable to shock nearby residents. In January 150 gypsies camped on the old Oakengates Foundry car park and were moved on. In May others were moved from land next to a bingo hall, and there were six families with their horses camping near the Lodge Road site, with their goats browsing TDC's carefully planted roadside shrubs and young trees. A few months later three new sites for a gypsy encampment were put forward to Wrekin District Council — Granville colliery, Hadley Road in Oakengates, near the Ironbridge bypass, and a car park in Madeley. WDC turned them all down. That other group of citizens for whom a home was difficult to find, came under attack from fellow Telfordians. Motorcyclists used the Silkin Way to the danger of unmotorised users. As it was not a public highway they were reported to wear no crash helmets, sport no numberplates, observe no speed limits, and sometimes to ride three to a bike. TDC was blamed in the press for not erecting clear signs banning motorcycles.

## Bouquets too

However there were bouquets as well for the development corporation. American electronics firms voted Telford as one of the most professional development agencies, ahead of all the other British new towns. The Japanese evidently thought so, too, and two more firms came, Seiko Epson to produce computer printers and employ 100 people and NEC to buy a 48-acre (19.4 hectares) site for the manufacture of video cassette recorders and with a view to an eventual workforce of 900. The factory was officially opened in November 1989 by the Princess of Wales.

EEC anti-dumping legislation added an interesting dimension. It was aimed at stopping low-cost goods pouring into Europe from Japan. This sharpened Japanese interest in setting up manufacturing capacity in Europe, and in making companies buy more components from European sources, since goods manufactured in a European Community country would still be taxed if more than sixty per cent of the parts were from Japan. By now Telford had the highest concentration of Japanese manufacturing in the United Kingdom, and in May acquired its seventy-third foreign investment. 'Competitive rents and greenfield sites that turn other areas green with envy', said a TDC spokesman in explanation. Even British firms were taking advantage of these assets, and the older established industries were enjoying the dawn of prosperity. Blockleys announced a new £8 million plant to double turnover and a £1 million contract for bricks for the Brighton marina. Its plans for further clay extraction in Hadley received a cool reception from residents. Ever Ready increased its workforce by 150. All these developments brought unemployment down to 15.5 per cent by August 1987, but the fact that 2,000 people, mainly women, applied for the 150 permanent and temporary jobs at Marks & Spencer — which opened in October — was indicative of the still difficult situation for many Telford families.

Meanwhile, during 1987 TDC published proposals for housing and some commercial development on 600 acres (243 hectares) of land in and around the old settlements of Overdale, The Rock, Dawley Bank and Lawley. The Lawley development involved first the opencast mining of coal on 185 acres (75 hectares) and the eventual building of 2,000 houses with open space and some offices on a total of 259 acres (105 hectares). This represented TDC's last big development project and brought immediate resistance from Lawley residents. There were more opencast proposals at Newdale, Arleston Hill and Ketley Sands. The Newdale operation went ahead, mining 250,000 tons of low-chlorine coal over twelve months and employing fifty people. Luxury homes on a thirty-six-acre (14.6 hectares) site at Apley Castle — a previous scheme had been turned down by WDC — received permission. At Sutton Hill residents formed a group to press TDC to do something about derelict housing on the estate. While many of these turned out not to belong to the development corporation, the call prompted TDC to look more closely at what might be done with some of its housing there that it found difficult to sell. It began to look for a developer to take over the housing, with startling results that became apparent a year later. About this time it was again mooted that TDC would ballot its tenants on which landlord — the local authority or a housing association — they preferred to have when TDC was wound up. More development corporation jobs were axed, and some left to swell the ranks of the various private firms being set up in the town.

## Thomas Telford's statue

TDC commissioned the sculptor André Wallace to fashion a statue of Thomas Telford which would be a centrepiece and an attraction in Telford Square, bounded by the development corporation's new office building, the county and magistrates' courts. Thomas Telford would have a good easterly view over lilyponds and flowerbeds down into the town centre. He was to be shown leaning on tall letters of his name, and with his coat hanging on the final D. An appeal for funds was launched among civil engineering companies. In the far south of the designated area Ironbridge's traffic difficulties now brought a renewed plea for another bridge across the Severn. Three possible sites were looked at, one was close to and replacing the inadequate Free Bridge, another much nearer the Iron Bridge, known as the Ladywood site, which protesters immediately condemned as detracting from the famous monument. Park-and-ride arrangements were run by the Ironbridge Gorge Museum on Sundays throughout the summer using vintage buses and coaches. The more normal bus services of the new town had earlier in the year been cut by a third because of losses. Now minibuses were introduced followed by privatisation of the bus company.

During 1987 the Clifton cinema reopened in Wellington in the upper portion of the old cinema, with a 300-seat auditorium. But shortly before had come the

announcement that a ten-screen cinema would be built at the town centre. This would seat 2,026 people with the largest auditorium holding 275. The town centre shops were already becoming prey to shoplifters. Police-inspired training for shop managers and assistants showed on video and by lectures how thieves operated and gave various measures to combat them. The town centre hotel planned to add another forty-six bedrooms in a £2 million project. Telford was now beginning to be a venue for exhibitions and conferences. The Telford and Shropshire Business Show was held in September, and a national engineering exhibition of advanced manufacturing technology used the Telford Racquets Centre. There came the first news of private interests seeking permission for a large retail centre, garden centre, petrol station and car parks at Ketley Dingle alongside the M54. This was not included in TDC's town plan, and neither it nor Wrekin DC believed that with the town and district centre facilities, it would be necessary, and was certainly not welcome.

*André Wallace's statue of Thomas Telford leaning on the letters of his and the town's name and surveying the town centre. Behind is New Town House, the development corporation's new home, under construction.*

The Ironbridge Gorge Museum Trust has steadily built up the essential elements of an East Shropshire coalfield Victorian settlement at the Blists Hill Museum, including shopkeepers, hotel staff, working men, women and children in period dress. The buildings came from Telford's earlier settlements and were re-erected at the open air museum. There is a foundry, a candle factory, sawmill, print shop and piggery among the industrial and commercial processes featured.

## Change of chairman

In October 1987 Frank Jones took over the chairmanship of the development corporation from Lord Northfield, who had done a twelve-year stint. Lord Northfield said, 'I am leaving on the crest of the wave. Telford is moving towards boom conditions, after years of building confidence in the new town and transforming its environment and facilities.' He enlarged on some of Telford's present attractions. 'Private investment is pouring in, unemployment is tumbling at last, sales of private housing are booming, the green environment is making us into a forest city. Facilities for all ages are of a high standard and our shopping centre is a runaway success.' He thanked and praised TDC's staff and his board colleagues, 'who have shared the grim days and are now enjoying the glad ones.' Lord Northfield had led a high-profile life as chairman, always in the public eye, approachable, leading from the front — if a trifle autocratically at times — and ready to take the brickbats as well as the bouquets. His political contacts in Whitehall had without doubt hastened the arrival of the M54, helped to secure the enterprise zone and probably influenced the successful outcome of the hospital issue for which his successor, as chairman of the county's health authority, had campaigned with great vigour.

During the past twelve years Telford's increasingly privately-financed house building programmes had almost all been constructed in brick. The vast majority of earlier buildings in the settlements before Telford had been built of local brick, reflecting the character of a region rich in clays. There had been or still were famous brickfields at Broseley just south of the designated area and the Severn, at Blists Hill, Coalmoor, Doseley, Lightmoor, Randlay, Langley and in the north at Hadley, Trench Lock, Snedshill, Ketley and Donnington Wood. Observant visitors and residents might see that often the same coloured or flecked bricks are used in both old and new buildings, and this reflected a definite policy on the part of TDC to suggest that developers where possible should link past and present through vernacular styles and brickwork.

*A private housing development a Aqueduct, built in the early 1980s viewed across a growing 'forest'.*

## Roundabouts galore

A TDC ploy was to make the roundabouts of the main arterial roads readily recognisable by placing some distinguishing feature on them. A ring of flag-poles, a special landscape composition, the concrete spire, a representation of a mine headgear, to name some of them. These were joined in late 1987 by a 16.4 feet (five metres) high representation in concrete of Thomas Telford's mason's mark. No doubt the story of Telford's many roundabouts is folkloric and told of other towns similarly blessed or afflicted with large numbers of them. But it was recounted with glee in Telford for years, especially by those older inhabitants who were seeing their familiar home territory so changed. The story goes that when planning the infrastructure, Telford's planners worked long hours in conference around a large table spread with maps and plans. They needed sustaining in the difficult work and drank endless mugs of coffee. Wherever a harrassed planner put down a mug, leaving a ring of brown moisture on a plan, there they placed a roundabout.

In his annual report to March 1988, Frank Jones was able to record growth in industry and commerce. Although permission to extend the enterprise zone had been refused, government had eliminated automatic regional development grants in Development Areas. This had left Telford free to compete for industry on a more equal footing with those favoured areas, relying on TDC's reputation for servicing new companies, and the town's by now very obvious attractions. Besides the 'throng of British firms', and the overseas companies, numbers of older established firms expanded or branched out into new fields of activity. Notable in the last category was GKN Sankey, which formed a new company with Jaguar Cars to manufacture car body pressings, with an additional 400 jobs at Hadley Castle. Among newcomers there was an increasing emphasis on plastics manufacture, the numbers reaching sixty companies, and despite the presence of the Plastics Processing Industry Training Board training centre at Halesfield, there was ironically soon a shortage of labour skilled in plastics work. Whether TDC had its tongue in its cheek is unclear, but mindful of this growing industrial strength in plastics, a suggestion was floated that any new bridge across the Severn should try and rival the panache of the first iron bridge — the first plastic bridge?

The Hortonwood industrial site, funded by sales of TDC industrial and commercial assets, was nearing completion, and there had been substantial growth in private industrial floorspace as well — now fifty-three per cent of the total was in private hands. The TSB management training centre was opened, as was the county library in the town centre. This was a handsome octagonal build-ing and loaned videos, cassettes and compact discs besides books. Next to it the ecumenical Meeting Point House had been started. A total of 679 houses had been built, and despite quite large price rises another 562 TDC houses were sold to tenants, making 3,442 or thirty per cent of the original stock of 11,513 dwell-ings. Sutton Hill was now fifty-five per cent owner-occupied. The reclamation total was 3,116 acres (1,262 hectares) and 1,667 mine shafts had been treated. The population of the town was about 113,000, and both the Telford Tigers ice hockey team and Telford United had had successful seasons and were bringing kudos to the town.

## Jubilee year

In January 1988, twenty-five years after the inauguration of Dawley New Town, a firm making plastic bin liners moved from cramped quarters and difficult labour conditions in Enfield. It summed up the reasons for its move — greater availability of labour, the central location for distributing products, availability of a suitable large factory at an acceptable price, and housing fifty per cent cheaper. The company recruited 300 workers in Telford. The eighth Japanese company to come, in electronics, had jobs for 160. At the end of January unemployment in the town was down to fourteen per cent.

As Telford's industrial boom took off, February lived up to its name of 'fill-dyke', the rain bringing land slips. A slip at Blists Hill blocked the Coalport road and cut power to 1,500 homes in Madeley. More serious was a potential slip on the Ironbridge bypass between Jiggers Bank and Buildwas which was to cost £1.75 million extra in concrete piles and more land for gentler slopes. A survey of the gorge's traffic presented a worrying picture. Some 750,000 visitors had come the previous year. The survey spoke of the damage to the environment and the misery of the inhabitants. There was opposition to a new bridge 'which would bring heavy lorries back to the area'. The opponents wanted the present bridge restored for local traffic only. They claimed that weight restrictions on the bridge were being ignored. There was talk of visitors in five-mile queues of traffic signing a 5,000-name petition for a new bridge. There was another traffic situation in north Telford. Several fatal accidents to cyclists had occurred on Queensway. Cyclists were banned from the road despite their protests that alternative routes were poor, and the county council agreed to collaborate in improving the other routes.

In March, TDC announced that two- and three-storey housing with flat roofs in Sutton Hill had been sold to a private developer for complete replanning and rebuilding. The chairman told the press, 'this development is one we did not get right . . . they were difficult to let and prone to vandalism'. In fact, many of the houses had been empty for three years. The developer demolished two residential blocks, garages and concrete walkways, put on pitched roofs, re-fitted the houses to modern standards and present-day expectations, and renamed the street Tudor Gardens from Severn Walk. The houses later sold well. The next month there was again a fire at the Central Ordnance Depot in Donnington. A nine-acre (3.6 hectares) building went up in flames, arson was suspected, and again there was some asbestos fall-out over Telford, although this was not as bad as from the earlier fire.

## Statue unveiled

The statue of Thomas Telford at the heart of the town centre was unveiled, Although some critics thought it 'gimmicky', a big majority found it amusing and friendly, and a welcome addition to the town. One TV cameraman was reported as not having found it so amusing. In trying to ensure that his subject was perfectly in place, clean and tidy, he was heard to say somewhat irritably to an assistant, 'if someone would just move that ***** coat we can start shooting'.

A simmering problem again surfaced, that of the ballot of TDC housing tenants to decide who should take over the houses on the development corporation's demise. Government had earlier suggested it might cut out the local authorities in favour of housing associations or groups of tenants, to which Wrekin DC reacted predictably. Now in May 1988, TDC announced that it would postpone a ballot for two years. Management meanwhile would be temporarily undertaken by housing associations. This led to strained relations between the two bodies, WDC taking high court action to stop the handover which it said was 'contrary to the wishes of the great majority of tenants'.

The retail park proposed by a large developer for Ketley Dingle was turned down by the local authorities but won planning permission on appeal, to the consternation of TDC and especially of Wellington, as the developers proposed to call it 'Wellington Park', regarded in the old market town as a 'sick joke' as its shopkeepers would suffer heavily. Wellingtonians had another cause for complaint. They believed British Rail was 'hell-bent' on downgrading Wellington station now that Telford Central was open, and inter-city trains no longer stopped there. Telford, always plagued by thoughtless vandalism, took more steps to fight back. A crime prevention panel was formed which was funded by local industry, attracted community support, and involved residents through neighbourhood watch schemes. A report from WDC gave the annual cost to the local authority of crime as £280,000.

## Britain in Bloom

In June 1988 Telford entered the Britain in Bloom competition where it was to gain invaluable experience for the two coming years when its successes were to set the seal of approval on the immense, detailed and expensive work of landscaping and gardening over more than twenty-seven years. Unemployment was now down to 12.5 per cent. TDC sought permission for housing at Bratton, Shawbirch and near Wellington. It also sought to extend the Hortonwood industrial estate by a further 112 acres (45 hectares). The development corporation proposed to build 250 houses at Horsehay with some industrial development on the old crane factory site, and a new public house on reclaimed land at Priorslee was planned. At Ketley Bank, British Coal applied for permission to opencast mine seventy-seven acres (thirty-one hectares) of 123 acres (fifty hectares) of development land for coal and fireclays. This was approved by the county council. After reparation the site would be used for housing and industry. Together with the major development site at Lawley, all these were manifestations of TDC's desire to leave behind it the necessary infrastructure and planning for the further development of the town, bringing it up to the 130,000 to 140,000 population target. All were to a greater or lesser degree contested by residents. Horsehay's difficulties were to be resolved by some reworking of the plans, Lawley's were to occupy a great deal of TDC time, in reworking to minimise local objections. An urban regeneration grant of £3.47 million was given for development of the Lilleshall land in the enterprise zone.

On the housing front, as land and house prices rose, young first-time buyers as everywhere in the country, were in difficulties. TDC was inundated with applications to buy by tenants anxious to become owners before prices rose further. The development corporation was also caught in the rising prices trap as costs of infrastructure, especially roads, escalated. Although unemployment was now under twelve per cent, in a survey by the West Midlands Low Pay Unit, Telford was listed as a low pay zone, and local councillors were quick to point out that there was still considerable poverty despite the buoyant economic times that the press headlined as 'Booming Telford' and 'Prosperous Telford'.

Priorslee Hall, TDC's home for twenty-five years, was put up for sale at between £2 million and £4 million. A jazz 'spectacular' was held by the Telford Society at the tennis centre, now called Telford Racquet and Fitness Centre. Meeting Point House, in the town centre next to the library, was opened — a multi-purpose building housing numbers of advice bureaux, a book shop, coffee shop, chapel, Christian councils and industrial and youth chaplains. For the August Bank Holiday Telford Show, a crowd of 10,000 was drawn to the town park. The ten-screen cinema opened its doors.

TDC again tried for an extension to the wind-up date. Mike Morgan, the general manager, told the press that they wanted the extra time in order 'to take the town to a point where it becomes self-sustaining'. This was later turned down. Increasingly during 1988 developments in industry, commerce and housing were being financed by the private sector. Much of the development was on land serviced and made available by TDC, and this could be released in an orderly fashion to keep up with corporate plan targets. But since the actual building work was out of its hands, TDC could no longer control the time-scale, and there were some delays. With the enterprise zone almost full, TDC stepped up its publicity campaign in other EC countries and to a wider audience overseas. To non-EC countries the United Kingdom was represented as a natural springboard for Europe after 1992 and the single market. As 1988 drew to a close the population was now nearly 116,000 and there were 52,762 jobs in Telford. The percentage of unemployed was 8.6.

## Property prices rise further

Huge rises in property prices greeted 1989, but development continued apace. There were two new hotel projects for the town centre. The retail park, now called Telford Bridge, was rapidly filling up. Some 300 jobs were created for office workers in the enterprise zone. Tatung took another 250 people, there were 100 jobs available at Dixon's Colour Laboratories, whilst Rists took on 120 people. A German company making nuts and bolts said it was coming to Telford because it was 'impressed by the clean and efficient image of the town, its central location, and the expert advice of TDC'. In its efforts to guide housing developments of all income brackets to sites throughout Telford, TDC had influenced the building of numbers of executive type houses of Mediterranean style facing south on a hill site at Sutton Hill, overlooking the golf course and Ironbridge Gorge.

The development corporation dropped its plans to hand over management of its houses temporarily to housing associations, but looked at the possibility of selling them as they became vacant to housing associations. The Clifton cinema closed for the second time, citing competition from the new Telford ten-screen cinema. Various sites were considered for M54 services but no decisions taken. With the Ketley Dingle retail park given approval by the Department of the Environment, the district council agreed with TDC that they would try and steer any further out-of-town stores to such places as Sutton Hill, Donnington and Muxton where their presence would not be detrimental to the town and district centres established so carefully with regard to trading requirements under the basic plan.

160

## Telford Hospital opens

After so much antagonism on the one hand and so much vigorous support on the other, Telford's hospital had been quietly built at Apley Castle. In January 1989 it opened its doors on a limited scale for elderly people transferred from Wrekin Hospital in Wellington. The major part of the 350-bed hospital was to be opened during the year with twenty consultants recruited, and with accident and emergency facilities, and medical and surgical wards. It would finally cater for up to 200,000 people, a much wider catchment area than Telford itself. In the event it was rapidly utilised by the public, so rapidly that at one point medical patients had to be referred to Shrewsbury.

*An aerial view of Telford's general hospital at Apley, named the Princess Royal Hospital. In its form and layout the hospital reflects human scale despite the complexity of its internal planning. Designed and built by the West Midlands Regional Health Authority.*

The next month Wrekin DC warned that unless there was to be a switch in emphasis in house building, there would be too few low-cost homes by 1991. Government gave WDC £4 million to compensate for the low rates from the enterprise zone. The sixteenth German company came to Telford. TDC handed over the repairs service for its 7,500 rented houses, and associated landscape maintenance to a housing association, and the Ironbridge bypass was at last opened. There had been some reluctance on the part of Shropshire County Council to adopt the road, built by TDC, because of the instability problems that had been encountered, and consequent anxiety over future maintenance costs. Now Ironbridge plans to give priority to pedestrians were announced, costing from £6 million to £8 million, involving an improved park-and-ride facility, and restrictions to traffic at peak times. A car park at Lightmoor was suggested. Local councillors worried that the plans would adversely affect Madeley and other neighbouring areas. Again the cry was for the Ladywood bridge to be built, but WDC backed a new bridge further towards the free bridge. Plans were finalised for a 150-bedroomed hotel by the racquets centre, emphasising the business confidence now manifest in Telford. The Shropshire Chamber of Industry and Commerce with headquarters at Halesfield, moved to Stafford Park, and now had over 300 company members.

On the sporting front, the possibility of a racecourse in north Telford was mooted, and 132 acres (53 hectares) of TDC land was set aside for it. Flat and National Hunt courses were envisaged. Initially the Jockey Club said it was not able to commit itself to any more racing fixtures at present and indicated that there were adequate racecourses within easy distance of Telford. A Stafford Park company engaged in research and development on artificial snow was featured in *The Times*. While ski resorts across Europe from Aviemore to the Alps were suffering the worst 'snow drought' for many years, the company opened an indoor *piste* in Telford where there was abundant snow of a kind. Of interest to anglers and conservationists, it was confirmed that Withy Pool in the town park was home to the rare European catfish, a hard-fighting predator introduced in the early 1950s.

*Offices and warehouses at Staffor Park, with the concrete spire o the roundabout at the entrance t the industrial area, placed as symbol of enterprise. Note the fir oak tree carefully preserved by th planners and incorporated into th landscape design.*

In May, Telford held its first International Day in the town park organised by WDC, with pavilions from Holland, Spain, New Zealand, Sweden, Japan and others. With perfect weather and free admission, 50,000 people sampled food and drink from overseas, and watched forty manned hot-air balloons competing for £3,000 prize money. During the same month the Prince of Wales opened the Museum of the River at Ironbridge. The Institute of Road Transport Engineers held its annual conference and display in the town. The government provided £230,000 to build fifteen small industrial units at Ketley business park which would create ninety jobs. An out-of-town supermarket was proposed at Trench Lock with 67,500 square feet (6,270 square metres) of retail space and 612 parking spaces.

## Shopping centre to be sold

Meanwhile TDC's assets in commercial and industrial buildings, and dwellings sold to tenants, were steadily being disposed of. Now the development corporation announced in June 1989 that the Telford shopping centre was for sale, and this despite the opposition of the local authority. The asking price was in excess of £80 million. Wrekin DC published its report *The Way Forward*, formulating how it wanted Telford to develop in the 1990s with an estimated

*New Town House was designed for Telford Development Corporation by Conder (Midlands). TDC's design brief called for a building of presence and dignity, with brick cladding and strong use of colour. It has a composite slate roof, a central atrium with boardroom and canteen facilities on the top floor. The detailed landscaping is typical of car parks in the town centre.*

population of 128,000 by 1996. The report took the town — and TDC — to task for various 'lacks' that it enumerated, notably 'unmet' housing needs and 'major social and cultural facilities'. It also thought social and economic benefits were spread unevenly in the town. In many ways the report pointed up TDC's contention that its work, given a development corporation's special powers that a local authority did not possess, were still needed beyond September 1991.

## The CTC and higher education

During the summer of 1989 another long-running Telford saga began. While it was evident that the university proposal was dead, steps were being taken to interest Wolverhampton Polytechnic in setting up an operation in Telford — an 'annex' at first, before development would lead to a full polytechnic in its own right. There was no opposition to this idea at all. But at the same time TDC announced firm plans to have one of the new and controversial city technology colleges, which while giving 11- to 18-year-old boys and girls a normal all-round education, would also concentrate on science, maths, technology and commerce. It would need longer hours and more weeks of schooling in a year than an ordinary school. There was a site at Old Park, and the school could be open in September 1991 with an intake of 180 first-year pupils and a sixth form direct entry of seventy. After four years it could have 1,000 pupils at a ratio of just over fifteen pupils to one teacher. The Mercers' Company was prepared to put up £1 million, and a similar sum would come from industry. Teachers, unions and Labour elements in the local authorities were all against, labelling the CTC divisive and elitist, and predicting that since there were spare places at the town's secondary schools, a school or schools would have to close.

Controversy continued in other fields. A proposed TDC development of 300 houses and a ski slope at Rough Park to the west of Woodside was opposed by residents, although backed by WDC. Government warned the local authorities to carry out their statutory duty in providing adequate gypsy encampments. All parish councils and the local authorities — in the words of the press — 'stuck to their guns' in refusing to contemplate a site for itinerants on their 'patch'. Plans for a new public house in Priorslee also were opposed by local interests, and it was moved slightly back from The Flash pool to appease them.

Industrial developments continued. Another German engineering company arrived, as did Swiss and Japanese companies which brought 450 jobs. The seventeenth Japanese company in Telford was a catering firm — to feed the other sixteen. The Land Registry started an £8 million office block at Old Park. There was a shortage of industrial and commercial units to let. TDC sold the shopping centre firstly to Taylor Woodrow Property Company 'for around £100 million to £110 million', but this sale fell through, and the second highest bidder, Universities Superannuation Scheme Limited, bought it. The property consisted of 635,000 square feet (58,992 square metres) of retail space in five large and eighty-one standard units, and 34,000 square feet (3,159 square metres) of office space. There were 3,230 car park spaces, an annual rental of £4 million, and planning permission for a further 86,000 square feet (7,989 square metres) of retail space.

*The northern edge of the town park as it comes into the town centre. Randlay residential estate and its allotments are in the foreground, then Randlay Pool and Blue Pool with the amphitheatre, the grass arena, various gardens and Spout Mound, with some of the Malinslee housing in the top left corner. Centre top is the racquets centre, ice rink and shopping centre, with Hollinswood flats and housing at right, and the business park beyond. A good idea of the 'forest' landscaping is given in the photograph.*

By December 1989 unemployment had dropped to seven per cent, and the population was 117,000. Telford had won the regional England and United Kingdom trophies of Britain in Bloom in the 'city' class for towns with over 70,000 inhabitants. In addition it won the Beautiful Britain award for new and extensive landscaping. According to press reports, the judges heaped praise on Telford's colourful entry and described the new town as 'a well-kept, clean and lived-in city'. In his annual report to March 1990, Frank Jones paid tribute to 'the enthusiasm and support of industry and commerce, the local authority and the people of Telford' in gaining the awards. Over a million square feet (92,900 square metres) of new factory space and 300,000 square feet (27,870 square metres) of office accommodation had been built in the year. House completions at 513 — some of which was low-cost housing at Aqueduct, Donnington and Leegomery — had fallen short of targets because of fall in demand. The Rough Park development near Woodside envisaged some two-bedroomed starter homes in a dual ownership scheme and there were plans for others at Brookside and Muxton. Rising interest rates had had some effect on British investment in the town, but overseas marketing had continued to pay dividends.

Now that the Granville colliery land had been reclaimed — the country park had opened in August — and the Lawley opencast coal mining operation was nearing completion, there remained only a few minor sites to complete TDC's huge land reclamation programme begun in the 1960s. The only missing link in the major roads programme was now the Horsehay bypass, scheduled for 1991. Improvements to minor roads, street lighting and footpaths were scheduled to be finished within eighteen months. But in TDC's view much still remained to be achieved, *vide* the Wrekin DC report. In the board's opinion this could best and quickest be brought about by the development corporation. The chairman made representations to government yet again for a further two to three years of operation, but there was no last-minute reprieve.

Meanwhile Telford New Town could look back on six years of unsurpassed economic growth.

*In July 1989 multi-national teams ran from Telford to St Etienne in France. Eurojog teams from France, Russia, Germany and Italy were joined by two British teams, Telford and Coventry. Here the Italian Ferrara team comes over the Iron Bridge at the end of time trials preceding the main event.*

# TELFORD DEVELOPMENT CORPORATION 1987 to 1989

By the end of the period covered by Chapter 10, the town's statistics were:

| | |
|---|---|
| Population | 117,080 |
| Dwellings | 45,270 |
| Average number of persons per dwelling | 2.58 |
| Houses built during period | 2,232 |
| Total employment | 58,190 |
| Manufacturing | 25,603 |
| Services | 27,941 |
| Other | 4,636 |
| Residents economically active | 52,693 |
| Number living and working in Telford | 45,687 |
| Percentage of economically active living and working in Telford | 86.7 |
| Percentage unemployed | 7.0 |

There were three marked changes in TDC's financial position. In late 1986 government wrote off approximately 75 per cent of the development corporation's debt (£440 million). This left a residual debt of £126.3 million. The success of the town brought substantial increases in property and land values, especially from the start of 1988. Both the volume and value of asset sales increased, making it possible to begin repaying remaining loans. There was an increasing emphasis on providing infrastructure so that the private sector could build factories, houses, shops and offices.

The debt write-off — made to other new towns as well — was because the money had been borrowed to finance non-income producing assets such as roads, land reclamation and the provision of public open space. At the time it appeared unlikely that the new towns would be able to repay these debts, but by March 1989 it had become clear that rising values would make it possible for Telford to repay a substantial part of it.

At this stage, TDC had assets costing £195.3 million, and in addition had spent £77.2 million on roads and £13.8 million on land reclamation.

Of the £195.3 million, a sum of £191.8 million related to completed assets:

| | |
|---|---|
| Dwellings | £89.9 million |
| Industry | £36.5 million |
| Commerce | £47.2 million |
| Other | £18.2 million |
| | £191.8 million |

The period saw, in addition to more high-technology firms, a growth in the numbers of plastics companies coming to Telford. These included Laconite Plastics (UK), PolyLina (UK), Sonoco Polysack (USA), Telford Extrusions (UK/Germany), TP Consumables (Japan), I K Precision (Japan), Borgers (UK/Germany) and Lignotock Manufacturing (UK/Germany). Other companies were Epson, printers and computers (Japan), Emile Tissot Food Ltd, food packaging (France), NEC Technologies (UK) Ltd, monitors, printers, cellular telephones (Japan), Kiyokuni Europe Ltd, precision metal components (Japan), Office International, office stationery, Marusawa Telford Ltd, precision metal components (Japan), Venture Pressings, body panels for Jaguar.

By 1989, employment in the electronic/electrical engineering sector had risen to 5,864, accounting for ten per cent of Telford jobs.

# 11 Consolidation and Demise 1990 to 1991

TELFORD — GROWTH OF DEVELOPMENT, 1990. *Compare this with the earlier maps on pages 61 and 122, representing 1963 and 1980 respectively.*

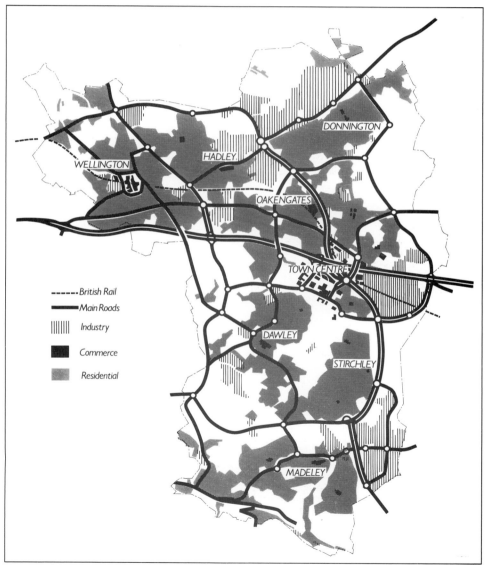

At the turn of the year the development corporation announced plans to hand over the first package of assets to the district council. Some 840 acres (340 hectares) of landscaped and open space would be transferred to WDC with a clutch of income-producing properties. 'This will ensure a high standard of maintenance without cost to the council's community-charge payers', said TDC's annual report to March 1990. The transfer was effected in June 1990 and included Dale End Park by the Severn, public open space mainly in south Telford, grassed areas in housing estates, play areas, park land, strips of miscellaneous land and pathways. To produce an income of around £250,000 a year, WDC received Dale End House, Madeley shopping centre, industrial premises in Stafford Park and Madeley, together with Stirchley Grange and two houses in the town park. A similar package with open space and income-producing assets in north Telford — to bring total income up to £600,000 a year — would be arranged for the next year, while the ten community centres in the new town were also scheduled to be handed over.

*Golfing at Great Hay, by Sutton Hill. The 18th century house is now part of the golf club and hotel complex. TDC built the golf course.*

Early in 1990 as well, TDC announced that the woodland in the Severn Gorge would be handed to a new body, the Severn Gorge Countryside Trust, which would own, manage and conserve the woods. Membership of the Trust would include representatives of the Ironbridge Gorge Museum Trust, the county council, Wrekin DC, Bridgnorth District Council and parish councils within whose boundaries the woods fell. Much of the land and properties which formed the Ironbridge Gorge Museum was still in TDC ownership. The development corporation had supported the museum financially from the beginning, and had maintained close liaison and concern for the success of the enterprise. TDC's museum assets would be transferred to a heritage trust acting as a holding body, which would in turn lease properties to the museum trust. TDC planned to endow the heritage trust with a sum of £4 million to ensure that the museum would be adequately funded.

168

## The CTC again

After continuing vociferous opposition, in February 1990 government gave its approval for the city technology college in Telford. It would be built on a fifteen-acre (six hectares) site at Old Park just west of the town centre's Telford Bridge retail park. The district council — against the college — objected that it would be on land needed for town centre expansion. TDC replied that there were still twenty-three acres (nine hectares) available for retail development and 128 acres (52 hectares) for commercial use. Her Royal Highness The Princess Royal came to Telford and officially opened the hospital, which was thereafter named after her.

Wrekin DC published a document entitled *Telford, A Town in Transition*. In it the district council called upon government moneys to the tune of £35 million in order to complete the town. This would be necessary 'to service and make available land for housing and industry, to maintain the town's growth momentum'. A theatre and arts centre, a crematorium, athletics track and polytechnic were listed as essentials. WDC estimated that an average of 1,370 jobs a year needed to be created to support the growing population. The next month, March, WDC's chairman called for TDC to continue beyond September 1991, stressing that the town needed another £70 million to £80 million invested to complete the infrastructure. Later in the same month came a suggestion from Shropshire County Council of a Telford Development Agency, a partnership between SCC, WDC and the Commission for the New Towns (CNT). This would fill the vacuum left by TDC, in providing serviced land for industry and commerce and continuing the work of attracting investment from outside. The Commisson for the New Towns, a government body, would be receiving the greater portion of TDC's assets in land and property. Its brief, particularly in the case of development land, was to realise those assets for government in the most advantageous way.

In fact, looking at the list of WDC's requirements in the town, the theatre project on the edge of the town park had not been abandoned by TDC although its application for government funding had been refused. As to the polytechnic, Wolverhampton Polytechnic would establish a temporary annex in a Stafford Park factory. The first intake of 200 students would begin courses in September 1990. The aim was to have 2,500 by the year 2000, with a heavy emphasis on business, information technology and computing courses. There were plans to move 'to a purpose-built home in the centre of Telford'. In March plans for a 400-metre synthetic running track at Oakengates leisure centre in Wrockwardine Wood were announced. They were backed by the county council, WDC, the Sports Council and TDC. Even the racecourse looked a little nearer realisation, when the promoter took the Jockey Club to the High Court over its refusal to allow him fifteen fixtures a year 'at the first new racecourse since 1927'. This was out of 120 new fixtures proposed by the Jockey Club. He lost his case, but there still appeared to be a good chance of fixtures for 1992, and TDC was keen to have a racecourse which would invest £10 million in the town and bring up to 250 jobs. Two months later planning approval was given for it, subject to satisfactory road access. An all-weather and a grass track were planned, with a grandstand, parade rings, saddling boxes, stables and parking for 2,100 cars. The organisers hoped that there would be a minimum of forty-five races a year.

During March, TDC had a town-wide 'blitz' on litter. Gales in February had spread rubbish into surrounding landscaped tree and shrub areas. A contract staff of forty-five was set to work. The operation highlighted the fact that the authorities — TDC and WDC — spent between them £400,000 a year on litter removal in the town. TDC announced that Telford would be entering the Entente Florale — the Europe in Bloom — competition, against towns in Austria, Belgium, France, Holland, Ireland and Hungary. A civic clock tower was erected in Telford Square close to the statue of Thomas Telford. The clock was donated by the high-tech Japanese firm Epson, which also announced a doubling in size of its factory with 100 new jobs. In the old industries, too, there was a resurgence in growth. Another 100 jobs and an investment of £10 million was announced by GKN, with a Ford contract for its engineering products division. The number of unemployed in Telford stood at six per cent.

*Telford Central railway station taken from the pedestrian bridge which links the station to the town centre. A train for London is at the platform.*

## Earth tremor

On April 2, 1990 an earth tremor which lasted five seconds shook buildings in Telford. There was no damage, but as always TDC and the new town had their share of other alarms, disappointments and successes as the year moved from spring to summer. A proposal to dump 'special waste' at the SCC's Granville tip had nearby residents worried, until assured that these would not be dangerous or toxic wastes. Priorslee Hall was empty and on the market. There was already planning permission for offices and a business park there. A property company proposed to add an eighty-bed private hospital, but this was refused by WDC on the grounds that it would be too close to housing and would engender too much traffic.

WDC expressed its unhappiness at the parking in the town centre. It said that at peak times, notably at Christmas, there were not enough spaces. A TDC plan for a leisure centre — a ten-pin bowling alley or some other family-orientated development — near the ice rink, would exacerbate the situation. The district council was worried that two- and even multi-storey car parks would have to be built in the future.

*Maturing landscaping with brick paving in late-1970s housing at Hollinswood.*

171

Telford Development Corporation carried out a survey. As at May 1990 there were 3,834 parking spaces for shoppers in the town centre, with a further 666 spaces at 'shared-use' car parks — with offices — a few hundred yards from the shopping centre, and making 4,500. Peak demand on Saturdays in the run-up to Christmas was around 4,050 spaces. Parking spaces for offices in the town centre amounted to 1,277 of which 666 were shared use. Peak demand for office spaces was 1,140, but of course office and shopping peaks did not always coincide. In addition there were 744 spaces for the recreation centres — the ice rink and racquets centre. At the retail park there were 750 spaces, with another 650 in the Sainsbury car park adjacent to the retail park. All in all, the survey concluded that the town centre was provided with adequate spaces for many years to come. While there would be occasions at peak shopping times when the car parks close to the shopping centre would be full, there were plenty of empty spaces not far away.

## The new bridge

Conservationists, many locals and English Heritage were solidly against the county council's proposal to build a bridge across the Severn at the Ladywood site, which SCC described as the best of three possibles. According to the county council the bridge would be a modest 'state of the art' structure of slender angled pairs of steel legs carrying a dual carriageway road in three spans. It would be 'quite low, elegant and unobtrusive'. The bridge was evidently designed to detract as little as possible from the Iron Bridge within sight, 400 yards up-stream. Quite apart from 'spoiling the view' of and from the famous monument, the locals were afraid it would bring more traffic to bedevil their lives. English Heritage stressed that the gorge was one of only eleven heritage sites in the United Kingdom. The national press waded in, mostly against the bridge. One newspaper described the 1779 iron bridge as 'Darby's elegant arch'. Several others attributed it to Darby, who appeared to have quite eclipsed the Shrewsbury architect, Pritchard, who actually designed it, almost certainly with Darby expertise in iron constructions. The alternative to the Ladywood bridge would either be a new bridge close to the 1909 free bridge between Ironbridge and Coalport or a rebuilt free bridge which for two years now had had to be augmented with a Bailey bridge. Later in the year a public enquiry was held and in December the DoE verdict went against the county council's Ladywood bridge, although the case for a new bridge in a different location was accepted.

In the summer of 1990 all kinds of projects were put forward. As the Ironbridge museum was 'too big to see in one day', the trust proposed a 'Victorian' hotel at Blists Hill with a 100-seater tea room, and a sixty-bed conventional hotel with holiday cottages. A cable television company came with a proposition to invest £18 million in giving Telford a choice of thirty-two channels. After opencast coal mining at Horsehay, a public golf course was proposed. The go-ahead was given by WDC to the Muxton golf course and hotel from existing farm buildings. A ten-pitch gypsy encampment was proposed on the old Shutfield Works site at Lightmoor, despite some fears that there was a danger of contamination from arsenic and cadmium. WDC approved the site but this was fought by the parish council. Meanwhile gypsies camping illegally at Muxton were moved on. The latest addition to the town park would be a heavily scented and textured garden especially for blind people, but for the enjoyment of all, including those who were wheelchair-bound. TDC put forward a proposal to build a fifty-bedroomed tourist hotel at Cuckoo Oak, Madeley, together with a thirty-bedroomed home for the elderly. Such was the confidence in Telford that there was also a suggestion of a hotel with 150 bedrooms by Telford's central railway station. Confidence was manifest in the announcement by Wellington's public school, Wrekin College, that Japanese would be taught.

Housing developments were mooted in Priorslee, east of the main road from the M54 Castle Farm interchange and Limekiln Bank roundabout. Here a total of 250 acres (101 hectares) was available — 94 acres (38 hectares) owned by TDC with planning permission, and the remainder belonging to Lord Stafford, for which planning permission had yet to be sought.

## Major growth point

Even with unemployment in June at 5.2 per cent, the authorities believed that jobs were now growing faster than people to fill them, and there was a need to stimulate house building, particularly of lower-cost homes. Nevertheless, when the GKN/Jaguar enterprise advertised 128 jobs, more than 1,000 turned up to recruitment centres and 5,000 enquiries were received.

It was evident that Telford was a major growth area for an entire region, and had attracted, and continued to attract many millions in investment. With the continuing sale of TDC properties, quite apart from those given to Wrekin DC, and the museum and countryside trusts, it now seemed likely that around £300 million of the sum written off by government would be recouped and thus all the massive developments of TDC over twenty-three years were going to cost the taxpayer £150 million. As a TDC spokesman somewhat jocularly but tellingly put it — 'the cost of 100 yards of the Channel tunnel'. TDC was confident that at least a couple of substantial foreign companies would move to Telford by the time it was wound up. There were still four or five possible sites of fifty acres (twenty hectares). One of these, close to the Hadley Castle plant, was taken up by a joint venture company between Italian motor manufacturer Fiat, and Nippon Denso, an auto component company part-owned by Toyota, which was in the process of building a car plant near Derby. There would be 500 new jobs by 1995. Another Japanese firm, making power tools, came to Telford with need of a workforce of 250.

A row which involved TDC and other new town corporations surfaced during the summer. The National Audit Office stated that the setting up of consultancies should have been more closely monitored by the Department of the Environment. It particularly called into question redundancy payments made to staff who continued to do much the same work but for a new employer. The principle had been clear at the time, that TDC's workload was as big as ever, and it needed the experience and skills of those 'privatised' staff, who knew its problems and work. No blame attached to the development corporations. The DoE admitted to the NAO that it had had insufficient experience of management buyouts at the time, to issue guidance to the development corporations.

In the latter part of the year the city technology college finally overcame the considerable opposition. Its detractors had pointed out that 2,000 places at comparable schools in Telford were empty. Others had said that the £8 million of government money for the college should have been put to improving the teaching of science and technology in existing schools. The county council

applied to the High Court for a judicial review, were refused permission, and appealed against that decision without avail. The college was named the Thomas Telford School, a headmaster appointed and pupils recruited. It would take 168 eleven-year-olds and eighty sixth-formers in September 1991.

## WDC's draft plan for Telford

Wrekin District Council published its draft plan for Telford until the year 2001 with a population of 140,000, and invited the public to comment. In addition to the industrial sites already developed and with expansion possibilities, WDC identified two areas of Lightmoor, Red Hill and Hadley Park as potential centres of employment. The plan envisaged up to 13,000 new houses, most to be built on land already approved for development. New housing sites allocated were at Hadley Park, 250 houses; Lightmoor, 500; East Priorslee, 500; The Hem just below Nedge Hill, 250; Telford Way, St George's, 40; Wellington Road, Muxton, 60; and Arleston Manor, 60. A 'green network' covering 5,680 acres (2,300 hectares) in the town would be kept as of 'ecological, aesthetic or recreational value to the community', while large areas on the edges of the town — the Telford Countryside Fringe — would remain rural during the operation of the plan. Except for a retail site planned at Lightmoor, new shops and services would go to the town centre and district centres. New leisure and cultural activities were envisaged for the town centre. The plan promised some road improvements on what was acknowledged to be an excellent road system, and the feasibility of a rapid transport system, probably a tram system, would be reviewed.

*The business park, Telford town centre, showing the footbridge to Telford Central railway station, the M54 and the road systems connecting with it.*

The role of the proposed Telford Development Agency was clarified. It would be funded to the tune of £150,000 each by the county and district councils and the Commission for the New Towns. It would promote Telford in the UK while supporting the West Midlands Development Agency as 'a supranational attracter of jobs'. The Shropshire Chamber of Industry and Commerce would also play a role. CNT would act as the agency's trustee of all government assets with a view to total disposal by a date as yet unspecified. The commission described its own function as that of carrying out 'the government's privatisation policy of new town assets'. The development potential was still 2,000 acres (810 hectares) of which half was industrial and commercial land and the rest housing, the polytechnic, a theatre and other cultural activities. The task up to 2001 was to create another 19,000 jobs. CNT would have an office in Telford which would also deal with Redditch. It would work closely with the district council's economic development unit, and would, WDC hoped, in its staff retain some of the skills and knowledge of TDC.

While its heirs debated and planned, TDC with more than a year of life yet to go, continued to work towards its goals and leave its 'estate' in good order. At the same time the town it had created continued to live its ever more fulfilling life. The Telford Show, the first without a TDC subsidy, was a success with 15,000 people and good weather, but remained delicately balanced financially and too dependent on good weather for success. Commercial interests planned a twenty-eight lane bowling alley and a night club for the town centre, and TDC was investigating the possibility of a skateboard area in the town park. The 250 houses at The Hem — mentioned in the WDC plan — were a TDC proposal on a sixty-nine acre (28 hectares) site of which thirty-seven acres (fifteen hectares) would be houses and the rest woodland. Just north of this on the southern slope of Nedge Hill, leaving the picnic spot untouched, would be a campus of 'buildings of quality' where it was hoped that agricultural, micro-electronic, pharmaceutical and biotechnological research would be carried out. It was an area of ninety-six acres (thirty-nine hectares) in total, of which fifty-five acres (22.3 hectares) would be built over. Residents of Stirchley and Brookside resolved to fight the developments on the grounds that Telford needed all the green places it now had. This was part of a growing feeling, voiced at the public meetings on the WDC plan. Oakengates residents also passed resolutions that there should be no new developments in their town.

*Telford town centre in bloom during the Entente Florale competition which the town won against contenders from Britain and other European countries. The photograph shows the external shopping square fronted by shops with offices above.*

## Winning the Entente Florale

Crowning Telford's achievements in landscaping and gardening, in September the town won the Entente Florale for towns of over 70,000 population against stiff competition from many other European countries. For Lawrence Hotchkiss, plantsman and long-serving member of the landscape department, as well as for other staff members, this result represented an appreciation of years of work on the landscape of Telford. In October the National Westminster Bank moved some of its insolvency and debt-recovery operations to Telford. All 230 staff from London were given the chance to move but there was naturally some local recruitment. More of the bank's operations are expected in 1992/93. In Stafford Park the Wolverhampton Polytechnic's annex was officially opened with 300 students enrolled.

Towards the end of 1990 the French nappy company, Peaudouce, closed with 190 job losses. A packaging firm, citing trading conditions, shed 83 jobs. Glynwed put 70 workers on a 32-hour week. Other factories went on short time, and the number of jobless rose. But there were movements the other way, notably the Swiss firm, Landis & Gyr, manufacturers of energy management systems, taking 85,000 square feet (7,897 square metres) at Hortonwood with a requirement of 200 people.

Much has been written of the vulnerability of new towns to deep recession. Certainly Telford suffered inordinately during the early 1980s as it had had to rely for many jobs on the last of the great metal-forming industries of former years, and many of these went to the wall if they had not modernised themselves and their products. In any recession to come, as now seemed likely, TDC's long-practised policy of encouraging a maximum spread of different types of industry could only stand Telford in good stead. For it was hoped that economic recession would not hit all sectors equally and at the same time.

There was still some primary industry in the form of opencast coal mining, and the more permanent brickmaking. Heavy engineering was represented by companies such as a diversified GKN, Glynwed, Johnston Pipes, and Pelloby Cranes. A wide range of plastic products from film to car bumpers, including many small specialist components, were manufactured. A tremendous spread of electrical and electronic products came from dozens of companies diverse in size and speciality — photocopiers, computer printers, radio/cassette/CD players, printed circuit boards, and precision instruments. Office furniture and equipment, clothing, carpets, food manufacturing including 'gourmet' meals and chocolate, and hot air balloons were representative of the great variety of general manufacturing. Apart from the Central Ordnance Depot that still employed some 3,000 civilians, the Inland Revenue activities were now well-established and recruiting locals, as was the Land Registry. The Plastics Processing ITB, the TSB training centre, the National Westminster operations, Windsor Life Assurance and other service organisations testified to the 'hedging-of-bets' policy of TDC. As employers of local labour there were no fewer than six three-star hotels, the general hospital, the shopping centre, the retail park, and all the services to the community — insurance, solicitors, architects, accountants, builders and many others.

Looking ahead to the next three years, recession or no, the newly-appointed Training and Enterprise Council, one of a countrywide network set up by government to involve industry and commerce directly in training, saw Telford as having a large pool of jobless women available as a workforce.

## Housing ballot announced

TDC announced that the tenants of its 5,000 or so houses would in March 1991 be balloted as to whether they wished their properties to be handed over to WDC or a housing association. Where individual houses were concerned, tenants could choose directly. With blocks of flats, these would go on a majority vote of the tenants. It would be a 'once and for all' ballot, so that if a tenant moved out, the incoming tenant would not be able to change his landlord.

The perennial problem of the gypsies was no nearer a solution. The Shutfield Works site was still a possibility. A site at Allscott for twelve pitches was under consideration by WDC despite loud local objections. Maddock's foundry site at Oakengates was put up for sale. It had gypsy caravans on it and there was TDC land adjacent. They were moved on by the law. The owners of Telford shopping centre announced plans to demolish the old Sainsbury store and put in a further thirty-three shops and stores. With car thefts from the town centre running, according to some estimates, at one a day, closed circuit television was to be installed to monitor the car parks, while a security firm would look after the car parks close to the cinema where many of the thefts occurred. To add to the sporting and recreational possibilities, planning permission was given for a full-scale equestrian centre at Woodhouse Farm, Red Hill, together with a seventeen-bedroomed hotel and a restaurant. Electrification of the Wolverhampton to Shrewsbury line was under review.

*Old people's single-storey housing at Hollinswood, close to the local centre and surgery, and within easy walking distance of the town centre shopping complex. Designed by TDC Architects' Department.*

*The shopping centre complex in Telford town centre, showing the proximity of car parking to the shops. A sunny sitting-out place with hanging baskets of flowers in the foreground.*

The turn of the year saw more and more Telfordians, through their parish councils, expressing their unease at plans for 140,000 in the town, suggesting that they wanted a limit to the green spaces to be taken for housing, industry and commerce. A population of 130,000 seemed to many 'to be more realistic'. Wrekin DC revealed its Telford strategy of job promotion, training, employment and tourism in January 1991. 'WDC must successfully market its (Telford's) strengths such as a strong national and international image, an attractive range of development sites, a first-class communications network, competitive land costs, an efficient workforce and an attractive environment.'

*A view from Hollinswood towards the town centre, with the local centre among trees in the foreground, including the new public house, 'The Woodcutter'. In the middle distance are flats, and at right the Inland Revenue building, Matheson House.*

As spring approached came news that the Environment Secretary was looking at the possibility of building the new Severn bridge alongside the free bridge. As to the racecourse, it seemed that thirty-three fixtures would be transferred from another racecourse in the same ownership, and that the building of Telford's own racecourse would go ahead. The garden 'of the senses' for the blind and the handicapped was now open and well used. Priorslee Hall was still unsold and there was speculation that it might be the site of the polytechnic.

## The dismantling of TDC

TDC's chairman, Frank Jones, was widely reported in the press, looking at the development corporation's role until the end of September 1991. He emphasised that TDC would continue at full power the work of attracting investment. TDC remained the owner of substantial amounts of land for industry and housing, and would organise planning permissions, continue with infrastructure and be able to hand on to the Commission for the New Towns its development land as ready as possible for sale with planning permission and services. He believed that TDC's development strategy would be a guide for CNT and that 'the town will continue to benefit from new investment and growth after TDC has gone.'

It was remarkable, the chairman thought, that TDC had seen the 1968 Madin plan, although modified and modernised, through to a near-conclusion twenty-three years later. He stressed that major development at Lawley, Muxton, Apley and Priorslee would continue in the future. He reiterated that the packages of land and assets handed over to the local authority were 'a fair way of achieving change, and if TDC's sums were right, there need be no change in the standard of land maintenance'. He continued, 'remember that Telford has an international reputation as a place where the quality of the environment has helped to bring prosperity'. He reminded Telfordians that in *The Task Ahead* published in 1984 with the county and district authorities, a target of 53,000 more jobs by 1993 had been set. No fewer than 61,000 new jobs had been achieved by the end of 1990.

In talking about the wide spread of modern and high-tech industry and commercial enterprises in the town, Frank Jones said, 'I don't think this town will ever again suffer the scale of damage which gave us the worst unemployment in the Midlands a few years ago'. He confirmed that CNT, with large land holdings would be the key player in the Telford Development Agency, in bringing new investment. He forecast that numbers of TDC staff with expertise in marketing and promotion would be transferring to the commission. 'I believe Telford will retain its dynamism,' he said.

Finally, TDC's chairman had a request to make to the Wrekin District Council. While he acknowledged that the name Wrekin was regarded with much affection locally, he believed it was little known outside the West Midlands. On the other hand Telford was now known internationally. He asked that, when Telford Development Corporation had gone, there should be another TDC — Telford District Council.

# TELFORD DEVELOPMENT CORPORATION 1990 to 1991

By the end of March 1991, the town's statistics were:

| | | | |
|---|---|---|---|
| Population | 119,000 | Residents economically active | 53,429 |
| Dwellings | 45,975 | Number living and working in Telford | 47,346 |
| Average number of persons per dwelling | 2.59 | Percentage of economically active living and working in Telford | 88.6 |
| Houses built during period | 1,287 | Percentage unemployed | 9.5 |
| Total employment | 61,040 | | |
| Manufacturing | 26,883 | | |
| Services | 29,121 | | |
| Other | 5,036 | | |

In the last years of TDC's life, three themes continued — significant asset sales, repayment in 1990 of all remaining debt due to government, and provision of infrastructure for the private sector to build factories, houses and offices.

Once the rented housing has been transferred to Wrekin District Council or a housing association, and all public open space to WDC or trusts within the town, together with balancing packages in income-producing properties, TDC's assets to be handed over the the Commission for the New Towns (CNT) will be worth approximately £20 million. These comprise industrial property in Hortonwood, and a few hundred houses where the tenants applied to purchase before 18 September 1990. They were retained on the basis that TDC would complete sales to tenants.

However, the most significant asset to be inherited by CNT will be approximately 1,975 acres (800 hectares) of development land. At March 1991 prices this land is worth approximately £200 million.

## Land use table
Comparisons of land use figures for the Telford designated area in 1966 and 1990, in rounded figures of acres, with hectares in brackets.

| | 1966 | | 1990 | |
|---|---|---|---|---|
| Residential | 3,710 (1,502) | Developed | 6,872 | (2,782) |
| | | Undeveloped | 1,282 | (519) |
| Industrial | 1,490 (603) | Developed | 4,481 | (1,814) |
| | | Undeveloped | 855 | (346) |
| Commercial | not known | Developed | 1,017 | (412) |
| | | Undeveloped | 203 | (82) |
| Agriculture and mining | 7,710 (3,121) | | 500 | (202) |
| Open space | 570 (231) | | 1,021 | (414) |
| Woodland | 580 (235) | | 1,300 | (526) |
| Derelict land | 5,251 (2,126) | Planted and safe, or naturally regenerated | 1,780 | (721) |
| Totals | 19,311 (7,818) | | 19,311 | (7,818) |

## Landscaping
Over the years, 3,471 acres (1,405 hectares) of land were reclaimed for buildings and open space, and 3,000 mine shafts located and made safe. Six million trees and 12.5 million shrubs were planted, together with 6.5 million daffodils and narcissi, 2.5 million crocuses, and half a million grape hyacinths. More recently, annually some 40,000 tulips and 10,000 hyacinths have been set out. Each summer throughout the town some 50,000 bedding plants are planted, and there are 800 hanging baskets and 300 troughs and tubs of summer flowers.

## Industry
At March 31, 1991, there were just over 300 companies and firms. At December 1990, 115 overseas firms provided 9,210 jobs or fifteen per cent of the total. Within these figures twenty-two Japanese firms provided 2,947 jobs or 4.8 per cent of the total.

New companies included Audio Visual Furniture Ltd, Busch (UK) Ltd, vacuum pumps, Mitutoya (UK) Ltd, precision tools, Landis & Gyr, electronic meters.

# 12 Opinions and Verdicts

Building a new town such as Telford needs money, effort, dedication, faith and support, all sustained over many years — in this case twenty-eight years. It takes, too, disruption, old ways annihilated, people's lives affronted, others' lives renewed with fresh beginnings and new loyalties. It engenders co-operation, pacts, good working relations, successes. Equally it brings antagonism, resistance, envy and failure. And always there is so much change — big and drastic changes which are more than some people can stomach.

With so much emotion created, effort expended, how do the builders of Telford New Town now regard their work? Have they fashioned it ill or well? Do they believe it works for all Telfordians? How does it sit in the fair county of Shropshire? The questions multiply, both for those who worked for the two development corporations and who were intimately concerned in planning and building the town and its communities, and the members of the board who guided, directed, cajoled this instrument of government — the development corporation — in forcing ahead, often in the face of considerable local and national apathy and opposition.

There are questions that councillors of the local authorities might also ask now that Telford is so largely being handed over to them. They and their councils played a big part over those twenty-eight years, acting in general as the people's watchdog, championing them in their views and causes. If the local authorities and TDC did not always see eye to eye, so much the better — it could be argued — since the final compromise decisions had the combined weight and authority of the bodies behind them. As they wait to inherit Telford, how do they regard the town? Will they have the funds and the professional expertise to continue the necessary growth of the town? As important, will they be able to provide the visionary element so evident in TDC's leadership at crucial times?

Finally, there are the inhabitants of this new town themselves, the enthusiastic and the reluctant Telfordians. They are of many backgrounds — from old mining settlements, from the market town, from Birmingham and the Black Country, from all over middle England, from Wales, London and the south-east. And from rural Shropshire, too. They run the gamut of age and income groups. How do they regard their town? With pride and affection? With resentment or indifference? Does it fulfill their needs for solid attractive housing, a good variety of jobs, excellent and convenient shopping, easy and quick commuting, a fine range of social, cultural and sporting opportunities within their means, and a green and pleasant environment? For in the end, the town 'belongs' to them, and especially to the younger generations, so many of them actually born in Telford, raised in Telford, and now living in Telford and raising a second generation of Telford-born.

## Appraisals by TDC people

A sample of views from TDC board members and senior staff, past and present, reveals some regrets, some hopes for the future, but in general an overall satisfaction with the town, its centre, the light and airy industrial areas, the later housing, and the landscaping throughout, particularly the forest element that year on year makes its beneficent presence more obvious. At a time when the nation is about to embark on a number of new national and regional forests, here a new forest is already part way to maturity. Most believe that there is room within the designated area for a comfortable 135,000 to 150,000 population, with a figure of 140,000 as the most likely. They do not think this will overcrowd the town or take away too much of the green and open space. They believe the three-tiered shopping system needs the extra population to ensure that the local and district centres and the town centre are all reasonably profitable. Similarly, more people will make further cultural and sporting facilities more viable. That is the general view within which there are numbers of more detailed comments and the occasional minority dissent.

Lord Northfield visits Telfords from time to time. He believes there is a need for more people quite quickly, and emphasises the extraordinary transformation in living standards that the new town has achieved. While Telford is recognised as a boom town, he is always happily aware that local identities have been preserved, that the new housing and industrial developments were carried out sensitively. He is particularly pleased with the town park's friendly incursion into the town centre, but would like to see more small shops of the 'boutique' type, and more intriguing walkways where the park meets the town centre, and where people would stroll on summer evenings. This development would be consistent with his long campaign when he was chairman of TDC to bring 'romance' to the town.

*Telford Bridge retail park on the fringe of the town centre. TDC's planning brief prescribed the planning form, architecture and use of materials.*

Frank Jones recalled how Shropshire in the early days of the new town much resented 'the cuckoo in its nest'. He hoped and expected that opinions had changed as Telford now brought wealth to the county, and villages in the countryside surrounding the new town had all benefited without being swamped. Active encouragement of a broad base for industry and commerce had been essential, but he thought that more office jobs were needed to keep a good balance. Sales of TDC housing had been exceptional, and that, together with the development of a strong private sector, had helped Telford become a town with a good spread of income groups. Frank Jones thought that if more rented houses were needed it would be up to government to build them. He still hoped that a theatre would be built in the town centre before too long.

*Priorslee primary school, designed by Shropshire County Council' Architects' Department. It is complex plan giving rise to an architectural expression well-suited to the new residential area it serves.*

## Self-motivating

Busy with details of TDC's demise while maintaining development at 'full throttle', Mike Morgan emphasised that the development land would be capable of being maximised very quickly since it would largely be ready serviced and with planning permission. Any future marketing of the town would need to stress the geographical location and the sheer quality of the industrial, commercial and living environments. He was optimistic that Telford would become self-generating before too long, drawing companies and people to it by the example of those already in the town and evidently prospering. He pointed out that around 11,000 of Telford's workforce drove in to work each day, mostly from Shropshire, indicating the measure of the town's influence on its surroundings. On housing, Mike Morgan felt that TDC's policy, after the early residential units in south Telford, in 'blurring' TDC rented housing and owner-occupation dwellings at the lower end of the market, had been successful bearing in mind budgets and density restrictions. None of the newer developments had a 'council estate' feel to them. Talking of car parking in the town centre, he believed that if in the future more was genuinely necessary, then low-level decked systems would be the answer. Finally he had one regret and one near-regret. The first was that the worldwide marketing of Telford had not begun earlier, the second was a backward look to the pioneering days of TDC. 'The early years were very exciting because we were breaking fresh ground. Now it is more a matter of applying professional skills and seeing things through — inevitably a little less exciting,' he said.

His predecessor as general manager, Joe Boyce, thought that with hindsight the three-tier shopping was fine in theory, but its execution and timing in Telford caused too much suffering on the part of shopkeepers in the district centres, and that the trend to superstores had in some measure thrown the system out of kilter. He also believed that the relationship of home and work, as far as easy access was concerned, had not been completely thought out and executed. While the road system was excellent and the town built for the motor car and lorry, other forms of transport had not been fully catered for. Early cycle paths had revealed a problem of security, both to cyclists and to properties backing on to those paths. Bearing in mind that a majority of families might have only one motor car — often taken to work by the breadwinner — adequate public transport was necessary for mothers, for the old and the young. Joe Boyce was sad that the rapid transport systems talked of in the past had come to naught. Any future public transport system would need to be better integrated with inter-regional bus and rail services than had so far been the case. He disagreed on the ultimate size of Telford, putting forward a population figure of 150,000 to 160,000 as a 'threshold' necessary for all the essential services built into the town to be fully utilised. Pressure for development up to and possibly beyond would be irresistible given the youthful population adding its own natural increase and the in-built dynamism of the town. He thought there would eventually be 'a gentle expansion' outside the boundaries.

Emyr Thomas also believes an optimum 150,000 population necessary to utilise services and for the provision of full artistic, cultural and sporting facilities. On the early residential units, he reminded critics that those are now thriving communities which are stoutly defended in every way, including their architecture, by those who live there. He regretted the decision not to build the western primary road as a dual carriageway, taken after the drastic reduction in population targets by

185

government in the 1970s. As Telford developed, especially on the western side where much of it is scheduled, the lack of the originally-planned ring road to motorway standards would be felt. Emyr Thomas also believed that a tramway or monorail system of own-track rapid-transit transport would be a huge boon. The big challenge to Telford that he saw was for its people to provide sufficient leadership from all strata of society — people prepared to work for the new society that Telford was creating, people who valued their surroundings and were prepared to look after them. Looking to the future, he saw the possibility of new villages in the countryside acting as satellites to Telford. He thought the new major road systems such as the dualling of the A5 beyond Shrewsbury, the new motorways to connect with the M40 and M42, would bring great benefit to the new town.

As chief engineer of TDC for many years, Laurie Buckthorp also regrets the 'emasculation' of the U motorway, although he believes the infrastructure — 'built to last as our Victorian forebears built' — could cope with much greater numbers than at present projected. He first saw the East Shropshire coalfield during the Second World War, and having lived for twenty-eight years in Wellington, has seen every change. He paid tribute, too, to the changes wrought by Wrekin District Council. He felt that acceptance of Telford was speeding up in Wellington, which had been solidly against the new town in the early days. He thought that TDC, with funding for infrastructure and a wide range of facilities, had instilled 'a bit of life' into the older communities and encouraged them to help themselves. He believed that Telford was already a good mix of development and open space, and he wanted to see the green fringe preserved, and felt that a population of 130,000 was about right.

## Councillors

Councillor Iris Butler was born and bred in the mining village of St George's, and she is typical of numbers of local authority councillors who have sought to work actively with the development corporation in gaining the best for their voters from the new town. She admits that as far as her own village is concerned, 'half of me wanted no change in St George's'. But she became swept up in the excitement and challenge of the huge changes taking place, many of them, as she says, for the better. While she has seen familiar places disappear or alter beyond recognition, and has accepted this, she now believes that any further 'infill' — taking green spaces — must be very carefully controlled. As a WDC councillor she is certain of the need for low-cost housing and more rented accommodation.

Although a Londoner, Councillor Jack Turner of Shropshire County Council and previously on the district council, has lived in Telford — in Lawley Bank and Dawley — for many years. He testifies that the 'by and large' good relationship between local authorities and TDC had contributed to the success of the town. He believes firmly that TDC's undemocratic nature was its strength in getting things done, and that it did a good and professional job, particularly in servicing industry. He was against the city technology college, seeing it as a return to a 'grammar school' and seriously diminishing the viability of other secondary schools by taking their bright pupils. He also thought that the station building, which should be as the Victorians had built them — prestigious, grand and welcoming — is insignificant and that WDC and TDC both failed there. As a dedicated Telfordian he would like to see electrification of the railway line, a helicopter pad and a crematorium.

The Holbrook family's house at Madeley was one of the first fifty compulsorily purchased and demolished for the Madeley bypass. 'But that didn't cloud our judgment of the new town,' said Mrs Holbrook. Les Holbrook, an SCC councillor, has been a member of TDC's board for fifteen years. He was born in Madeley and married a girl born in Ironbridge and raised in Dawley, thus disproving the old saying that Dawley/Madeley marriages never happened because of the sharp rivalry between the towns. Living now in Oakengates, believing 100 per cent in Telford and the benefits it has brought, the Holbrooks nevertheless say that Oakengates town centre has suffered despite its new roads and refurbishments. People, they say, are still very loyal to their own small patch. They can be heard to say, 'we went up to Telford at the weekend'. Les Holbrook believes it only right to keep local loyalties, but acknowledges a loyalty also to the bigger area. His children and especially his grandchildren accept Telford as 'their town'.

## Lightmoor some years on

The community at Lightmoor encountered many difficulties, not least legal and financial problems, and gaining planning permission to run businesses. There are now fourteen families living on twenty-seven acres (eleven hectares). A second phase of eight families joined the first, bringing an architect/planner, a civil engineer and two bricklayers among them. The houses are timber framed, face full south, are heavily insulated, with heat exchanger recovery systems and solar panels. The community put in its drains and roads with its own hands, built a water purification plant and septic tank. Much of the twenty-seven acres is third grade agricultural land with some regenerated coal tips. Seven shafts had to be capped. Computer software, cabinet-making and timber animal houses are among the businesses run in Lightmoor. One family keeps a smallholding, many grow their own vegetables and fruit. Co-operation at all levels and for most work about the community is the order of the day. The financial and social wellbeing of the people depends on the community. 'It's a paradise for children', said Gerwyn Lewis, one of the original pioneers, who works for the Green Wood Trust in Coalbrookdale, 'and life is tough and good for the rest of us. But it's a test of how secure marriages are.'

## Marvellous marriages

Millie Parry was born in a small terraced house at Snedshill ninety years ago, one of ten children of a miner at Woodhouse Colliery. She remembers the pigs and chickens in the back yard, the big vegetable garden and the home-brewed ale. In the 1920s times were hard and her brothers had to leave and find work elsewhere in England. Although the surroundings in those days were pit mounds, decaying industries and pollution, she does not remember finding them depressing. 'It was only that we had to leave to find work'. Her husband was from St George's and worked as a chauffeur for the Lilleshall Company. She worked at Priorslee Hall in those days, and later served tea for twenty years to TDC staff in the same building. On the close local loyalties, she recalls how one sister started courting a boy from Lawley Bank. Her parents tried to put a stop to it but in vain, and the marriage went happily ahead. Millie has spent all her life within a mile or two of her birthplace, only marginally affected by the momentous happenings round about. She remembers with affection the places of yesteryear and gets lost in Telford's town centre. Her overriding pleasure in the new town is that it has enabled the girls of all the villages to 'make marvellous marriages with boys in good jobs'.

Living in St George's, Des and Elsie Guy are both from established East Shropshire coalfield families — she was born in the village, the daughter of a miner at the Grange Colliery, he is from The Nabb. They have also seen their childhood countryside changed, and their friendly, close-knit village expanded to take in many 'foreigners'. They admit that incomers have become interested in the village and contributed to its life. Like many of similar age group in the north Telford settlements they have — sometimes grudgingly — come to accept the new town and use its new facilities with pleasure, in their case, the cinema and swimming pools. But they do feel 'a little smothered' by Telford, and hope that no more of their green spaces will be taken for housing and industry.

John Lees was born and raised in Hadley. On both sides his family had been on the coalfield for generations. His father worked at Maddock's foundry, his grandfather was a nailmaker and cobbler. On his mother's side there had been painters at the Coalport china works. John 'picked the tips' as a boy, then joined The Staffordshire Regiment, and when stationed in Germany found, in a booming economy, that the Germans were throwing out good solid but outmoded furniture as they purchased new. There was no market for it there, so the municipal lorries collected it up to dispose of it. He bought himself out of the Army, went back to Germany with a truck, went round before the municipal lorries, and collected up the free discards to sell in Telford, setting up business in 1976. His business has prospered, he has moved into importing and exporting, but still runs a big centre for second-hand furniture in Oakengates, and employs fifty people, some from old settlement families but many new Telfordians, too. Now in his early forties, John Lees says that Telford has been good to him. He likes the 'town in a forest' aspect and finds communications first-rate. If there is a downside to life in Telford, both he and his wife Theresa, born in Wellington, find people a little more preoccupied with their own affairs, a little less friendly than in the past.

Another Wellingtonian is Neil Griffiths, whose father's family goes back to the 1740s in the Shrewsbury and Wem area. In his early thirties, he married a girl from Donnington, and they now live at The Rock. Neil has worked for TDC for twelve years, and recalls how at school in Wellington in the 1970s he was hardly aware of the new town or concerned about it. Its huge scale was a surprise to him, but like many of his generation he has taken the advantages and assets of the new town and made full use of them. He finds the variety and quality of available housing extraordinary. He believes the landscaping is Telford's greatest success and 'we've yet to see the best'. Neil would like to see more cultural life, especially more live music — rock and pop for him. He recalls an occasion which he feels reflected the new town's spirit. On a fine summer Sunday afternoon the Shropshire Youth Jazz Orchestra played in the town park bandstand while up to 5,000 people strolled in the sun and listened.

## Foreman bricklayer

David Eccleston comes from an old Madeley family and his wife Beryl is from Ironbridge, where they now live. As a foreman bricklayer he worked all over Telford, on schools in Woodside, Madeley and Wellington, on new housing in

Brookside, Dawley and Hollinswood, and on renovation work in Coalbrookdale, Ironbridge and Madeley. He now lectures on building in Shrewsbury. Having helped to build the new town he is always interested in developments, and finds the landscaping wonderful, the rawness gone. The Ecclestons enjoy shopping in Telford town centre, especially the free and easy parking. They find the district centres 'a little run down' and are sad that so many of the shops for 'ordinary folk' in Ironbridge have disappeared in favour of outlets for tourist wares. They are followers of Telford United, are proud of the grand effort of winning the Entente Florale, find bus services poor, and more crime and vandalism than in the past. They tend to have their friends among the old Ironbridge and Madeley families. Not so their daughter, Merle, who was at school in Madeley, and who now teaches at a school in Stirchley. Her friends are from widely-differing backgrounds and live all over Telford.

*Looking from the edge of the town centre towards St George's on the skyline. In the foreground is The Forge interchange on the M54. In the middle ground is modern office development privately financed on former Lilleshall Company land within the enterprise zone. The buildings at right are on the site of the Priorslee blastfurnaces.*

A privately-financed and built factory at Hortonwood, where the landscaping has just been planted in front of a cool and elegant steel-framed and steel-clad building.

## Incomers

Martin Brookes describes himself as a 'newtownophile'. After a spell in Harlow New Town in Essex, he and his wife Shirley came to Dawley New Town in 1964 when he opened up a dentist's practice. They lived in Little Dawley before moving to Sutton Hill in 1970, to one of the private development houses next to the golf course. Shirley Brookes became one of the pioneer teachers in Sutton Hill, struggling at first with a class of forty-one. Sutton Hill rapidly filled up. For many it did indeed represent the prospect of a new life in better surroundings. It was somewhere to start afresh. But at first life was pioneering with mud, dust and some hostility outside.

Some families moved back to whence they had come, most stayed to see conditions improving all the time. 'Now they say with great pride — "I was a pioneer",' said Martin Brookes. Both testify to the rapid growth of a strong community, helpful and friendly, from which those who put in most gained most. 'Now you have the parents of couples who came from Birmingham or the Black Country retiring here so as to be near their families.' With so many born-and-bred Telfordians growing up, wanting to live and work in the town, the Brookes expressed concern that rented accommodation and starter homes might be lacking. They want to see more schemes such as the low-cost homes built at Rough Park, Woodside.

Rona and Rowland Sheldon had two small daughters, a small house and no garden in Warley, West Midlands. They were an 'overspill' family, coming to Sutton Hill in 1968. A third daughter was born there in 1970. Through church and school they soon entered into the pioneering community and made friends. Rona joined keep fit classes and a choir, took part in Brownies and Guides. Rowland worked as a plumber during the building of Woodside, and now runs his own heating and ventilating business. They moved to Little Dawley twelve years ago. Their daughters all live and work in Telford, one is married and at Aqueduct, the other two at Ketley Bank and Randlay. From Little Dawley they have good walks in countryside — notably along the Silkin Way and at Lightmoor — without getting into a car, and hope that this will long remain. They do their shopping locally in Dawley, and in the town centre, and like to go 'browsing' in Shrewsbury once in a while.

*The opening ceremony of Telford Development Corporation's village green at Lawley, built and land-scaped in advance of the residential development already planned but not yet begun. Schoolchildren stocked the lake with fish.*

## A better chance

'We wanted to give our children a better chance,' said Don and Margaret Smallwood, who moved from Smethwick to Brookside in 1979. They rented a brand-new house and Don commuted to GKN in Smethwick initially where he was in production control. He then went into business with three video shops in Telford.

Later the Smallwoods opened a general store and off-licence in the district centre of Madeley from which they have just retired. Their children are grown up and live in Telford. Their daughter is a school teacher and in St George's, the eldest son is a carpenter who works for a small Telford builder, and twin sons work in the Madeley shop. Before beginning another enterprise the Smallwoods are exploring Telford, noting the changes, amazed at the greenness of the town, shopping at the town centre and delving into the extraordinary history of the East Shropshire coalfield.

*Aerial view of Telford town centre, showing the motorway box, the large areas of car parking spaces and the bus depot.*

*Windsurfing on Priorslee Lake in spring, with the NEC factory beyond, and a bulb farm's fields of daffodils and narcissi on the hillside.*

## The youngsters

Yvonne Wood's parents came from Birmingham to Sutton Hill in 1969. A tool-maker by trade, he opened a small factory in Ironbridge. Yvonne went to the Alexander Fleming primary school in Sutton Hill and on to the Madeley Court school. She worked as a dental nurse in two local practices for four years before completing a year's course to become a dental hygienist. She is married and lives in Aqueduct. Heather Angus's father was in the RAF based locally, and stayed when he left the service, to work in electronics at Halesfield and live in Sutton Hill. Heather went to the primary school with Yvonne, then to the Abraham Darby school in Madeley, and on to the University of Kent where she gained a degree in English and education. She is now a civil servant with the Land Registry in Telford. Colin Edwards also went to the same primary school and to the Madeley Court comprehensive. He did a catering course and joined the RAF as a cook, but decided against service life. He now works as a production manager for a Halesfield firm, is married to a girl from Broseley, and lives in Woodside.

Born and bred in Telford, all three have a huge affection for their town, and were always glad to get back after working or studying away. They especially talked of the fresh air and greenery. They tend to have friends who live all over the town and are from different backgrounds, and they find Telford friendly.

*Tranquillity and modern industrial elegance at Apley.*

They all spoke of the community spirit in Sutton Hill and their new home areas. Having been brought up in a place that was always changing, they agreed that they took the construction activity for granted and found it all exciting. They applauded such occasions as the Telford Show and other town park events, as being excellent for town morale.

While the cinema was wonderful they would like to see more cultural events and would support a theatre in the town centre. They praised the free car parking in shopping centres, but thought car parking on the estates left much to be desired. Car thefts and the level of petty crime generally they felt should be fought more vigorously.

Their biggest criticism of Telford was in the standard of public transport, pointing out that many young people did not have motor cars, and while they could sometimes cycle within a few miles of their homes, had normally to rely on the bus service. They too expressed the wish that future development would be sufficiently contained to leave Telford with its exceptional green areas for the enjoyment of future generations.

All in all, a practical and thoughtful set of opinions on Telford New Town, from those who built it and those who live and work in it. As Telford Development Corporation ceases to exist, how could and how should its extraordinary new town develop further? And should it and will it?

Grand Prix Européen de l'Entente Florale 1990

Britain in Bloom ~ United Kingdom Winners 1989

# *Epilogue*

Since demographic changes, economic cycles and political considerations have affected the growth of Telford so markedly in its short life, there can be no telling precisely what the future holds. But the broad outlines are certainly there. The development of more industrial, commercial and housing sites will take place as planned by the development corporation and now by the district council. More incomers to take up the jobs created, together with the native young Telfordians and their families, will most probably bring the population within the next ten to fifteen years up to around 150,000.

Such a population would be necessary in order to provide the final cultural and sporting facilities and infrastructure that so many townspeople are now asking for. A population of this size would certainly be vital to make any kind of own-track, rapid-transit transport system viable economically. That system could cut the congestion by motor cars already seen in some residential parts of the town, slow down the growth of two- and three-car families, and keep Telford's supremely good network of roads still wonderfully clear of thick traffic for many years. It could also help to ameliorate the Ironbridge Gorge's chronic tourist traffic jams. Such a transport system may even be important to the continued prosperity of Telford, for we do not know how the costs of fossil fuels and their pollution aspects will affect motoring in the future.

The people of Telford evidently set much store by the ready availability of woodland, grassland and open space for their use. And they have expressed concern that development may slash this recreational acreage. Looking at land use figures, even with the projected development it appears that they will have around 4,000 acres (1,620 hectares), and it will be up to Telfordians through their elected representatives on the district council to make sure that 'enough development is enough', when it comes to the taking of further green acres.

Certainly the variety of wildlife in Telford endorses the contention that there are plenty of varied habitats and open spaces. Wildfowl use the lakes and pools, nightingales sing in coppiced woodland, the occasional osprey soars over the river. Barn owls, short- and long-eared owls, curlews, lapwings, wrynecks and nightjars are seen and heard. Woodland birds come into Telford's growing forests to shelter in winter, including flocks of long-tailed tits. Fieldfares and redwings are attracted to thorn hedges for their harvest of berries. There are otters in the Severn, badgers in the gorge and in many other places, muntjac and roe deer, and of course foxes abound. Adders and grass snakes, great crested newts, bats at Stirchley in old industrial buildings, all swell the number of species. Butterfly watchers can see green hairstreaks, holly blues, white admirals and fritillaries, as well as the more common species. Telford boasts seven or eight species of orchid. There are salmon in the Severn, and most lakes and pools yield up carp, tench, roach and pike.

Telford has yet to acquire the full range of cultural activities that a town of its size and prestige should have. These will come, probably sooner than later, and the new town will become a complete town in the material sense. Is it yet an entity? The answer to that question must surely be — yes. But do all who live in the town believe that? In the settlements, new and old, is there evidence of the gradual welding of the individual small places into one town? Perhaps the word 'gradual' is the key. The older generations tend to keep their loyalty for the settlements that were there before Telford. The incomers of the middle generations are clear in their allegiance both to the residential unit to which they came, and the greater concept of the new town. They are transitional, but regard Telford with pride and affection. They say, when away, 'I come from Telford'. But it is by the young, no matter what their background, that the spirit of Telford will be finally forged. They are mobile, with a more cosmopolitan outlook in a town known nationally and internationally, and with many different nationalities living and working in it.

Perhaps there will even come a time when Shropshire, having seen what it thought of as a disproportionate share of its development moneys going into the new town over a quarter of a century, and having become more prosperous because of Telford, will be proud of its extraordinary new town.

As Britain's cities, towns and even some villages become distorted with too many housing and industrial additions on their peripheries, their centres in distress from an overload of vehicles and people, and their roads clogged with car commuters, perhaps the new towns lobby headed by the Town and Country Planning Association will at last be heeded. Perhaps a fresh and practical appraisal of the environmental and sociological worth of new settlements will be made.

When that happens the example of Telford, with its size and its ability to offer a wide spread of jobs, will prove of fundamental use. Ebenezer Howard in 1919 hoped that eight-five per cent of the workforce in his second garden city would live in the town, cutting commuting to a minimum, enabling the breadwinners to come home earlier, with ample time for their families and recreation. That percentage was not achieved. Yet in Telford, eighty-eight per cent of the economically active Telfordians work in the new town.

The story of Telford's struggles and triumphs shows the deep thought, careful construction and firm but understanding handling necessary in such a great enterprise, in striving to make a complete town in every sense.

# Bibliography

ALDRIDGE, Meryl, *The British New Towns*, Routledge & Kegan Paul, 1979

ASHWORTH, William, *The Genesis of Modern British Town Planning*, Routledge & Kegan Paul, 1954

BARRETT, Franklin A., *Caughley and Coalport Porcelain*, F. Lewis, 1951

BAXTER, R. M., *A History of Wellington*, 1949

BOWCOCK, E. W., *Shropshire Place Names*, Wilding & Son, Shrewsbury, 1923

CARTLIDGE, Rev J. E. Gordon, *The Vale and Gates of USC-CON*, Congleton

CROSSMAN, Richard, *Diaries of a Cabinet Minister*, Hamilton and Cape, 1975

DAWLEY DEVELOPMENT CORPORATION
   Annual Reports, 1964 to 1968; *The Master Plan for Dawley* (John D. Madin) January 1965; *Continuity Plan* 1967; *Madeley Draft Policy*, October 1967

DAWLEY UDC, *Dawley — The Official Guide and Handbook*, 1956

DE SOISSONS, Maurice, *Welwyn Garden City: A Town Designed for Healthy Living*, Publications for Companies, 1988

EYTON, W. R., *Antiquities of Shropshire*, John Russell Smith, 1856

FENTER, D. G., *Papers: Building Developments Carried Out in Telford by the Development Corporation*, Victoria County History Records

FROST, A. J., *The Story of Donnington and Its Parish Church*, 1978

GALE, W. K. V. and NICHOLLS, C. R., *The Lilleshall Co Ltd — A History 1764 to 1964*, Lilleshall Co Ltd, 1979

HADFIELD, Charles, *The Canals of the West Midlands*, Kelley, 1969

HAYNES, Rev C. M., comp., *Old Dawley and Pool Hill*, Countryside Publications Ltd, 1984

HOWARD, Ebenezer, *Garden Cities of Tomorrow*, 1902, Faber, reprint 1946

IRONBRIDGE GORGE MUSEUM TRUST, *Thomas Telford: Engineer. Proceedings of Seminar*, 1979

MILES, Malcolm, *Newport in the Second World War*

MILES, Ron, *The Iron Bridge at War. Journal of the Wilkinson Society*, No. 1, 1973

MORRISS, R. K., *Railways of Shropshire: A Brief History*, Shropshire Libraries, 1983

OSBORN, F. J. and WHITTICK, Arnold, *New Towns, Their Origins, Achievements and Progress*, Leonard Hill, London, 1977

PURDOM, C. B., *The Building of Satellite Towns*, J. M. Dent & Sons, 1925 and 1949

RANDALL, John, *History of Madeley*, The Wrekin Echo, 1880

RAYSKA, Urszula, and CARR, Anthony, *Telford Past and Present*, Shropshire Libraries and Telford Development Corporation

ROLT, L. T. C., *Thomas Telford*, Longmans, Green and Co, 1958

SHAFFER, F., *The New Town Society*, McGibbon & Kee, 1970

SHEPPARD FIDLER, A. G., *Dawley as a New Town*, Ministry of Housing and Local Government, 1962

TELFORD COMMUNITY ARTS, *The Hadley Book*, 1982

TELFORD COMMUNITY ARTS, *Oakengates in the Words of Oakengates People*, 1987

TELFORD DEVELOPMENT CORPORATION
   Annual Reports, 1969 to 1990; *Dawley Policy Plan*; *Employment and Income Report* (Social Survey), 1973; *'Help': Needs of Services for the Elderly in Telford*, 1975; *Landscape Master Plan*, 1971; *Madeley Wood — Policy for Rehabilitation*; *North West Telford — Context Study*; *Oakengates Centre*, 1971; *Research into Commuting*, 1972; *Shopping Study in Telford*, 1977; *Stirchley District Plan*; *Telford Basic Plan*, 1971; *Telford in the 1980s*, Emyr Thomas, General Manager, TDC, 1980; *Telford — The Task Ahead*, 1987; *Traffic Noise*, 1971; *Transport (Social Survey)*, 1973; *Wellington Centre* (John D. Madin) 1969; *Wellington Centre*, 1974

TRINDER, Barrie, and COX, Jeff, *Yeomen and Colliers in Telford*, Phillimore, 1980

TRINDER, Barrie, *The Industrial Revolution in Shropshire*, Phillimore, 1981

VIALLS, Christine, *Coalport and the Iron Revolution*, Cambridge University Press, 1980

VICTORIA HISTORY OF SHROPSHIRE, THE, Volume XI, ed. George Baugh

WALKER, S. T. & Partners, *Jockey Bank, Madeley Wood. A Policy for Rehabilitation*, Report for Telford Development Corporation

WIGGINS, W. E., *Ancient Woodland in the Telford Area*, Telford Nature Conservation Project

WILLIAMS, W. Howard, *The Industries of the Oakengates Area (An Historical Review)*, 1966

WREKIN DISTRICT COUNCIL, *Telford Local Plan, 1991 to 2001*

NEWSPAPER CUTTINGS. From the *Wellington Journal, Dawley Observer, Telford Journal, Shropshire Star*, 1963 to 1991

# Appendix 1

## Members of the two development corporations

### Dawley Development Corporation

| | | |
|---|---|---|
| Sir Reginald Pearson, Kt, OBE, MIMechE, MIProdE | Chairman | 1963 to 1968 |
| Alderman W. T. Bowen, JP | Deputy Chairman | 1963 to 1968 |
| The Rt Hon The Viscount Boyne, DL | | 1963 to 1968 |
| Mr J. C. Cadbury, MA (Cantab), FCI | | 1963 to 1968 |
| Mr I. Jones, JP | | 1963 to 1968 |
| Mr F. W. Kenchington, FRICS, FAI | | 1963 to 1968 |
| Mrs I. M. Wilson, MBE, BA (Cantab) | | 1963 to 1968 |

### Telford Development Corporation

| | | |
|---|---|---|
| Sir Frank Price, Kt, DL, FSVA, FCIT | Chairman | 1968 to 1971 |
| Mr J. R. S. Dugdale | Chairman | 1971 to 1975 |
| The Rt Hon Lord Northfield of Telford | Chairman | 1975 to 1987 |
| Mr F. J. Jones (Deputy Chairman 1986–1987) | (Chairman 1987–1991) | 1986 to 1991 |
| Mr I. Jones, OBE | Deputy Chairman | 1968 to 1974 |
| The Rt Hon The Viscount Boyne, DL | Deputy Chairman 1975–1982 | 1968 to 1982 |
| Mr J. R. Parry, MA, FRICS | Deputy Chairman 1982–1986 | 1981 to 1986 |
| Mrs E. J. Holt | Deputy Chairman 1987–1991 | 1975 to 1991 |
| Mr J. C. Cadbury, MA (Cantab), FCI | | 1968 to 1975 |
| Mr L. J. McCulloch, JP, FRICS | | 1968 to 1975 |
| Lt-Col R. C. G. Morris-Eyton, TD, BA | | 1968 to 1975 |
| Mrs I. M. Wilson, MBE, BA (Cantab) | | 1968 to 1975 |
| Mr H. R. Gibbons | | 1969 to 1975 |
| Mrs D. M. Walder | | 1969 to 1975 |
| Dr I. F. Gibson, PhD, BSc(Econ) | | 1975 to 1991 |
| Mr L. J. Holbrook | | 1975 to 1991 |
| Mr A. J. Hooke, BA | | 1975 to 1980 |
| Dr P. M. Vine, CBE, MA, LLM, PhD, DL | | 1975 to 1989 |
| Mr A. G. Curtis | | 1976 to 1979 |
| Mr M. J. Davies | | 1977 to 1991 |
| Mr R. A. H. Lloyd, TD, DL | | 1977 to 1989 |
| Mr R. Hall | | 1980 to 1988 |
| Sir Fred Hardman, MBE | | 1980 to 1991 |
| Mr R. I. Kenyon-Slaney | | 1980 to 1984 |
| Mr P. Court, FCBSI, FInstD, FBIM | | 1984 to 1991 |
| Mr R. A. H. Thomas, BA(Econ), FCA | | 1985 to 1991 |
| Mr R. A. Gammie, FRICS | | 1987 to 1991 |
| Mr J. Pendle, OBE, JP | | 1988 to 1991 |

### General Managers

| | |
|---|---|
| Mr R. Penrhyn Owen | 1963 to 1968 |
| Mr E. Thomas, CBE, LLB, LMRTPI, DL | 1969 to 1980 |
| Mr J. F. Boyce, FRICS | 1980 to 1986 |
| Mr M. D. Morgan, BSc(Est.Man), FRICS | 1986 to 1991 |

# Appendix 2

## *Principal events in Telford's history*

### 1963
Dawley New Town designated and development corporation established in January. Sir Reginald Pearson appointed chairman. John H. D. Madin & Partners, of Birmingham, appointed planning consultants.

### 1965
Dawley's draft master plan published in January. Gitchfield site for sewage works chosen. In July, West Midlands study on Wellington/Oakengates project and relationship with Dawley published. Site preparation begun in November at Tweedale industrial estate.

### 1966
Site preparation begun in March at Sutton Hill residential estate. 'Continuity' plan for southern part of town published in April. In July, Archbishop of Canterbury dedicated stone at Sutton Hill pastoral centre. September — first Tweedale factory handed over and site preparation begun at Halesfield industrial estate.

### 1967
In February, site preparation begun at Woodside residential estate, and month later first house occupied at Sutton Hill. The Queen visited Dawley in March. Madeley policy plan, Stirchley district plan and Dawley 'opportunities' plan published in November. In November, draft designation order for Dawley, Wellington and Oakengates published.

### 1968
March — Sir Reginald Pearson resigned and Sir Frank Price became chairman of Dawley Development Corporation. In February, Ironbridge and Severn Gorge policy plans published. Site preparation begun at Brookside residential estate. Madeley bypass opened in December. Designation order made enlarging new town to include Wellington and Oakengates, and change of name to Telford.

### 1969
January — renovation of Ironbridge shopping centre begun. In March, Telford Development Corporation published its basic plan, and in same month the first Woodside houses handed over. Plans for phase 1 of Telford town centre made. In September, phase 1 of Madeley district centre opened.

### 1970
In March, first US company, Eaton Yale and Towne, came to Telford. Site preparation started at Stafford Park in June.

### 1971
Sir Frank Price resigned and John Dugdale became TDC chairman. Landscape structure plan published. In October, the eastern central primary road, south, opened. The next month Wellington centre policy plan published, and draft order for M54 motorway.

### 1972
In January, the Dawley policy plan published. Work begun on M54 Wellington bypass. Private housing development begun at Stirchley. In June, first families moved into Brookside. The Brookside pastoral central dedicated in July.

### 1973
Tenth anniversary of new town. During March, TDC bought Telford United's ground. In July, phase 2 of Madeley district centre opened, and in September Hadley policy plan published. October saw phase 1 of Telford town centre opened. First continental European company, Merlin Gerin, came to Telford.

### 1974
Wrekin District Council established in April. The 5,000th rented home handed over. June — the 150th TDC-built factory completed. Next month site preparation begun for housing at Malinslee and in November at Aqueduct.

## 1975

Phase 2 of Telford town centre announced. North-west Dawley housing started in May. Cutback in population target to 145,000 to 155,000 by 1986. Apley Castle chosen as Telford hospital site. In November, John Dugdale resigned and Lord Northfield became TDC chairman. Heritage Year award for Ironbridge Gorge Museum. In December, context study for north-west Telford published, together with Ketley Bank area plan. M54 Wellington bypass and eastern central primary road, north, both opened. RIBA town centre competition.

## 1976

TDC initiated five-year plan. First houses handed over in Malinslee in March, and next month first office block opened in Telford town centre. In May, first houses occupied in north-west Dawley and Great Hay golf course opened. Restoration of Priorslee village begun in July. Dawley bypass opened the next month. Town centre competition won by A. G. Sheppard Fidler.

## 1977

Silkin Way opened in April. In July, population target moderated to 135,000 by 1986, and subsequently ten-year development strategy produced by TDC. August saw first houses at Leegomery occupied. In October, site preparation for housing begun at Shawbirch.

## 1978

In January, the Dawley/Donnington distributor road opened, and in February the Hadley bypass completed. Work started on phase 2 of Telford town centre in September.

## 1979

Government approval for first 500 houses at Priorslee. Great Hay leisure complex planned. Bicentenary of Iron Bridge celebrated in July and Museum of Iron opened. In July, the Madeley/Coalport road opened. November — last coal mine, Granville colliery, closed.

## 1980

In March, work started on southern part of north-east primary road. June saw opening of southern district road and handing over of first Aqueduct houses. In October, final go-ahead for M54 motorway. Inland Revenue announced its national development centre to come to Telford.

## 1981

Application for assisted area status refused in March. Work begun on M54 in June. Telford Opportunities Centre opened in September. The Queen opened phase 2 of Telford town centre in November. The same month Hadley district centre was completed.

## 1982

April saw updating of TDC's 1977 development strategy plan. The Inland Revenue building opened in June. Next month the 1,000th TDC rented house was sold, and work begun on the hospital site. Government announced Telford's enterprise zone in November.

## 1983

February saw first Japanese company, Hitachi Maxell, come to Telford. Lightmoor community proposed in March. Fire at Central Ordnance Depot in June. In September, first Telford Business Show held and racquets centre opened. M54 opened in November.

## 1984

Telford enterprise zone inaugurated in January. Official approval for Telford general hospital in the same month. February saw declaration of Telford as intermediate assisted area. In October the ice rink opened by Princess Anne. The West Mercia divisional headquarters completed in December.

## 1985

Plastics Processing ITB opened training centre in April, and Telford Central railway station begun. 'The Task Ahead' published by TDC with local authorities in July. Tatung factory (Taiwan) opened in same month.

## 1986

Town centre library begun in February. Telford Central railway station opened in May. In July, Ironbridge bypass started, district registry of Land Registry begun, and Meeting Point House dedicated. Magistrates' court and probation office opened in October. In September, TDC instructed to become 'facilitating agency' through privatisation of functions. Frank Jones appointed TDC's deputy chairman in November. December saw TDC's wind-up date confirmed as September 31, 1991, and Marks & Spencer announced its arrival in Telford. NEC Corporation proposed to build factory requiring 1,000 employees.

## 1987

Government wrote off £450 million of Telford's debt. Phase 3 of Telford shopping centre opened. Marks & Spencer opened in October, and in the same month Frank Jones became TDC chairman and Lord Northfield retired. November — Telford Bridge retail park proposed.

## 1988

Silver jubilee year. In January, Telford central library opened. April — statue of Thomas Telford unveiled, and Ketley Dingle retail park proposed. In June, Telford entered Britain in Bloom contest, Priorslee Hall for sale. Meeting Point House opened. In October, phase 3 of town centre inaugurated. In November, town centre's ten-screen cinema opened. The TSB management training centre opened.

## 1989

In January, TDC moved from Priorslee Hall to New Town House, and Telford general hospital opened on limited scale with full service to follow in October. In February, the Ironbridge bypass opened. Racecourse proposed in March. In May, Telford's first International Day was held, and the 5,000th rented house sold. The next month Telford shopping centre put up for sale, and Wrekin DC published 'The Way Forward'. Telford again entered Britain in Bloom contest and won its category. A city technology college (CTC) was proposed.

## 1990

During February the CTC was approved by government and building begun. The Princess Royal officially opened the hospital. In June, first transfer of TDC assets to Wrekin DC, with woodland in Severn Gorge to be handed to a new trust. In June, Telford entered Entente Florale (Europe in Bloom) and won its category. Public enquiry into new bridge across the Severn. Wolverhampton Polytechnic set up annex in Stafford Park in September. WDC published plans for Telford until year 2001. Telford Development Agency proposed. Housing ballot announced for spring 1991.

# Index

*Numbers in italic type refer to illustrations.*